W9-ARB-123

LOST
DECADES

LOST DECADES

The Making of America's

Debt Crisis and the Long Recovery

Menzie D. Chinn
Jeffry A. Frieden

W. W. Norton & Company

New York • London

For information about permission to reproduce selections from this
book, write to Permissions, W. W. Norton & Company, Inc.,
500 Fifth Avenue, New York, NY 10110

For information about special discounts for bulk purchases, please
contact W. W. Norton Special Sales at specialsales@wwnorton.com
or 800-233-4830

Manufacturing by RR Donnelley, Harrisonburg
Book design by Charlotte Staub
Production manager: Devon Zahn

Library of Congress Cataloging-in-Publication Data

Chinn, Menzie David.
Lost decades : the making of America's debt crisis and the long
recovery / Menzie D. Chinn and Jeffry A. Frieden. — 1st ed.
p. cm.
Includes bibliographical references and index.
ISBN 978-0-393-07650-9 (hardcover)
1. Debts, Public—United States. 2. Debts, External—United States.
3. Budget deficits—United States. 4. United States—Economic
conditions—2009– 5. Financial crises—United States.
I. Frieden, Jeffry A. II. Title.
HJ7537.C45 2011
336.3'4350973—dc22
2011012043

W. W. Norton & Company, Inc.
500 Fifth Avenue, New York, N.Y. 10110
www.wwnorton.com

W. W. Norton & Company Ltd.
Castle House, 75/76 Wells Street, London W1T 3QT

1 2 3 4 5 6 7 8 9 0

For
Laura
& Anabela

CONTENTS

FIGURES

PREFACE

The midterm elections were over, and the Republicans had made stunning advances. The GOP had picked up over seventy seats in the House of Representatives and seven seats in the Senate. Perhaps just as important, the Republicans had taken a number of crucial governorships from the Democrats, including the pivotal states of Michigan, Ohio, and Pennsylvania. The election was a dramatic reversal of the Democrats' landslide victory two years earlier, and was a particular blow to the president, who had swept into office in the midst of a devastating economic crisis.

Certainly the Democrats could be satisfied with some major legislative accomplishments, passed with their previous majorities. But now, a disappointing economy and stubbornly high unemployment rate had brought back to life a Republican Party that had appeared moribund two years earlier. For the foreseeable future, the Republicans, together with allies among conservative Democrats, would be able to block or force changes in just about any initiative the president had in mind.

The year was 1938, and the economic recovery from the Great

Depression was in deep trouble. Back in 1933, when Franklin D. Roosevelt became president, the country was in the fourth year of the
deepest depression in its history. The Roosevelt administration had
moved quickly and aggressively to try to bring the country's economy
back to life. Roosevelt and his fellow Democrats in Congress purged
the nation's banking system and imposed stringent new regulations.
They created an ambitious array of federal programs to put the millions of unemployed to work. And they initiated the first serious federal social program in American history, Social Security.

By 1936 the economy was recovering. The unemployment rate
had fallen to 14 percent, still high but down from where it was, 25
percent, when Roosevelt took office. Both national income and the
stock market were rising rapidly. In light of the upturn, the Roosevelt
administration resolved to tackle the federal government's budget
deficit, which in 1936 had reached nearly 5 percent of gross domestic product (GDP), a level unprecedented in peacetime. Delivering on
promises to trim the deficit, the administration cut spending by 20
percent and raised taxes by even more; within a year the budget was
practically back to balance. Meanwhile, the Federal Reserve tight-
ened monetary policy, apparently to avoid a resurgence of inflation.

In the aftermath of the fiscal and monetary retrenchment, in the
summer of 1937 the American economy collapsed into a steep recession. Industrial production dropped by one-third, the stock market
plummeted more than 40 percent, and the unemployment rate shot
back up to 19 percent. As the American economy slumped, the
administration's popularity faded rapidly. And the result of the 1938
midterm election reflected this loss of confidence in the federal government's ability to bring the nation out of the Depression.[1]

Today the United States and the world are slowly recovering
from the most serious international economic crisis since the Great
Depression of the 1930s. As was the case in the late 1930s, the causes
and consequences of the crisis are hotly debated. And just as then,
a great deal rides on an appropriate understanding of why and how
the United States got to where it is today. How could the world's richest economy go broke? How did the world's most powerful banks
collapse? Why would the most conservative government in modern
American history nationalize enormous portions of the U.S. econ-

omy? Why did millions of American families lose their homes, and millions more their jobs? Whose fault is it all?

We have a unique perspective on these debates. We have spent, between the two of us, more than fifty years working on debt crises. We have lived through and studied financial and currency disasters in Europe, Latin America, Asia, and Russia. We have witnessed firsthand, and analyzed in detail, the human, social, and political wreckage of irresponsible borrowing. We have watched country after country lose decades of economic progress to the austere aftermath of financial crises. But we never feared that we would see a classic debt crisis in our own homeland. And we never imagined that our country could face the prospect of almost two decades lost to misguided policies, an unnecessary crisis, and a daunting task of economic reconstruction. Nonetheless, there is value in our ability to compare the current crisis to those we have known and investigated. As we examine the events of the past decade, and look toward the decade to come, we can draw on a wealth of comparative and historical experiences to guide our analysis.

The United States is in the midst of the greatest failure of economic policy, and of financial markets, of recent times. This is the story of how and why it got there, and of what the nation must do to repair a wounded economy.

The crisis

The most serious economic crisis of the past seventy-five years began as the summer of 2008 ended. In August and September, credit markets everywhere entered a downward spiral that spun faster and faster until, in the first two weeks of October, it seemed that the world economy might be coming to an immediate end. During those dark weeks and months, an international economic order that had inspired faith bordering on rapture around the world appeared to have turned on its creators and strongest supporters. The United States, the very center of economic globalization, was gripped in a panic that threatened to destroy the world economy. The collapse seemed to surge out of nothing and nowhere. One week there was mild concern about a sluggish housing market in the American Sunbelt, the next week the whole world was staring over a precipice into the end of global capitalism. The world's strongest economy turned into the sick man of international capitalism. The American paragon of capitalist virtue, protector of the free-market faith, took over huge swaths of the private sector. What happened? How could this come to pass?

The United States borrowed and spent itself into a foreign debt crisis. Between 2001 and 2007, Americans borrowed trillions of dollars from abroad. The federal government borrowed to finance its budget deficit; households borrowed to allow them to consume beyond their means. As money flooded in from abroad, Americans spent some of it on hard goods, especially on cheap imports. They spent most of the rest on local goods and services, especially financial services and real estate. The result was a broad-based economic expansion. This expansion—especially in housing—eventually became a boom, then a bubble. The bubble burst, with disastrous effect, and the country was left to pick up the pieces.

The American economic disaster is simply the most recent example of a "capital flow cycle," in which capital floods into a country, stimulates an economic boom, encourages high-flying financial and other activities, and eventually culminates in a crash. In broad outlines, the cycle describes the developing-country debt crisis of the early 1980s, the Mexican crisis of 1994, the East Asian crisis of 1997–1998, the Russian and Brazilian and Turkish and Argentine crises of the late 1990s and into 2000–2001—and, in fact, the German crisis of the early 1930s and the American crisis of the early 1890s. We can best, and most fully, understand the current debt crisis by understanding the dozens of debt crises that have come before it. What causes such crises? What can we learn from the paths to them, through them, and out of them?

To be sure, the most recent American version of a debt crisis was replete with its own particularities: an alphabet soup of bewildering new financial instruments, a myriad of regulatory complications, an unprecedented speed of contagion. Yet for all the unique features of contemporary events, in its essence this was a debt crisis. Its origins and course are of a piece with hundreds of episodes in the modern international economy.

For a century American policymakers and their allies in the commanding heights of the international financial system warned governments of the risks of excessive borrowing, unproductive spending, foolish tax policies, and unwarranted speculation. Then, in less than a decade, the United States proceeded to demonstrate precisely why such warnings were valid, pursuing virtually every dangerous policy it had advised others against.

Most analysts of the crisis miss this central point. Each of the many accounts published since 2008 has focused on one or another limited aspect of the crisis. Some follow the financial meltdown and response blow by blow, yielding vivid insights into the personalities and institutions involved. Other accounts emphasize the role of financial regulators in the collapse, documenting the influence of Wall Street over the deliberations in the halls of Washington, D.C. Yet others explain how the financial crisis caused so deep a global recession. Our analysis starts with the macroeconomic drivers of the experience, includes the political pressures, incorporates the regulatory enablers, and puts the crisis into a comparative and historical context, drawing parallels and lessons from the dozens of similar episodes from the past.

The American crisis immediately spread to the rest of the international economy. The world learned a valuable lesson about global markets: they transmit bad news as quickly as good news. The American borrowing binge had pulled much of the world along with it—drawing some countries (Great Britain, Ireland, Iceland, Spain, Greece) into a similar debt-financed boom, and tapping other countries (China, Japan, Saudi Arabia, Germany) for the money to make it possible. The collapse dragged financial markets everywhere over a cliff in a matter of weeks, with broad economic activity following within months.

Impact and implications

The global crisis raises the specter of global conflict. As governments scramble to protect their citizens, their actions can be costly to their neighbors: a bailout favors national over foreign firms, devaluation puts competitive pressures on trading partners, big deficits suck in capital from the rest of the world. The 1929 recession became a depression largely because of the collapse of international cooperation; the current crisis may head in that direction if international collaboration similarly fails.

With or without broader international complications, the United States faces hard times. The country lost the first decade of the twenty-first century to an ill-conceived boom and a subsequent bust. It is in danger of losing another decade to an incomplete recovery and economic stagnation.

In order to not lose the decade to come, the United States will have to bring order to financial disarray, gain control of a burgeoning burden of debt, and re-create the conditions for sound economic growth and social progress. None of this will be easy. The tasks are made more difficult by the fact, which we have learned to our alarm, that all too many policymakers and observers cling to the failed notions that got the country into such trouble in the first place. If Americans do not learn from this painful episode, and from others like it, they will condemn the nation to another lost decade.

ACKNOWLEDGMENTS

Many individuals helped us with the preparation and improvement of this book. Viral Acharya, Barry Eichengreen, Nancy Frieden, Thomas Frieden, Joseph Gagnon, Peter Gourevitch, Richard Grossman, James Kwak, David Lake, Peter Robinson, and David Singer read all or parts of the manuscript and gave us valuable comments. Marvin Phaup, Andrew Sum, and Arthur Kroeber assisted with particular portions of the project. Charles Frentz, Marina Ivanova, Jonathan McBride, Rahul Prabhakar, and Albert Wang provided important research assistance.

LOST
DECADES

Welcome to Argentina:
How America Borrowed Its Way
into a Debt Crisis

Latin Americans tell of when, in difficult times, a local dictator defended his rule before a skeptical nation. "When I took office," he insisted, "we stood on the brink of an abyss. But since then, we have taken a great leap forward!" The bitter story circulated in the early 1980s, as Latin Americans faced the worst debt crisis in their history. Beginning around 1970, the countries of the region had borrowed hundreds of billions of dollars from banks in North America, Europe, and Japan. The frenzied borrowing kept the economies going. Brazil built up the developing world's biggest industries; Mexico went from being an oil importer to a major oil exporter; Chile's Pinochet dictatorship spurred the rise of huge private conglomerates. The borrowing also drove speculative bubbles in finance and real estate, but in these prosperous times some disproportionate enthusiasm was understandable.

In August 1982 came the great leap into the abyss. Squeezed by rising interest rates on their debt, and falling prices for their oil exports, the Mexican government announced that it could not make payments on its $80 billion foreign debt. Within weeks, loans dried up to all of Latin America, and soon to all of the developing world. Heavily indebted countries spent the next decade struggling through the aftermath of the crisis.

After 2001, Americans took a similar march toward their own indebted abyss. They borrowed trillions of dollars from foreigners and used the money for a national binge of consumption, financial excess, and housing speculation. Seven years later came the great leap off a financial cliff. In August 2008, borrowers and lenders alike looked down and saw nothing but air.

Deficits, round one: the 1980s

America started its journey to the brink almost thirty years earlier, when the country engaged in its first massive foreign borrowing of the modern era. In 1981, Ronald Reagan signed into law one of the largest tax cuts in American history. Over the next four years, the Economic Recovery Tax Act of 1981 reduced federal tax revenues by nearly half a trillion dollars (almost a trillion dollars in 2010 terms).[1]

Although it was clear that these tax cuts would immediately increase the government budget deficit, the Reagan administration argued that the tax cuts would soon pay for themselves and eliminate the deficits. The tax rate was too high, the argument went, so that reducing it would spur economic growth and the overall tax take enough to balance the budget. The idea was that there is a point at which the tax rate is so high that it actually discourages economic activity and reduces government tax revenues. The result would be a curve, with tax revenue rising up to the point where exorbitant taxes make the economy stagnate, after which point tax revenues start to fall. The curve was called a "Laffer curve" after conservative economist Arthur Laffer, who is alleged to have drawn it on a paper napkin for Dick Cheney, Donald Rumsfeld, and some other Republican politicians in the 1970s. The Laffer curve became a major justification for persisting with aggressive tax cuts even as budget deficits ballooned.

Paul Volcker was chairman of the Federal Reserve at the time. Unlike Laffer and many of the administration's economic policymakers, Volcker was a pragmatic moderate who favored macroeconomic restraint. He had been appointed by President Jimmy Carter in 1979, largely to contend with persistently high inflation. Volcker did in fact concentrate on reducing inflation, with great success, and soon became the country's most prominent advocate of fiscal and monetary prudence. From his vantage point at the Federal Reserve, Volcker watched the erosion of the government's budgetary position after 1981 with dismay. He reflected later,

> The more starry-eyed Reaganauts argued that reducing taxes would provide a kind of magic elixir for the economy that would make the deficits go away, or at least not matter. . . . The more realistic advisers (everything is relative) apparently thought the risk of a ballooning deficit was a reasonable price to pay for passing their radical program; any damage could be repaired later, helped by a novel theory that the way to keep spending down was not by insisting taxes be adequate to pay for it but by scaring the Congress and the American people with deficits.[2]

The "starry-eyed Reaganauts" were wrong, and the Reagan tax cuts drove the federal budget into deficits larger than anyone had imagined possible. Experience demonstrated that while a Laffer curve might exist in theory, taxation in the United States—which after all has one of the lower tax rates in the industrial world—was far below the level at which reducing taxes would increase tax revenue.

Federal budget deficits averaged $200 billion a year during the 1980s, topping out at $290 billion in 1992. For the eight years of Reagan's presidency and the following four of the presidency of George H. W. Bush, the federal deficit averaged nearly 5 percent of GDP. An international financial policeman such as the International Monetary Fund would regard this level as quite dangerous, especially in good times. In fact, when the European Union set an upper bound on deficits for those countries regarded as reliable enough to join the euro zone, the limit was 3 percent of gross domestic product (GDP). By this standard, the United States had drifted well beyond the boundaries of fiscal responsibility.

As the federal government borrowed heavily to cover its deficit, the federal debt went from under $1 trillion in 1981 to over $3 trillion in 1993, well more than doubling on a per-person basis. For the first time since World War II, the government's debt was rising as a share of the economy, from a low of 26 percent of GDP to 49 percent. The deficits also, in the words of David Stockman, who ran the Office of Management and Budget for Reagan, "so impaired, damaged, fatigued, and bloodied" the political system as to turn it into something "like the parliament of a banana republic."[3]

The United States was looking like a banana republic in another way: its government was borrowing much of the money it needed from foreigners. While the United States had been a developing debtor nation in the distant past, those days had appeared long gone. Before the Reagan deficits, when the American government needed to borrow, it borrowed from Americans, by selling bonds to American investors. Economists who worried about the effects of this government borrowing were concerned that it would "crowd out" private borrowing. With more risk-free Treasury bonds to buy, Americans would buy fewer stocks and bonds of private companies. The companies would find it more expensive to borrow—nobody could get lower rates than the government—and this would inhibit private investment. But this is not what happened in the 1980s. For now, when the federal government looked to borrow, foreigners were just as likely to do the lending as Americans. This did not reduce, but in fact increased the amounts of capital available to the United States. Indeed, one of the reasons why the failure of the Laffer curve did not bring down the Reagan economic policies more generally was that the burgeoning budget deficits were covered by borrowing from abroad.

The U.S. government was able to borrow so much from foreigners because of the explosive growth of international finance over the previous decade. After the economic catastrophes of the 1930s, investors and financial institutions everywhere retreated to their home markets. For forty years, lending was almost exclusively domestic. Americans lent to Americans, Germans to Germans, Argentines to Argentines. But eventually memories of the terrible losses of the 1930s faded, new communications and electronic technologies made it cheaper and easier to do business across borders, and banks looked for new ways to make money. Over the course of the 1960s international finance revived gradually, picking up pace over the 1970s. By the early 1980s the gradually rising tide of global finance had become a flood: while the international financial system held barely $100 billion in the early 1970s, by the early 1980s it had surpassed $2 trillion.[4] Finance and investment had become globalized.

Financial globalization allowed the Reagan administration, and the Bush administration that succeeded it, to borrow over $100 billion a year from abroad to finance their budget deficits. European and Japanese investors, eager to buy American investments, snapped up most of the Treasury securities the federal government issued. Foreign lending allowed the deficits to grow without much of a direct effect on the stock of capital available to American firms and households.

Foreign borrowing helped fuel economic growth through the 1980s and allowed Americans to spend more than they earned. However, the country's growing foreign debt was not unmitigated good news. While borrowing from abroad was a boost to American economic activity, eventually the debts would have to be serviced. It was not clear that the price was worth paying, that getting money from foreigners now justified having to pay more to foreigners in the future. Some of the concern was with how the borrowed money was spent, for if it was being squandered, then certainly it was not a good deal.

There were good reasons to worry about where the money from large-scale foreign borrowing was going, and in fact much of the spending ended poorly. As budget deficits stimulated the economy, and capital poured into the country from abroad, waves of money swept through the financial system and into real estate. Housing prices soared, especially in rapidly growing parts of the nation, in the South and Southwest. With oil prices at historic highs in the early 1980s, oil-producing regions such as Texas grew particularly rapidly. Politicians rushed to get out of the way of the booming financial markets: the Reagan administration and Congress passed a flurry of laws reducing regulations on banks and other financial institutions.

But the financial frenzy eventually fizzled, especially as home prices began to decline in the previously booming states. The collapse of oil prices after 1985 hit Texas especially hard, given its dependence on the petroleum industry. The result was a wave of mortgage delinquencies and, eventually, bank failures. The failures were concentrated in the savings and loan industry. These financial institutions, long focused on housing loans, had been substantially deregulated in the previous few years, so that they were making riskier loans than they were used to. Many of the banks' own finances turned out to be shaky if not fraudulent, and the government regulators turned out to be sorely lacking. The result, between 1986 and 1995, was the failure of more than half of the country's savings and loans, over a thousand institutions with total assets of more than half a trillion dollars (about a trillion 2010 dollars).

As in many financial crises of the past, the savings and loan crisis revealed a pattern of shady financial dealing, influence-peddling, corruption, and outright illegality at the intersection of the real estate and financial markets.[5] One of the most spectacular instances concerned the Lincoln Savings and Loan Association of Southern California, whose owner, Charles Keating, contributed over $1 million to the campaigns of five U.S. senators—subsequently called the "Keating Five"—who intervened repeatedly on behalf of what turned out to be a largely fraudulent financial operation that ended up costing taxpayers $2 billion. The disaster even touched the White House: Neil Bush, son of then Vice President George H. W. Bush and a director of the failed Silverado Banking, Savings, and Loan Association in Colorado, was officially implicated in questionable conflicts of interests. Silverado's failure cost taxpayers over $1 billion. It took more than ten years to resolve the savings and loan crisis, at a cost to taxpayers of more than $150 billion.[6]

Although foreign money kept flowing into the United States, by the end of the 1980s the fiscal laxity of the decade was raising alarms of several sorts. The nation's debt, overall and to foreigners, was at disturbing levels and rising rapidly. The savings and loan fiasco showed, as had hundreds of capital flow cycles in the past, that these financial boom times could easily go bust. And while future generations could hardly complain about the burden that continued federal deficits were imposing on them, there were enough Americans worried about this that pressures mounted to rein in the Reagan- and Bush-era deficits. The money the American government borrowed from foreigners still had to be paid back, and the borrowing could not go on forever without causing concern.

From deficits to surpluses: the 1990s

Over the course of the 1990s, Washington struggled to come to grips with the burgeoning mountain of debt. In the 1992 presidential election, Democrat Bill Clinton defeated incumbent George H. W. Bush in large part because of discontent with Bush's management of the economy in the aftermath of a short recession. Bush was also penalized in some quarters for raising taxes to confront the deficit. Nonetheless, the Clinton administration that took office in 1993 made getting the federal deficit under control its principal economic policy goal. The government cut spending and raised taxes, despite the political unpopularity of both sets of measures. The politics of deficit control became particularly complicated after 1994, when the Democratic administration shared power with a Republican House and Senate. Nonetheless, over the course of the 1990s, the Clinton administration and Congress gradually, painfully, worked their way toward deficit reduction.

In 1993 the federal debt stopped rising as a share of GDP, and soon it began declining. Rapid economic growth did some of the work, as did the reduction in military spending once the cold war ended. However, the main story was that for the first time in many years, the government made politically difficult spending cuts and tax increases. As the twentieth century came to a close, the country finally—definitively, it seemed—had put the troubled legacy of deficits and debt behind it. Indeed, the economy was in the midst of a brisk expansion, driven in part by enthusiasm for new high-technology industries.

By 1998, the U.S. government was in an unaccustomed position: its deficits had disappeared. For the first time in forty years, the federal government was covering its expenses. After decades of budget deficits, the government ran a fiscal year 1998 surplus of $69 billion;

by 2000, the surplus was up to $236 billion. At this rate, the Congressional Budget Office estimated, the national debt would be paid off by 2006—for the first time since 1835.[7]

The growing surplus led to new debates, this time about what to do with it—whether to use the money to pay off the public debt, or to make provisions for Medicare and other government programs that were heading toward their own financial straits, or to use it for new spending programs, or to cut taxes. The *Wall Street Journal* editorialized, "it's time to start worrying about the booming federal surplus," and argued vigorously that the surplus justified tax reductions: "A tax cut is the only way to stop the politicians from spending us back into deficits."[8] The newspaper's editorial position was ironic for a conservative icon: it had been forgiving of Republican budget deficits but was now hostile to Democratic surpluses.

Those worried about the surpluses included the man who was by then chairman of the Federal Reserve, Alan Greenspan. Greenspan, appointed by Ronald Reagan in 1987 to succeed Paul Volcker, was a fiscal and monetary conservative like Volcker; but Greenspan was a longtime disciple of militant free-market ideologue Ayn Rand, and had a strong belief in minimal government involvement in the economy.

Greenspan, like the *Wall Street Journal* editorialists, worried that surpluses would put more money than was economically healthy into the hands of the government rather than the private sector. He told Congress that "a major accumulation of private assets by the federal government . . . would make the federal government a significant factor in our nation's capital markets and would risk significant distortion in the allocation of capital."[9] Greenspan's fear was that as the federal government ran bigger and bigger surpluses, it would invest the money in financial markets, which would eventually give the government control over many important investments. It would be better to reduce the surpluses, Greenspan argued, to get capital back into private hands. While more government spending could have done the job, this conflicted with Greenspan's small-government view; he distinctly preferred tax cuts.

Other observers expressed concern that as government debt was paid off, the Federal Reserve would run short of the Treasury securities it uses to guide monetary policy. In order to intervene in money markets to push interest rates up or down, the Fed typically buys and sells Treasury bonds. But if the federal government isn't borrowing, the Treasury does not issue many new bonds, and so the Fed does not have the ample supply of Treasury securities it normally uses to carry out its policies. "The Street doesn't have them to lend anymore," complained one market analyst, as observers speculated that the Fed might be reduced to using World Bank debt or some equally poor substitute to affect the money markets.[10] While the federal surpluses were welcome, they also led to vigorous debate over the appropriate way to deal with them.

Doubling down: from surplus to deficit, 2001–2007

George W. Bush put an end to the surplus debate within months after taking the presidential oath of office in January 2001. The Bush administration arrived in Washington with clear plans to take advantage of the large surpluses in order to reduce taxes, even if this created new deficits. The Republicans now controlled the presidency and both houses of Congress, and they quickly enacted a series of tax cuts. Part of the reasoning was driven by the desire to stimulate an economy that was stagnating in the wake of the collapse of a previous boom in information technologies (IT). The "dot-com bubble" had burst in early 2000, and neither the stock market nor the economy more generally had fully recovered. The administration hoped the tax cuts would help. It redoubled its commitment to deficit spending after the terrorist attacks of September 11, 2001, arguing that stimulative macroeconomic policies were justified in this environment. Tax cuts, budget deficits, and loose monetary policy could keep the country out of recession and get it growing again.

The turnabout in the government's finances was immediate and dramatic. In the spring of 2001 the Treasury estimated that it would repay $57 billion of federal debt in the third quarter of that year (June–September); six months later it announced that it would instead have to *borrow* $51 billion in those three months. As the *Economist* magazine noted, "The $108 billion difference between the two numbers is one of the largest plunges in the government's fiscal position ever recorded."[11]

Deficits during the George W. Bush administration quickly reached and exceeded the Reagan-era deficits. The administration started with a surplus of $236 billion in 2000. The tax cuts shrank federal government revenue by some $400 billion a year, reducing it from 21 percent of GDP in 2000 to 16 percent of GDP in 2004. By then the federal deficit was $413 billion—a dive into red ink of about $650 billion. Over the eight years of the Bush administration, the budget deficit averaged about 3.5 percent of GDP a year, a number matched in peacetime only by the Reagan administration (see figure 1). When George W. Bush took office, the federal government's debt owed to the public had been reduced to $3.3 trillion, 33 percent of GDP; when he left office, it was up to $5.8 trillion, 41 percent of GDP.

In the space of a few years, the Bush administration reversed the accomplishments of a difficult decade of budget-balancing, achieved with often painful spending cuts and tax increases. It bequeathed trillions of dollars in additional debt to future generations. But it also set off a broad-based explosion in borrowing more generally, and especially in borrowing from abroad. For as the federal budget

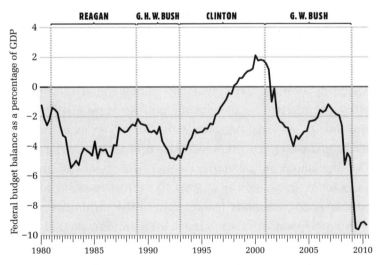

Figure 1. From deficit to surplus and back again: U.S. federal budget balance as a percentage of GDP, 1980–2010. Source: Bureau of Economic Analysis.

went from surplus to deficit, it dipped deeper and deeper into the enormous pool of capital that is the international financial system, borrowing ever greater amounts from abroad. Between 2000 and 2008, foreign holdings of federal government securities—bonds of the Treasury, and of other federal agencies—nearly quadrupled, increasing by $3 trillion.[12] By the end of 2008, the federal government owed foreigners almost $4 trillion; foreigners owned about two-thirds of the government's publicly held debt.[13]

Many in the administration felt that borrowing so much from foreigners was no matter, and perhaps even a good thing. Foreigners, they said, had so much faith in the U.S. government that they were willing to lend to it at very low interest rates. As debt fever spread to the private sector, and American banks and their customers began piling up debts to the rest of the world, the administration and its supporters argued that this simply reflected international confidence in the United States. After all, the American economy was one of the healthiest in the world, rife with profit opportunities; why shouldn't foreigners want some of the action?

Moreover, the fact that much of the foreign money flooding into the United States belonged to foreign governments looking for a place to park their currency reserves was yet another opportunity knocking on America's door. The United States could take advantage of the unique role of the U.S. dollar in world monetary affairs, of its "exorbitant privilege," as French policymakers had called it bitterly in the 1960s. The country could act like a banker to the world, attracting deposits at little or no cost due to its reliability and the centrality of its currency. Why not profit from the good reputation?

Some went so far as to assert that the country's borrowing spree was not the country's responsibility. In March 2005, Ben Bernanke was a member of the Federal Reserve's Board of Governors, the central bank's managing body; he would soon be appointed chair to succeed Alan Greenspan. Bernanke argued that burgeoning foreign borrowing was *not* mainly the result of "economic policies and other economic developments within the United States itself" but rather of extraordinarily plentiful international credit: "a significant increase in the global supply of saving—a global saving glut."[14] In this view, it was first and foremost foreign hunger for American assets that caused the debt buildup.

The availability of easy money from abroad certainly facilitated borrowing, but this argument is one-sided: foreigners hardly forced debts onto unwilling or unwitting Americans. After all, other rich countries with good international standing (Canada, the Netherlands, Germany) did not take advantage of their creditworthiness to turn themselves from creditors into debtors. It takes both lenders and borrowers to launch a borrowing boom. Americans—and especially the U.S. government—made conscious decisions to borrow abroad, starting in the most recent round with the fiscal deficits that burgeoned after the tax cuts of 2001.

And while deficit spending might have been justified for a while after 2001, the immediate justification did not last long. By 2003 the U.S. economy had clearly recovered and then some: Democratic Senator Kent Conrad (N.D.) complained that the economic policies were "a little like a drunk going on a binge. It feels good for a while, but you all know the hangover is coming."[15] Indeed, the country had just gone through twenty years of difficult and contentious struggles over deficit spending, which seemed to have been resolved with the emergence of surpluses in the late 1990s. Yet the deficits continued and even grew. Why, after so much pain and suffering to put the federal government's fiscal house in order, did the Bush administration ramp up the deficits well beyond what was needed to counter the 2001–2002 slowdown?

Political deficits

Like the earlier Reagan-Bush deficits, the George W. Bush deficits were primarily the result of large-scale tax cuts. Some supporters of the 2001 tax cuts resuscitated the Reagan-era argument that they would soon pay for themselves. Laffer-curve logic was often repeated by the younger Bush in justifying his tax cuts and deficits: "The best way to get more revenues [sic] in the Treasury is . . . [to] cut taxes to create more economic growth." President Bush's budget director reiterated that "the tax cuts . . . are not the [budget] problem. They are, and will be, part of the solution."[16] Despite the rhetoric, by 2001 there were virtually no remaining true believers in Laffer-curve and related arguments.[17] Why then the sudden descent back into uncontrolled deficit spending?

It is no coincidence that since 1980, Republican administrations have run substantial deficits, while the intervening Democratic administration was responsible for the only significant deficit reductions (and surpluses). Few Republican thinkers believe the economic argument for deficits, but many are explicit about the political goal involved: to restrain spending by their Democratic opponents. Milton Friedman, the Nobel laureate who was the intellectual godfather of Reagan-era Republican economic policy, stated it pithily: "the only effective way to restrain government spending is by limiting government's explicit tax revenue." The prominent conservative pundit Irving Kristol repeated, in the *Wall Street Journal*, that "tax cuts are a prerequisite for cuts in government spending." And Republican Senator Rick Santorum (Pa.) was pointed in 2003: "I came to the House as a real deficit hawk, but I am no longer a deficit hawk. I'll tell you why. . . . Deficits make it easier to say no."[18]

Republicans cut taxes to create deficits that restrained their opponents. They had little reason to restrain their own deficit spending. The strategy had worked well before. The Reagan and Bush administrations' mountains of debt severely limited the options available to the Democratic president to whom they bequeathed the debt, Bill Clinton. The George W. Bush administration had every reason to believe that its own debt accumulation would similarly constrain any future Democratic administration. As it turned out, it was right, although not precisely as it had planned.[19]

The Bush administration hoped to realize broader electoral benefits from its economic policies, in addition to the purely partisan political advantage. Tax cuts were politically popular, especially with the middle-class Americans who have traditionally been torn between the two parties. They would have been less politically attractive if they had been matched with spending cuts, especially in programs popular with middle-class voters, such as Medicare and Social Security, or with such powerful groups as the farm lobby. Fortunately for the administration, spending cuts were not necessary as long as the spigots of foreign capital remained open.

The rest of the country gets in the foreign-borrowing act

The U.S. government's foreign borrowing was just the start. The tax cuts boosted consumer spending, while the fiscal deficits spurred the economy more generally. Americans began borrowing to supplement their incomes, in expectation of future economic growth. And foreigners were willing to lend to Americans, even—perhaps especially—to American households. Foreigners had been investing in the United States at a reasonable clip during the late 1990s, but that capital inflow was particularly focused on investments in America's high-technology sector.

This was different; now most of the foreign loans that were not going to the government were going directly or indirectly to households, to allow them to increase their consumption of everything from consumer electronics to housing. American banks dipped increasingly into international capital markets in order to lend more and more to American households. They channeled much of this into housing and consumer finance. The impact of this increased borrowing on the American middle class was powerful—and, importantly for the government, electorally appealing.

Foreigners lent trillions to the U.S. government and trillions more to private American citizens and businesses. The most general measure of a country's foreign borrowing is its current account deficit. This measures the difference between what a country earns on its goods, services, investments, and other activities, and what it spends to buy such things from foreigners. Whatever a country does not pay for out of its income, it has to borrow—just like a company or a family. The current account deficit can thus be seen as a simple but reasonably accurate picture of how much capital, in the form of loans and investments, a country is receiving from the rest of the world. Over the course of the 1990s, with great foreign interest in American investments, the current account deficit averaged about $100 billion a year, rising toward the end of the decade as foreigners put money enthusiastically into high-technology investments during the dot-com boom. But this was dwarfed by the capital inflow of 2001–2008, when the current account deficit averaged $600 billion a year. This measure of America's foreign borrowing totaled about $5 trillion between 2001 and 2008. By then, nearly one-third of all the country's home mortgage debt was owed to foreigners as well.[20]

Any way you count, the United States was borrowing massively from abroad after 2000. The flow of capital to the country averaged about 5 percent of GDP over these years—a proportion comparable to the foreign capital inflow to Mexico, Indonesia, Brazil, Thailand, and other developing-country debtors when they are at the peaks of their borrowing. The United States was sucking in capital from the rest of the world, fueling its economic growth with funds borrowed from abroad.

The two deficits, fiscal and current account, pumped up American purchasing power. Increased consumption possibilities spread broadly throughout the economy. As the government spent more, the recipients of its largesse benefited. As the prices of homes rose, so did the ability to borrow against them, leading middle-income homeowners to more spending money. As credit became more readily available, even to those previously excluded from financial markets, more people could live better on borrowed money.

This debt-financed consumption had attractive political features for the party in power. For thirty years, working-class and middle-class Americans had seen their incomes stagnate, while the country's rich and super-rich had gotten ever better off. Over that time, the wealthiest 10 percent of the country's households had seen their share of the nation's income rise from one-third to half—which meant, of course, that the other 90 percent had seen their share drop from two-thirds to one-half of the country's total income.[21] In this context, it was easy to understand why there was so much latent anger over the gap between the rich and the rest. Access to easy credit and easily financed consumption helped take the edge off this resentment.[22] After all, who could worry too much about the distribution of income, or holes in the country's social safety net, when everybody had credit cards?

And as the capital inflow drove up housing prices, homeowners saw their principal assets rise in value. A president who had, after all, lost the popular vote in 2000 had many reasons to encourage the budget deficits, private borrowing, and consumption boom that developed after 2001. Tax cuts and deficit spending allowed the Bush administration to do two politically desirable things: increase its support, and limit the maneuvering room of the Democrats. The current account deficit permitted a politically popular boom in consumption. There were powerful political arguments for spurring, and encouraging, foreign borrowing by the government and by the country generally.

Where the money came from

For every borrower there is a lender; where were America's? Who in the world was so eager to invest in the United States, and why? After all, the phenomenon of so much of the world's capital flowing into the United States was a bit like water running uphill. Capital normally moves from rich countries, where capital is plentiful, to poor countries, where capital is scarce. The scarcity of capital in poor countries means interest rates are much higher there than in rich countries, and these higher rates draw foreign money in. But this was different: much of the money coming into the United States originated in countries whose people were much poorer than Americans, such as China. Why?

Three broad classes of investors financed the Bush boom. The first was the most traditional: wealthy individuals. Europeans, Japanese, and others were eager to add more American assets to their portfolios. The U.S. economy was growing twice as fast as the European average, and three or four times as fast as the economies of Germany and Japan. While the dot-com bubble had burst, taking with it a lot of foreigners' paper profits from the 1990s boom, the U.S. economy was still attractive. It was also safe, not a trivial consideration in the aftermath of a series of recent, catastrophic financial crises. Investors had chased higher returns in Latin America, East Asia, Turkey, and Russia, only to be hammered with huge losses and the two biggest defaults in history, of about $100 billion each, in Russia in 1998 and Argentina in 2001. Low-risk American loans seemed well worth the lower return. So hundreds of billions every year flowed into the United States from private investors in Europe, Japan, and elsewhere.

The second kind of investor in the United States came from oil-exporting countries in the Middle East. Many oil-rich governments establish endowments in which to save the enormous surpluses they accumulate, to be used in difficult times or when their oil runs out. Some of these "sovereign wealth funds," as they are called, tend to be cautious, for they are investing for the very long haul. For them, too, the security of the United States was particularly attractive.

A third kind of investor was another type of government fund, controlled by East Asian countries to hold their huge foreign currency reserves. Foremost among these was China, for less than obvious reasons. It is easy to see why the Middle Eastern countries with vast oil wealth and few people accumulated enormous reserves, but China is a poor country with a huge population whose income per person is barely one-fifteenth that of the United States. China certainly did not have capital to spare; instead, the government accumulates foreign reserves primarily to keep China's exports competitive on world markets.

For thirty years, since China's regime partly opened the country to the world economy, the government has emphasized producing manufactured goods for export to Europe, Japan, and North America. One key to this strategy has been maintaining a weak currency. China accomplishes this by intervening in the foreign exchange market by buying dollars with its own currency, the renminbi. This pushes up the value of the dollar relative to the renminbi, and keeps the Chinese currency weak.

Normally, exporters take the dollars (or other foreign currencies) they earn and exchange them for local currency to spend at home. When they do this, they raise demand for the local currency, which then goes up in value. This makes exports more expensive—but it also increases the real purchasing power and standard of living of the people, who can now buy more with their money. The process, when it takes place, is an example of an automatic economic adjustment: the currency of a country running a trade surplus tends to go up in value, making its goods less attractive and reducing the trade surplus.

But the Chinese government did not want the country's trade surplus to decline. If it let the market rule the supply of and demand for the Chinese currency, the renminbi would have gone way up in price.

This would have made Chinese goods more expensive to foreigners. And the Chinese government had staked its future on constantly increasing the country's manufactured exports. With hundreds of millions of farmers eager to work in the cities, the regime figured it needed to create 10 million new urban jobs a year.[23] In addition, the private and public, foreign and domestic, export-industry factory owners were politically important to the government. All this militated for keeping the Chinese currency weak.

A government can keep its currency weak by "intervening" in the market for its currency, and by "sterilizing" the inflow of money from export earnings. As the exporters sell the dollars they earn for renminbi, the government buys up the dollars; then, instead of selling the dollars to somebody else, it invests them abroad. In the case of China, the government parked hundreds of billions of dollars in export earnings abroad. Then, to prevent the resulting increase in renminbi from driving up inflation, the government offset that effect by forcing banks to lend out less.[24]

China was joined by a tier of rapidly industrializing export powerhouses running from South Korea, Hong Kong, and Taiwan through Singapore and Malaysia. These governments, too, were looking for safe investments—and while not indifferent to profits, they were more interested in security than in the rate of return. So even though their money could easily have earned a higher rate of return at home than in the United States, the governments of these relatively poor countries invested in America.

East Asian exporters and some sovereign wealth funds run by major oil exporters wanted a safe and secure place to park dollars. American government debt was a perfect investment for them. And so, between 2001 and 2008, foreign governments did most of the lending to the U.S. government. By 2008, two-thirds of the $6 trillion in federal debt was owed to foreigners, and three-fourths of that was owed to foreign governments and their agents. China and Japan had each put about a trillion dollars into Treasury and other government securities, and other Asian exporters another half trillion.

While foreign governments invested their money primarily in loans to the U.S. government, other foreign investors wanted to lend to or invest in private enterprise. The government's budget deficit was the catalyst for the borrowing spree, which dipped largely into money from foreign governments. But within a couple of years, foreign private lenders and investors were centrally involved, especially in American private borrowing for the housing market. The United States had become the biggest international borrower in world history.

Foreign money and the national economy

So what was the problem? Foreign borrowing is as old as the world economy, and in the distant past the United States had been a major foreign borrower. The founding fathers themselves were intimately acquainted with the costs and benefits of a country's foreign debt. America's national and state governments borrowed heavily to finance the War for Independence and the first years of the new nation. By 1790 the debt was about $40 million, equal to more than one-fifth of the country's GDP (a comparable share today would be about $3 trillion). About one-fourth of the debt was owed to foreigners. Alexander Hamilton, the nation's first Treasury secretary, insisted that the government repay all these debts, owed by states and the national government alike. Debt repayment, although costly and controversial, signaled the reliability of the new nation to future lenders and made further borrowing possible.

America's thirst for foreign loans lasted over a century and was central to its economic development. The rapidly growing nation borrowed more internationally than any other country during the nineteenth century, and financed much of its growth with foreign money. One of the country's most urgent priorities was developing its transportation infrastructure, and much of this was done with foreign money. Early on, foreigners, mostly British, provided half of the $8 million needed to build the Erie Canal.[25] When Europeans saw its enormous success—the canal paid for itself within a few years after its 1825 opening—they eagerly lent to other American states to finance new canals and set up new banks. By 1841, the states owed about $200 million, about half to foreigners; as a share of GDP, this $100 million was roughly equivalent to a trillion dollars today.

As the nation continued to grow, Americans borrowed from European lenders to build many of the canals, railroads, mines, and mills that allowed the country to develop. Indeed, many of America's principal financial institutions got their start bringing American borrowers and European lenders together. J. P. Morgan's father launched the family's financial business by moving to London and selling American investments to Europeans. August Belmont emigrated to New York as the Rothschilds' American agent and soon became one of the country's leading financiers. While Europe was where the money was, America was where many of the most profitable investment opportunities were. All through the nineteenth century, foreigners lent to and invested heavily in the United States. And the nation's borrowing experience illustrates the fact that there is nothing inherently wrong with foreign loans.

"A national debt, if it is not excessive," Alexander Hamilton said, "will be to us a national blessing."[26] And Hamilton was right: foreign borrowing can make eminently good sense. It makes money available to people who can use it, from people who would rather invest it than use it. If the loans are applied wisely, they make both borrower and lender better off. Corporations borrow to expand production; students borrow to go to college. As long as a corporation makes more from the expansion than it has to pay in interest, both borrower and lender profit. As long as a student's earning power is increased by more than the interest rate, both he and the lender—and perhaps society—are better off.

Foreign borrowing, like any borrowing, makes sense if the borrowed money is used productively. Inasmuch as it increases the ability of the borrower—individual, firm, government, nation—to service its debt, it can pay for itself and pay handsomely for the creditor as well. The borrowed money doesn't have to do this directly; it can increase productivity indirectly. When a state or national government borrows to improve roads, ports, or schools, for example, the hope is that this will speed economic growth indirectly, so the government can repay the loan out of increased taxes on a larger economy.

Bad bets and bad debts

Theory or no theory, anyone with even a passing knowledge of history or finance knows that the history of finance is littered with debt crises, episodes in which a country borrowed heavily but then collapsed into financial distress. The world has seen many credit cycles, both domestically and internationally, with spectacular booms and busts on national and international financial markets.

All through the nineteenth and early twentieth centuries, rapidly developing countries borrowed regularly from European investors, and just as regularly collapsed into debt crises. The Great Depression of the 1930s caused terrible debt problems everywhere, and virtually every debtor nation defaulted on its debts. When international lending revived in the late 1960s, international banks poured hundreds of billions of dollars into developing countries—especially in Latin America. This, too, ended in crisis after the 1982 Mexican default. But once that passed, lending resumed—until a new round of crises hit financial markets, from Mexico in 1994 to East Asia in 1997–1998 to Russia, Turkey, Brazil, and Argentina from 1998 through 2001.

Even American foreign debt had its disasters. The country's first major borrowing boom, in the 1820s and 1830s to build canals and set up banks, ended very badly. For while some of the money went to viable, profitable projects, some also went to questionable public works and weak banks. In 1841 and 1842, in the midst of a deep recession and financial crisis, many states could not pay their debts; some repudiated them. In fact, the State of Mississippi has refused to honor these debts for over 150 years. The creditors have not forgotten: the British Council of the Corporation of Foreign Bondholders regularly reminds the state's governor that "the Council cannot acquiesce in an unjustifiable default merely because it has been successfully maintained for many years." The Council does note, somewhat forlornly, to its members that "the State of Mississippi does not reply to communications from the Council."[27]

But that was then, and the United States today—the State of Mississippi aside—is not Thailand or Turkey. Most investors expected America's foreign debt to be different because the United States did not seem to suffer from the problems that have plagued other troubled debtors. Remember that both debtors and creditors profit if the debts are used productively; and if any country seemed sure to use money productively, it was the United States.

However, there are no sure bets in finance, and there are many reasons why the uses to which borrowed money is put can turn out to be less productive than expected. First, there is uncertainty about the rate of return on an investment. It is not always clear that a particular project will be worthwhile—the price of exportable resources goes down, or mines don't pan out, or factories can't stand up to the competition.

Second, the effective interest rate on the loan can change. This might be because the interest rate is adjustable, as many interest rates are these days. It might also be because the interest rate is fixed while prices decline, which makes the *real* interest rate—the interest rate compared to the rate of inflation—that much higher. In both instances, lenders and borrowers are hit by unexpected events that make the loans less attractive and less likely to be paid.

The crisis of the 1930s drove down the return on debtors' investments, even while it raised the effective interest rates they paid. During the Depression, prices of most goods dropped precipitously; farm and raw materials prices declined especially rapidly. This hit particularly hard at heavily indebted farmers in the United States and developing countries abroad. Meanwhile, the cost of paying off debts stayed the same. Debtors in the millions were unable to service their debts; soon the banks that had made the loans were insolvent, financial systems collapsed, and economies collapsed with them. In the early 1980s, developing-country debtors were particularly hard hit when the Federal Reserve pushed up American interest rates to over 20 percent, because the debtor nations' loans were at variable interest rates and these rates went up accordingly.

Debts can go bad when lenders and borrowers make debt decisions for reasons that have little to do with the financial feasibility of the debt. Bank loans, for example, are often made by individual loan officers who may be long gone from their current position when the loans go bad. If loan officers are promoted on the basis of the quantity of loans they make and not their quality—for it will be years before their quality is known—they have incentives to push

loans even onto borrowers whom they know are not really creditworthy. Borrowers, too, can have reasons to take on debts they
know they cannot service; they can declare bankruptcy, get out from
under their obligations, and still enjoy the debt-financed lifestyle for
a time.

Another source of bad loans is "moral hazard," behavior undertaken in the expectation that if anything goes wrong, somebody will
step in to bail the debtors and creditors out. Banks may make questionable loans, and companies and households may take them, if
they believe that they are implicitly insured by a government concerned about the systemic implications of widespread debt defaults.
Banks regarded as "too big to fail" may take risks which banks that
actually could fail would not.

Some loans made for reasons that are not purely financial involve
"herding," the tendency of lenders to "follow the leader." When some
financial institutions are making money on loans to Latin America,
or to high-tech start-ups, or to young homeowners, there is pressure on other financial institutions to chase the money. It is hard to
explain to shareholders why a bank is passing up profit opportunities that other banks seem to have found. So new lenders rush in,
pushing loans out the door as fast as they can. But just as financiers
can flock together in making new loans, so can they flee en masse at
the first sign of trouble.

The East Asian crisis of 1997–1998 demonstrated how quickly
financial fads and fashions can turn. Early in 1997 East Asia was
the darling of international investors, with investments flowing into
the region at the rate of nearly $100 billion a year. But in the summer
of 1997, asset and housing booms in the region began to go bust.
A financial crisis erupted, and by the end of the year capital was
flooding out of every country in the area. Within two years over
$200 billion had fled. Often investors deserted a country for no other
reason than that the country was within a thousand miles of a financial trouble spot. Herding helped in good times, but the harm it did
undoubtedly outweighed its benefits.

The modern world economy has seen dozens of cycles of debt
and debt crises. Typically the borrowing starts slowly, as the best-
informed or most adventurous lenders move in. Over time new

lenders—less well informed—follow the leaders and add their money. Eventually the lending accelerates into a boom, in which lenders need to lend ever more to keep expanding and borrowers need to borrow just to keep up their debt service payments. Ultimately it all comes to an end, usually with a crash, and lending dries up until enough of the debt is forgiven, or forgotten, or both. There are good reasons to be wary of foreign borrowing, for it can go wrong if used poorly, or if overtaken by unforeseen events, or if poorly motivated.

America was different . . .

To most international lenders, none of these concerns seemed relevant to the United States. The world's most dynamic economy was built on productive investments. Its free-wheeling markets made sure that only profitable investments survived. Its financial transparency guaranteed full information and a minimum of surprises. And its sophisticated regulators knew when and how to manage markets least and best. If there was a safe place to invest, the United States was it.

But not everyone was convinced that America's foreign borrowing was going to end well. Starting soon after 2001, prominent economists Maurice Obstfeld and Ken Rogoff wrote paper after paper arguing that the United States was "on an unsustainable trajectory."[28] Lawrence Summers warned an International Monetary Fund audience in October 2004 that America's position represented "a system that is uneasy in its consequences and unlikely to endure indefinitely as debt accumulates."[29] Menzie Chinn wrote in 2005, "U.S. citizens and foreign governments *do* need to worry about the current account deficit. . . . There is a looming crisis."[30] Nouriel Roubini and Brad Setser argued, in a widely discussed paper late in 2004, that "the tensions created by this system are large, large enough to crack the system in the next three to four years."[31] For those who saw trouble on the horizon, the only real question was whether the path downward would be sudden or gradual—a "hard landing" or a "soft landing," as the debate went.[32] The warnings proliferated as deficits grew and debts accumulated.

But the warnings largely came from academic observers, and very little of the concern wore off on the general public, or the general investing public, or on policymakers. To some extent this was because the data were confusing and contradictory.[33] To some extent it was because academic supporters could also be found with the less alarmed view that this level of American foreign borrowing "is not only sustainable, it is perfectly logical" and that "the system will last."[34] But many observers simply refused to believe that the United States could borrow its way into trouble. And sitting politicians had little reason to question their good fortune in presiding over an economic expansion and consumption boom.

The United States was not alone in the exuberance of its foreign borrowing. A phalanx of rich countries had, like the United States, found that economic success made them popular with investors and lenders. Most prominent among those that joined the United States in the borrowing boom of the early 2000s were the United Kingdom, Ireland, and Spain. They all, like the United States, borrowed heavily from the rest of the world.[35]

The United Kingdom has long had, or fancied it had, a special relationship with the United States, and indeed its borrowing spree was especially similar to that of the United States. Between 2000 and 2007, the United Kingdom averaged a current account deficit of $50 billion a year, borrowing an average of 2.4 percent of GDP from the rest of the world every year. American foreign borrowing was about double that as a share of GDP, but British borrowing was substantial. Similarly, while the U.S. government was averaging deficits of 3.6 percent of GDP between 2002 and 2007, the British government was close behind at 2.8 percent of GDP. Both countries had deregulated their financial systems in major ways over the course of the previous twenty years, and London and New York were the two global leaders of financial innovation and experimentation.

Across the Irish Sea, an even more exaggerated version of the American drama was being acted out. After digging itself out of a large debt crisis in the early 1980s, Ireland became one of the fastest-growing economies in the world. By 2005, the Celtic Tiger was one of the world's richest nations, far ahead of its former colonial master, Britain. This prosperity was built on a highly educated, English-speaking workforce, on productive high-technology manufacturing, on membership in the European Union, and eventually on adoption of the euro. On the basis of this extraordinary economic success— after all, Ireland had been a poor country for most of its history—the country began, like the United States and the United Kingdom, to suck in capital from the rest of the world.

And Ireland did borrow. The current account deficit averaged about $4 billion a year between 2000 and 2007, equivalent to a thousand dollars per inhabitant per year, or 2 percent of GDP. But this is only part of the story. Over the course of the 1990s, Ireland turned itself into an international banking center to rival Switzerland and Luxembourg. Hundreds of financial institutions set up shop in Dublin, and Irish banks expanded aggressively abroad. As Ireland flourished as a financial center, the four big Irish banks borrowed more and more internationally to lend to the booming local economy. In 2003, Irish banks owed about $12 billion to the rest of the world, but by 2007 they owed $130 billion, equal to nearly two-thirds of the country's GDP, or about $100,000 for every household in Ireland.[36]

Spain, too, joined the ranks of the world's borrowing nations in the new millennium. Spaniards borrowed about $1 trillion abroad after 2000, and the pace of borrowing quickened as time went on: in 2007 the current account deficit was over 10 percent of GDP, a staggering figure. The booming economy drew in capital, and also drew in people, half a million immigrants a year.

Spain and Ireland had one important difference from the United States and the United Kingdom, and one important similarity to each other: the euro. Foreign lenders had good reasons to be wary of Spain and Ireland, which had gone through financial difficulties many times over previous decades (and centuries, in the case of Spain). But membership in the euro zone gave the two countries a new attractiveness. They were growing extremely rapidly, in part because the euro facilitated their trade and investment ties with the rest of Europe. And foreign lenders had good reason to believe that the Spanish and Irish economies were now protected by the broader euro umbrella. These more peripheral countries were now so closely linked to such core euro member states as Germany, France, and the

Netherlands that the new European Central Bank, and its member governments, would have to ensure that other member governments could pay their debts. Finally, with price stability enshrined in the European Central Bank's mandate, anxieties about inflation in either country disappeared.

In the event, American foreign borrowing turned out not to be that different from other countries' foreign borrowing. Beneath all the complexities of modern financial innovation and regulation (and its absence), the American experience was like that of borrowing nations past and present. Foreign debts made the good times better; they made the bad times worse. There have been tidal waves of international capital flows to and from borrowing nations for centuries. But there has rarely been a capital flow cycle quite so enormous in its upswing as the American borrowing boom of 2001–2007, and there has rarely been a crash quite so dramatic or so global as the American collapse of 2008.

No one factor on its own could have caused a crisis of this magnitude. The capital inflow might have been managed more effectively; the borrowed funds could have been used more productively; financiers may have had reasons to behave more prudently; regulators should have recognized the implications of the risks they were allowing banks to take. In what follows, we trace how all these forces came together to bring down the American and international financial system. We start by delving into the origins and effects of America's foreign borrowing binge.

Borrowing, Boom, and Bust:
The Capital Flow Cycle

In the early 1990s, Thailand went through a tremendous construction boom. As tens of billions of dollars flooded into the country, lending to real estate firms soared. Builders doubled the amount of office space in Bangkok in just over three years. Cranes lined the skyline, and new suburban developments sprouted all over town. But by early 1997, the building boom was in trouble. In February, one banker reported bluntly on the state of the real estate market: "There are no transactions." One-fifth of all the housing units built in the previous five years was empty. One-fourth of all the office space in Bangkok was vacant. Stock prices of real estate companies were down nearly 95 percent. Thai banks found that nearly half of all the loans on their books were bad. Within a few months, Thailand crashed into the gravest financial crisis in its history.[1]

And so it went in the United States. In 2004, the suburbs of Las Vegas and South Florida were booming with building activity. New developments were mapped out and built, prices were soaring, banks were eager to lend, people were impatient to buy. By 2010, a drive through these suburbs was surreal: neighborhood after neighborhood was empty. Either the new housing had never been occupied, or the formerly enthusiastic new owners had defaulted, been foreclosed on, and moved out. The boom had gone bust, and it dragged the rest of the American economy—and the world economy—with it.

How did America's foreign borrowing spree go so awry? What made our debt-financed boom turn out as badly as those of Thailand, Mexico, Russia, Argentina, and dozens of other countries in the past? What was it about the $5 trillion Americans borrowed from foreigners between 2001 and 2007, or the way they borrowed it, or the way they spent it, that proved so unsound?

Federal deficits and Fed policy

America's latest bout of foreign borrowing began in 2001 with the federal government suddenly shifting from having a massive surplus to accumulating a massive deficit. As the government dipped into international financial markets, eventually borrowing a couple of trillion dollars, the deficit spending had three broad effects. First, in cutting taxes by hundreds of billions of dollars a year—an estimated $2 trillion over a decade—the government gave taxpayers that much more money to spend. Second, borrowing by the federal government sustained, even increased, government spending during the 2001 economic slowdown. This put money into Americans' hands to help stimulate the economy. Third, the deficit allowed the government to increase military spending in the aftermath of the September 11, 2001, attacks, especially after the invasions of Afghanistan and Iraq. Thus, federal foreign borrowing increased both public and private spending.

The Federal Reserve's policy of driving interest rates lower than they had been in decades was the next major spur to American borrowing. The Fed's principal tool of influence on the economy is its benchmark interest rate, the Federal Funds rate, which is what banks charge each other for money. Most people can't get the Federal Funds rate, but when banks pay less, or more, for their money, they adjust the interest rates they charge consumers and businesses accordingly. So the Fed's interest rate policy has a profound impact on the economy through its effect on borrowing and lending. If the economy is in the doldrums, the central bank can stimulate it by reducing interest rates and encouraging borrowing, which increases spending. If the economy is "overheating," risking inflation, the Fed can restrain it by raising interest rates and discouraging borrowing, which reduces spending.

The most widely accepted guideline for interest rate policy is one devised by John Taylor, a distinguished Stanford University macro-economist. In 1993 Taylor proposed a relatively simple rule that central banks can follow to achieve price stability, low unemployment, and policy credibility. This "Taylor rule" adjusts the interest rate in line with changes in the inflation rate and the rate of economic growth, and is generally seen as defining an appropriate target for a reasonable monetary policy. A monetary policy that is too "tight"—with interest rates too high—could slow economic growth, while a monetary policy that is too "loose"—with interest rates too low—could lead to excessive borrowing and inflation. Over the course of the 1990s, monetary policy had generally been restrained and in line with the Taylor rule. For example, from 1995 to 2000, the Fed kept the Federal Funds rate at about 3 percent above the rate of inflation: inflation averaged 2.5 percent a year, while the Federal Funds rate averaged 5.5 percent. When George W. Bush was elected president, in November 2000, the rate was at 6.5 percent with inflation at about 3.4 percent.

Alan Greenspan was in charge of the nation's monetary policy at the time. After his initial appointment as chairman of the Federal Reserve by Ronald Reagan in 1987, he was reappointed by George H. W. Bush in 1991, reappointed again by Bill Clinton in 1996, and again in 2000. Greenspan, a lifelong Republican, had close ties, as we mentioned earlier, to Ayn Rand's "Objectivist" movement, which champions a radical individualist view of society. Rand herself argued, in a 1964 book called *The Virtue of Selfishness*, for "full, pure, uncontrolled, unregulated laissez-faire capitalism."[2] Nonetheless, Greenspan served under President Clinton and seemed committed to monetary moderation and fiscal prudence. It came as a surprise to many when, despite his traditional fiscal conservatism, Greenspan supported George W. Bush's 2001 tax cuts and the large deficits they caused.

Soon after the 2001 Bush tax cuts went into effect, Greenspan's Fed began bringing interest rates down precipitously. By September 2001 the benchmark rate was about 3 percent; in December it went below 2 percent and kept falling. The central bank justified the policy because growth was slow in the aftermath of problems in the high-technology sector and after the terrorist attacks of September 11, 2001. This seemed reasonable. But the Fed kept pushing interest rates down.

Long after the economy began growing again, through most of 2003 and 2004, the Federal Funds rate stayed around 1 percent— the lowest rate in more than forty years. Greenspan raised the rate above 2 percent only in December 2004. Meanwhile, inflation was substantially higher than the prevailing interest rate. From 2002 through 2004, while the Federal Funds rate averaged 1.4 percent, the Consumer Price Index averaged 2.5 percent growth, so that the central bank's main interest rate was well *below* the rate of inflation. When an economy has "negative real interest rates"—that is, interest rates less than the inflation rate—lenders are effectively giving money away, and people have tremendous incentives to borrow.

The Federal Reserve was breaking the Taylor rule: a Taylor-rule Federal Funds rate would have averaged almost 3 to 4 percent between 2002 and 2004, rather than the barely 1.4 percent that was in place.[3] This was an extraordinary episode in American monetary policy, during which the central bank purposely held interest rates below the rate of inflation for several years. Although it is always hard to know what goes on at the Fed, some cynics felt that Greenspan was trying to make sure that President George W. Bush would reappoint him when Greenspan's term ended in 2004. Certainly Greenspan's unexpected support for large-scale deficit spending, coupled with the uncharacteristically lax monetary policy, suggested an attempt to curry favor with the administration. In the event, Bush renominated Greenspan for an unprecedented fifth term as Fed chair in May 2004. And the low interest rates of 2002–2004 certainly helped secure the reelection of President Bush, who, after all, had lost the popular vote in 2000. As if to confirm the suspicions of the cynics, interest rates began rising again after the 2004 presidential election.

With interest rates at historic lows, and foreigners still eager to lend, Americans themselves borrowed in ever larger amounts. The total indebtedness of Americans—to each other and to foreigners—had been generally stable or slowly rising during the 1990s, equaling about 2.6 times the country's GDP by 2000. Between then and 2007, the country's total debt soared by $22 trillion, rising to over 3.4 times output. In those seven years, the debt of the average American rocketed from $93,000 to $158,000.[4] While this was spurred by the burgeoning gross debt of the federal government—which went from $5.6 trillion to $9 trillion in those years,[5] from about $20,000 per person to about $30,000 per person—private borrowing was galloping ahead as well. And while much of the financial action involved Americans lending to Americans, the scale of the borrowing was only made possible by the inflow from abroad.

Foreigners supplied much of the money that was allowing Americans to live beyond their means. Lending to the U.S. government was direct: foreigners simply bought Treasury securities. But foreign lending to individual Americans was largely indirect, intermediated through a complex financial system and a dizzying array of complicated financial instruments. In some cases, American banks borrowed from foreign banks or investors, using the additional funds to relend to American households. In other cases, American loans were packaged into bonds and other securities that were then sold to investors. In this latter process, called "securitization," an American investment bank might bundle together thousands of mortgages or credit card debts to underwrite a bond issue to be sold to investors, including those abroad. The bonds in question would compensate the investors out of the interest payments these thousands of homeowners and credit card holders made on their debts. The bond was a good deal for the foreign lenders, as it allowed them to diversify their holdings among many mortgages and credit cards, and gave them access to loans they regarded as high earning and safe. The ultimate borrowers, the homeowners and credit card holders, had no idea that much of the money they were borrowing eventually came from Germany, Kuwait, and China, but that was the reality.

Who was doing all this borrowing? The United States had been running a current account deficit—that is, borrowing from abroad—

before 2000, but the proportions were smaller and the purposes to which the money was put were quite different. In the several years before 2000, the principal foreign debtors in the United States were private corporations and households, each of which was borrowing from abroad an amount equivalent to about 1 percent of GDP—the government was in surplus, and so it was not borrowing. But after 2000 there were two crucial changes. First, the total amounts borrowed skyrocketed, so that by 2003–2007 they were triple and quadruple what they had been ten years earlier. Second, the borrowers changed dramatically. Now the government was the largest single user of borrowed money. And as interest rates plummeted and private individuals were drawn into the financial frenzy, households doubled and tripled their foreign borrowing. Meanwhile, corporations actually went into surplus, financing their activities out of profits.[6]

The fact that America's foreign borrowing was going exclusively to the government and to private households was a warning signal. International financial institutions, such as the International Monetary Fund, typically advise developing countries that borrowed funds should go into investments that raise the nation's capacity to produce, and so to pay off its debts. Government budget deficits and residential housing are unlikely to be productive; if the IMF saw a developing country using foreign debt to fund budget deficits and housing construction, it would raise red flags. And in fact the head of the Bank for International Settlements, the central bankers' central bank, did voice his concern early in 2006. Noting that the money America borrowed was going to federal deficits and residential investment, he observed, with typical understatement, "This combination does not raise US productive capacity." It meant, he said, that "major macroeconomic risks are at high levels and rising" and warned of "potential abrupt adverse changes in the financial environment."[7] But almost nobody was listening. Living on borrowed time was too appealing.

On borrowed funds

American households borrowed ever more, even surpassing the government in foreign borrowing in 2005. Americans borrowed to buy

cars and computers, racking up credit card debt to go on vacation
and go out to dinner. Between 2000 and 2007, consumer credit rose
by a trillion dollars, from $1.5 to $2.5 trillion.[8] And Americans borrowed to buy houses—especially to buy houses. As interest rates
declined, tens of millions of Americans took advantage to refinance
their mortgages or to buy new homes.

Household borrowing drove a remarkable growth in the housing market and a striking rise in housing prices. The average price
of American homes, as measured by the widely used Case-Shiller
index, was generally stable over the 1990s, but it skyrocketed after
2000 (see figure 2). Mortgage lending soared from about $750 billion
in 2000 to over $2 trillion a year between 2002 and 2006. As more
loans were written, average housing prices doubled in the country's
major cities between 2001 and 2006—and rose by much more in
some places. Merrill Lynch estimated that half of all new private-
sector jobs created after 2001 were related to housing, and as one
observer noted, "For all intents and purposes, real estate *was* the
economy."[9]

The housing boom was particularly pronounced in the South and
Southwest. The population there was growing three times as fast

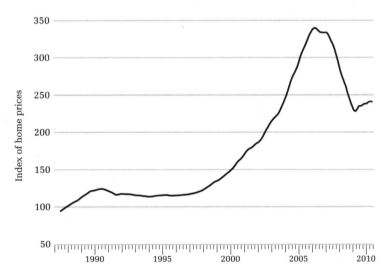

Figure 2. The housing boom. Case-Shiller home price index for ten
major cities, seasonally adjusted, 1987–2010. 1987 = 100. Source:
Standard & Poor's.

as in the rest of the country, by two million people a year. In South Florida, people camped out overnight to be at the head of a line of thousands to buy into a new development in Wellington, near Palm Beach. Over three thousand people showed up for the development's grand opening, and the developers sold $35 million worth of homes in one weekend. A few miles south, in Weston, Florida, more than eight hundred hopeful buyers paid a thousand dollars apiece just to enter a lottery for a chance to buy one of 222 new townhouses; every last one sold within seven hours.[10] Scenes like these were repeated in Phoenix and San Diego, Tampa and San Antonio. And home prices skyrocketed accordingly: between 2000 and 2006, the median price of a home in Miami went from $150,000 to over $400,000; in Las Vegas, from $135,000 to $310,000.[1]

Despite the soaring prices, more Americans than ever found it easy, and cheap, to borrow to buy a home. The expansion of home ownership swelled the ranks of the homeowners, and the gain in housing wealth made existing homeowners better off. Making it easier for American families to buy their own home—or at least to live in a home whose mortgage was in their name—has been the goal of many American politicians. The appeal of this to politicians was reminiscent of a previous era in British politics. In the 1980s, Margaret Thatcher's government sold off many of the country's public housing units to their residents. Among other things, this created a large new group of homeowners who were more likely to vote for Thatcher's Conservative Party.[12]

The George W. Bush administration crafted its own variant of the Thatcher policy, called the "ownership society." While there had been a push to expand home ownership under the Clinton administration, particularly in historically disadvantaged neighborhoods, the Bush administration's new efforts were much broader.[13] It championed private ownership in general and home ownership in particular. As President Bush told the National Association of Home Builders in 2004, "Home ownership gives people a sense of pride and independence and confidence for the future. . . . [W]e're creating . . . an ownership society in this country, where more Americans than ever will be able to open up their door where they live and say, welcome to my house, welcome to my piece of property." The president was greeted with enthusiastic chants of "Four more years! Four more years!" from the home builders in attendance.[14]

Rising home prices and easy money drove a broader increase in other consumer spending. Those who already owned their own homes could take advantage of ready credit and the higher value of their homes to refinance their mortgages at lower payments and take cash out. The more housing prices rose and the lower interest rates got, the more existing homeowners could borrow against their homes. This in turn would allow them to spend more—transforming a home, as the saying went, into an ATM. By one estimate, for every thousand-dollar increase in a home's value, a family who would otherwise have had trouble borrowing could increase consumption spending by $110. As the national median house price shot from under $140,000 in 2000 to nearly $250,000 in 2006, the borrowing and housing booms allowed a median cash-strapped family to spend $12,000 more than otherwise—enough to buy a car, or take several vacations, or to remodel that now more valuable home.[15]

Banks and other financial institutions profited handsomely from the borrowing boom. Whether they brought foreign lenders together with domestic borrowers, or originated mortgages and consumer loans, or innovated intricate financial instruments, there was much more work to be done and much more money to be made. Increased financial activity inflated the size of the financial sector, which added over a million jobs and increased its share of the country's GDP from 7.0 to 8.3 percent in the ten years leading up to 2007. The earnings of people in finance—especially at and near the top— soared along with housing and stock prices. Whereas the salaries of engineers and financiers with postgraduate degrees were roughly equivalent until the middle 1990s, by 2006 financiers were making one-third more than engineers. By then, one careful study estimated, financiers were overpaid by about 40 percent. The financial services sector was much bigger than it needed to be; every year, people in finance were earning at least $100 billion more than was economically justified.[16]

Foreign debt–fed spending by Americans sucked in imports, more than doubling the country's trade deficit from 2001 to 2006. By then, Americans were buying abroad over $750 billion more than they were selling abroad. The big story here was a surge in imports, from $1.4 trillion in 2001 to $2.4 trillion in 2007.

Swelling imports were great for consumers, who found stores filled with inexpensive goods from abroad, but they devastated American manufacturing, especially producers of labor-intensive goods who competed most directly with imports. Between 2000 and 2007, the country lost almost three and a half million manufacturing jobs, nearly one-sixth of the total. Computer and electronics manufacturers shed a quarter of a million jobs. Garment and textile producers were particularly hard hit, losing over 300,000 jobs, more than one-third of the total. Burlington Industries of North Carolina, once the world's largest textile producer with over forty plants around the world, went bankrupt, and by early 2005, the sector was losing a factory a week, along with 1500 jobs.[17]

A predictable bubble

The massive inflow of funds, the bloated financial sector, the surging imports, the orgy of consumption, the bubble in the housing market: all this was eerily familiar to anyone who had lived through, or observed, earlier debt crises. America was looking like any one of dozens of developing countries that had borrowed themselves into the poorhouse over the previous forty years.

Latin Americans might recall their borrowing in the 1970s and early 1980s, before their debt crisis began in 1982. Governments spent far more than they took in, and used foreign funds to fill the gap between spending and taxes; the Argentine and Mexican governments borrowed about half of what they needed from foreigners. The banking systems, which handled much of the capital inflow, swelled; those of Chile and Argentina doubled and tripled their share of the economy in a few short years. Housing prices soared; they increased by nearly tenfold in Chile over a little more than a decade. Stock markets boomed. And then it all came crashing down after August 1982, driving Latin America into a lost decade of depression, hyperinflation, and slow growth.[18]

The same pattern was repeated fifteen years later in East Asia. Hundreds of billions of dollars flooded into the region's rapidly growing economies. By 1995, countries like Thailand and Malaysia were borrowing amounts equal to more than 8 percent of GDP every year, using foreign money to finance one-fifth and more of their total investment. Thai banks tripled their real estate lending between 1990 and 1995, as the property market boomed. All over the region there were spectacular increases in housing prices, in stock market indices, and in the size of banking sectors. But in 1997 it all collapsed. By the time it stopped falling, the Thai stock market was down almost 80 percent from its pre-1997 peak.[19] This roller coaster ride was repeated in the middle and late 1990s in Russia. And at roughly the same time in Turkey. And in Mexico again in the early 1990s. And with an extraordinary vengeance in Argentina in the 1990s, leading up to a spectacular implosion in 2001.

America's housing and financial booms, and its gaping trade deficit, followed a well-worn script, one acted out by dozens of countries sliding down the slippery slope of this capital flow cycle. Large-scale foreign borrowing caused all of these domestic pathologies.

Anatomy of a boom

When a country's government, people, and firms borrow abroad, capital flows into the country, which increases the ability of local residents to buy goods and services. Some of what they buy are hard goods, such as cars and consumer electronics. In the American borrowing boom, the connection was often direct, as easy money helped consumers finance purchases of these big-ticket items.

More spending on computers, clothing, furniture, and other things that can be traded easily across borders increased imports by 50 percent between 2001 and 2005. Meanwhile, exports grew very slowly, so that by 2005 the trade deficit was well over $700 billion. The average American family of four was buying $30,000 worth of goods and services from abroad every year, while the country was only selling $20,000 worth abroad per family. The difference was paid with borrowed money.

Borrowers also spend borrowed money on things that can't easily be traded internationally: housing, financial services, medical care, education, personal services. Increased demand for these goods and services simply drives up their prices. Their supply also increases, but not quickly enough to meet all of the increased demand—it takes a long time for the supply of single-family homes or doctors to grow. Just as foreign borrowing causes a surge in imports, it causes a surge in the relative prices of housing, restaurant food, medical care, and other services.

Those living through a borrowing boom see these developments in a number of ways. People have more money to spend, and things from abroad seem cheaper, for example, imports and vacations. At the same time, goods and services that do not enter world trade get more expensive. This can be a boon to some, such as home-owners whose properties rise in value. But it can also lead to soaring prices for health care, education, and transportation. Higher prices for these services also drive up the price of manufacturing at home, again making it hard for local producers to compete with foreigners.

Economists capture this process by dividing everything in an economy into two types of goods and services. One type of good can easily be traded across borders: clothing, steel, wheat, cars. Because these goods are traded, their prices cannot vary much from country to country (leaving aside trade barriers and transportation costs). The value of these "tradables" tends toward an international price, times the exchange rate. The Mexican price of steel is simply its world price times whatever the peso is worth today.

A second kind of good or service has to be consumed where it is produced; it cannot be traded at all or easily. These "nontradables" are mostly services, such as haircuts and taxi rides. The prices of nontradable services can vary widely, since there is little international competition, for instance, in haircuts. Travelers know this intuitively: cars cost pretty much the same everywhere, while haircuts and taxi rides can be much cheaper in some (especially poor) countries than in others. The main nontradable is housing, and shelter is a crucial part of every household's budget—in America, it accounts for about a third of consumer spending.

A borrowing boom raises the prices of nontradables, such as financial services, insurance, and real estate. This is good for those who work in these industries, and for people who own nontradables, such as housing. But the surge in imports, and the rise in other prices, is bad for producers of tradables, such as manufactured goods and agricultural products.

This is precisely what was happening to the United States after 2001. Nontradables sectors boomed, while tradables sectors lagged. Between 2000 and 2007, prices of services rose by 25 percent, while prices of durable consumer products declined by 13 percent. The import surge and the rise in nontradables prices savaged the manufacturing and agriculture sectors, which together lost nearly four million jobs. But finance, insurance, and real estate were growing at more than three times the pace of manufacturing, adding over a million jobs in five years.[20]

Sometimes foreign borrowing drives the country's currency up directly. Foreigners lend to Americans by buying American bonds, mortgages, and other securities. To do so they also have to buy dollars, so the dollar's value rises. The stronger currency makes imports cheaper in domestic currency, and locally produced goods more expensive to foreigners. Local residents buy more imported goods, local producers sell less of what they make, the trade deficit grows, and national producers of traded goods complain. Back in the early and middle 1980s, when the Reagan administration's budget and current account deficits led to a rise in the dollar's value by more than 50 percent, imports soared and exports collapsed, millions of manufacturing jobs were lost, and demands for protection from foreign goods skyrocketed.

Economists capture both of these effects—on the currency, and on the relative prices of tradables and nontradables—with the concept of the "real exchange rate." This takes into account both the "nominal" exchange rate—a currency's stated value in terms of another currency—and the relationship between prices at home and abroad. A currency's real exchange rate can rise, or appreciate, in one of two ways. First, prices can stay the same while the currency rises in nominal value. If the dollar goes up from 1.0 to 1.2 euro while American and European prices stay the same, Americans can buy 20 percent more with their dollars in Europe. The second way is for the currency to stay the same while American prices and wages rise by 20 percent. Then, again, Americans can buy 20 percent more in Europe with their dollars because European prices are now that much lower than American prices.

The American trajectory after 2001 was in line with the typical experience of a country embarked on a major foreign borrowing binge, with some variations. In developing countries, borrowing booms are often accompanied by a spike in the ostentatious consumption of luxury cars, foreign liquor and perfume, and expensive electronics by affluent consumers who take advantage of the easy money to buy imports they couldn't normally afford—or to travel abroad. When Latin America is in the expansion phase of one of its debt cycles, the airplanes to Miami and Los Angeles are crowded with Latin American tourists. On the way back to Buenos Aires or São Paulo, the Argentines and Brazilians cram the baggage holds and overheads full of American televisions and computers that now seem ridiculously cheap to them. Americans didn't need to travel any farther than the nearest Wal-Mart to fill their homes with foreign goods. Meanwhile, as borrowing increases the amount of money people have to spend, they use some of this increased purchasing power to buy financial assets and real estate. So stock prices and housing prices rise dramatically.

The United States was right on track.

The Bush boom bubbles

By 2005, the joint effects of America's foreign borrowing and loose monetary policy were everywhere. The capital inflow swelled imports and pumped up demand for nontraded goods and services. Nontradables sectors, especially financial services, insurance, and real estate, expanded rapidly. Low interest rates allowed consumers to buy more goods on credit, and more households to buy a home. Those who already owned their home found that rising housing prices and low interest rates made it irresistible to borrow and consume even more. The same was true about the spectacular rise in the stock market and in financial investments more generally: as households saw their retirement and other savings rise, they had every reason to consume more and save less.

Rising home prices, falling interest rates, and soaring consumption fed on each other. Families whose homes were more valuable saw themselves as wealthier, and greater wealth justified more spending. There was nothing fictitious about this new-found wealth, for the family could use it to borrow and spend even more. Millions of Americans found that they could make use of a financial arrangement that was becoming commonplace, a home equity line of credit, to borrow against their now more valuable home. The new money could then be spent on home improvements, new appliances, or a vacation. As one Las Vegas resident told his wife in 2005, "Honey, I told you we'd live in a million-dollar house some day. . . . I just never thought it would be this one."[21]

But by 2005 the housing boom seemed clearly to have turned into a bubble.[22] Housing prices were rising virtually everywhere, and in some areas they had reached levels that were almost certainly unsustainable. For example, by early 2006 the median home price in San Diego was $500,000. But a standard index of affordability, which calculates how many households could afford the basic cost of living in their homes, reveals that barely one San Diego household in twenty could afford to live in the region's median home.[23]

As early as September 2003, the country's most prominent real estate economists, Karl Case and Robert Shiller, were warning that the country might be in a housing bubble. At that point their conclusion was only guardedly pessimistic.[24] By the middle of 2005, Shiller was more definite, arguing in a prominent *New York Times* article that "the housing craze is another bubble destined to end badly."[25]

It seemed clear to many that the United States was waltzing down a path well worn by other countries that had ended up in serious crises. The economic expansion had become a boom, and the boom had created a bubble in the housing and financial markets. And, in fact, many economists and other observers started sounding alarm bells about the panoply of potential problems, of which the housing bubble was just one. At least as worrying were the fiscal deficit, the current account deficit, the burgeoning foreign debt, the consumption boom, and the swollen financial markets.

Many of the cautionary notes came from impeccable sources. Raghuram Rajan took leave from teaching finance at the University of Chicago's business school to serve as chief economist of the IMF for much of the boom period, from 2003 until 2007. In August 2005, at an annual gathering at Jackson Hole, Wyoming, he was explicit about the risks inherent in financial globalization. While the rise of finance had brought undoubted benefits, he argued, "the financial risks that are being created by the system are indeed greater" than in the past. He pointed out that while free-wheeling and internationally linked financial markets can draw economies up together, they can also pull them down together, which could conceivably cause "a catastrophic meltdown."[26]

New York University economist Nouriel Roubini warned so often, and so alarmingly, of trouble to come that journalists dubbed him "Dr. Doom." Late in 2006, he told an audience that the United States faced "a once-in-a-lifetime housing bust, an oil shock, sharply declining consumer confidence and, ultimately, a deep recession . . . homeowners defaulting on mortgages, trillions of dollars of mortgage-backed securities unraveling worldwide and the global financial system shuddering to a halt." Dr. Doom went on to point out that "these developments . . . could cripple or destroy hedge funds, investment banks and other major financial institutions like Fannie Mae and Freddie Mac."[27]

As housing prices began to decline late in 2006, warnings of impending doom proliferated. Early in 2008, with housing markets already in trouble but long before the scale of the crisis was clear, economists Ken Rogoff and Carmen Reinhart were arguing that the United States showed clear signs of a classic capital flow cycle leading to a financial crisis. Rogoff knows crises: like Rajan, he served as chief economist of the IMF (from 2001 to 2003). One of the Reinhart-Rogoff papers asked, "Is the 2007 U.S. sub-prime financial crisis so different?" and gave a resounding "no" answer. Rogoff and Reinhart pointed out that "the run-up in U.S. equity and housing prices," often regarded as bellwethers of an impending collapse, indeed "closely tracks the average of the previous eighteen post World War II banking crises in industrial countries."[28]

But for every Cassandra warning of impending trouble, there was an Apollo to neutralize the dire predictions. Some were blinded by their own economic or political interests, others by partisanship or ideology.

Special interests and special pleading

Why did the Bush administration ignore all the warnings, and all the signs that the economy was in an unsustainable bubble? To be sure, no government likes to put the brakes on a hard-driving economy. One of the most famous phrases in all of economic policymaking is that of William McChesney Martin Jr., chairman of the Fed from 1951 to 1970, who described the job of a central banker as being "to take away the punch bowl just as the party gets going."

In the case of the roaring Bush boom and bubble, some powerful interests had a major stake in keeping financial and housing markets rising. The lending boom and deregulation swelled the financial system like never before, in ways closely linked to housing markets. American bankers had written millions of mortgages whose viability was predicated on continually rising housing prices. If housing prices leveled off, or even fell, many of these mortgages would go bad and drag the creditors with them.

political economy of housing itself was closely related: much of the increased lending and spending went into housing, so that home builders and related industries made spectacular profits, as did those in the real estate business. The construction industry, including home builders, is well organized and well represented in Washington. The industry is historically close to the Republican Party—three-fourths of its federal political action committee (PAC) contributions between 2000 and 2006 went to the Republicans.[29] When, in 2005, a presidential panel recommended reducing subsidies for home builders and homeowners, the housing lobby swung into action and effectively killed any talk of reform.[30] A little later, the National Association of Home Builders, one of the country's principal business political donors, threatened to halt all of its congressional contributions in response to a perceived lack of congressional willingness to support the lobby's proposals, a move that led one citizen's watchdog to remark, "What the home builders have done is expose the underbelly of the connection between money and politics."[31]

Realtors, too, are highly political—the National Association of Realtors is typically the largest single PAC contributor to national candidates—and leans strongly toward Republicans. Even Freddie Mac and Fannie Mae—two government-sponsored agencies that support the housing market by buying up mortgages from banks that originate them—made massive political contributions, some $170 million during the boom decade.[32] Academic studies have confirmed the general impression that mortgage lending became increasingly politicized as the boom progressed. One such analysis found that campaign contributions and lobbying by the mortgage industry, along with the importance of real or potential subprime mortgage borrowers in a congressman's district, had a powerful impact on congressional voting behavior toward the housing boom, and that this impact gained strength as the boom went on.[33]

The administration had to take electoral considerations into account too. Many of the states benefiting most directly from the building boom were politically important, either because of their size or because they were hotly contested between the parties: Florida, Colorado, Arizona, Nevada.

And as the boom continued, it was not just that influential interest groups had come to rely on the formula established after 2001; it was that any interruption in the process was a threat. Many of the newly written mortgages had been made to borrowers who were barely able—if able at all—to service their debts, in the expectation that rising housing prices would make the properties worth more, hence more creditworthy. This bet would pay off, however, only if housing prices continued to rise. And much of the growth of the financial system had been built on the edifice of new housing-finance instruments that depended on the underlying value of the mortgage loans. If the mortgages that served as foundation to the financial edifice went bad, the entire building risked collapsing, floor by floor. So the housing boom had not only been lucrative; it had made the profitability, perhaps even the very survival, of major industries reliant on its continuation. A substantial slowdown risked bringing down the entire house of cards. Any government would contemplate this possibility anxiously, especially one that was reliant on political support from the regions where the housing boom was strongest, and from industries most dependent on a continuation of the boom.

And so defenders of faith in the Bush boom abounded, typically in and around the Bush administration. Early in 2005 in the *Washington Times*, James Miller III, who had served as Ronald Reagan's budget director, lauded "the efficient U.S. arrangements for housing finance" as "the envy of every other country." The trillions going into home loans reflected the accumulated wisdom of a competitive financial system: "Gone are the days of mortgage credit crunches and exorbitant mortgage rates spreads. American homeowners . . . are assured of a steady, liquid, and generally affordable supply of mortgage credit. And investors, both domestic and foreign, are provided a flow of debt- and mortgage-related securities that are highly liquid, transparent, and secure."[34]

Also in 2005, Alan Reynolds of the Cato Institute disparaged the "economic pessimists, who try to persuade us terrible things are about to happen. A perennial favorite is the 'housing bubble' about to burst, with a supposedly devastating impact on household wealth. . . . In short, we are asked to worry about something that has never happened for reasons still to be coherently explained. 'Housing bubble' worrywarts have long been hopelessly confused. It would have been financially foolhardy to listen to them in 2002. It still is."[35]

A few months later Larry Kudlow, the *National Review*'s economics editor, wrote a column titled "The Housing Bears Are Wrong Again," whose subtitle claimed that the housing sector was "writing [a] how-to guide on wealth creation." In it, Kudlow dismissed "all the bubbleheads who expect housing-price crashes in Las Vegas or Naples, Florida, to bring down the consumer, the rest of the economy, and the entire stock market."[36] In the subsequent three years, the housing sector oversaw the destruction of trillions of dollars in household wealth; and housing prices in Las Vegas and Naples, Florida, declined by over 50 percent, bringing down the consumer, the rest of the economy, and the entire stock market. And despite Miller's faith in the mortgage market, the lack of transparency and liquidity in the securities being snapped up by investors, domestic and foreign, very nearly brought down the entire international financial order.

The fact that many of the optimists worked for the housing industry might have been a tip-off. One, David Lereah, then the chief economist of the National Association of Realtors, published a book in 2005 called *Are You Missing the Real Estate Boom?* and re-released it in February 2006 with an even less subtle new title: *Why the Real Estate Boom Will Not Bust.* Of course, Lereah's advice devastated those who followed it. Nonetheless, as he told *BusinessWeek* several years later, after leaving his position with the housing lobby, "I worked for an association promoting housing, and it was my job to represent their interests."[37]

Nonetheless, most Americans found it more appealing to sit back and enjoy the rapid growth, rising housing prices, and supremely bullish stock market. Certainly the government had little reason to rein in the celebratory consumption binge—especially as a controversial war in Iraq threatened the administration's popularity. In any case, the United States was hardly alone in living in a financial and housing bubble.

America has company

People in other parts of the world had also discovered the attractions of debt-financed consumption. Local regulators also encouraged new financial opportunities and new financial instruments. And they all went through the same sorts of experiences as the United States.

The government and people of the United Kingdom, like their American brethren, borrowed heavily from abroad to increase consumption—as in the United States, British investment as a share of GDP actually went down between 2000 and 2007. The country's imports skyrocketed while exports stagnated, so the trade deficit shot from $50 billion in 2000 to $180 billion in 2007. "Getting cheap goods from Asia," remarked one economist, "has boosted purchasing power so UK consumers have gone on a big spending binge—on many services."[38]

Meanwhile, the housing market in the United Kingdom was going through a boom even greater than the American one: the average price of a house sold in the United Kingdom skyrocketed from £80,000 in 2000 to £180,000 in 2007, an increase of 125 percent. In dollar terms, at market exchange rates, the increase was even more staggering, from $130,000 to $350,000. The average house in London cost nearly £500,000 by 2007, nearly $1 million; housing prices over the decade rose more than four times faster than people's incomes. In two-thirds of the country's towns, housing was priced beyond the financial reach of average government workers.[39]

The financial markets in the United Kingdom bubbled upward with its home prices. The City, London's financial center, had become the engine of growth for the entire economy. The City alone employed nearly 350,000 people and was adding workers at the rate of nearly 100 a week. By 2004 the country's financial sector already accounted for nearly one-third of the nation's economy, its economic output double that of British manufacturing.

Ireland was, if anything, embarked on an even more remarkable debt-financed consumption boom. As tens of billions of dollars poured into the Irish banking system from Asia and the rest of Europe, and thence into the Irish economy, familiar patterns emerged. The financial services and construction sectors grew ever more outsized. By 2007, nearly one-third of Irish workers were in construction or finance—about double the proportion prevailing in the recent past. In 1997 there were 245,000 people employed in the construction and financial services sectors, about 15 percent less than in industry; by 2007, this was up to 568,000 workers, just about double the number of those employed in manufacturing.

Irish borrowing turned the country into a major financial center and created a housing bubble that put all others to shame. Between 1997 and 2007 the *average* house price in Dublin shot up from $115,000 to $550,000. This was remarkable for a medium-size city in a small country with an ample supply of buildable land. By 2007, the average house in Dublin cost two and a half times as much as the median house in America's metropolitan areas, and substantially more than the median house in the New York metropolitan area. Most of this housing bubble was financed abroad—the net indebtedness of Irish banks to the rest of the world went from 10 percent of GDP in 2003 to 60 percent in early 2008.[40] And it was accomplished without any unusual financial developments—no subprime mortgages, no novel approach to securitization. It was just an old-fashioned housing bubble, fueled by old-fashioned foreign borrowing.

Spain, too, built its housing and financial bubble much the old-fashioned way, borrowing a trillion dollars and more abroad. And as with the other deficit nations, the lion's share of the borrowing went into a housing boom and bubble. The cost of housing rose so rapidly in Spain that there was serious concern about pricing much of the population out of the market. This led to the proliferation of "mini-flats," apartments of 30 square meters (about 320 square feet), and their aggressive promotion by the country's housing minister. Even this was no guarantee of affordability; in a distant suburb of Madrid, mini-flats were going for nearly $200,000.[41]

It was not just membership in the euro zone that made foreigners eager to lend to Spain and Ireland; the monetary policy of the European Central Bank in Frankfurt encouraged Spanish and Irish households and firms to borrow. Both Spain and Ireland had relatively high interest rates before the euro was created in 1999; afterward interest rates in the two countries moved quickly down toward euro-zone levels. On top of this, after 1999 euro monetary policy was set, for the euro zone as a whole, by the European Central Bank in Frankfurt. Between 2002 and 2005 the Central Bank, like the Fed, kept interest rates very low—2 or 3 percent when inflation was about 2 percent. This meant that real interest rates—taking inflation into account—were around zero for the average euro-zone country. But Spain and Ireland were growing faster than the rest of the new euro bloc, and their prices were rising faster than elsewhere. This meant that in Ireland and Spain, where inflation was 3 or 4 percent, real interest rates were negative. In Spain, for example, while mortgage interest rates had been around 11 percent in the late 1990s, by 2005 they were down to 3 or 4 percent—roughly the same as inflation. As in the United States, this gave people a powerful incentive to borrow as much cheap money as they could, to buy houses that were rising in value 10 percent or more every year.

At the height of the building boom, as in Ireland, one Spanish worker of every seven was employed in housing construction. Half a million new homes were being built every year—roughly equal to all the new homes in Italy, France, and Germany *combined*—in a

country with about 16 million households. The amount of housing
loans outstanding skyrocketed from $180 billion in 2000 to $860
billion in 2007. Over the ten years to 2007, housing prices tripled,
second only to Ireland among developed countries; by then, the
average house in Madrid cost an unheard-of $400,000.

Plenty of people sounded alarms, abroad and in the United
States, that these bubbling economies were headed for trouble. But
it was hard for national governments basking in the light of booming economies to take the alarms seriously. Between the economic
and political influence of bankers and home builders, the electoral
importance of those who were benefiting from the expansion, and
the political requirements of incumbency, it was easy to keep the
machine going, even if the best mechanics were warning about its
weaknesses. After all, there had been warnings before, and sometimes they hadn't come true. Perhaps this capital flow cycle, this
borrowing boom, was not like the ones that had come before it; perhaps it would keep going without crashing and burning.

"We are different"

People in the United States, United Kingdom, Spain, Ireland, and
the other big borrowing nations were not the first to believe—or to
want to believe—that they would escape calamity, that they were
different.[42] Generations of politicians, in scores of countries, have
convinced themselves that warnings of economic dangers are over-
blown. Capital flow cycles of the sort the United States was experiencing are enormously enjoyable to almost everyone, especially
governments that can take the credit for the upswing. Forewarnings
of impending problems are never welcome, even though in retrospect it would probably have been wise—and even self-interested—
for governments to take them seriously. Public opinion, and voters,
are rarely kind to governments that oversee earth-shaking crises. So
why do politicians ignore intimations of impending doom?

Good times often reinforce themselves, not least in the minds of
politicians. When the economy is growing, they tend to credit their
own talents; when the economy hits the skids, politicians tend to
blame outside forces. And when an economy is growing particularly

strongly, and attracting trillions of dollars from investors around the world—whom, one assumes, are putting their money where their beliefs in quality are—and history's most sophisticated financial system is trumpeting the wonders of advanced risk management, then it is easy to convince oneself that previous cycles that ended badly are no guide to current developments. Our economy is sound. Our people are unusually productive. Our economic management is extraordinarily competent. Our institutions are uniquely secure.

Such beliefs are common, however, to almost all such capital flow cycles, including those that ended unambiguously badly. The tendency to ignore warning signals is nearly universal and goes back hundreds of years.[43] Denial often lasts long after the fact, when in retrospect it seems obvious to everyone that they had experienced an unsustainable boom. After most recent debt or currency crises, at least some of the policymakers in office at the time of the crisis continued to insist that the problem was with irrational speculators, or politically motivated opponents, or misinformed foreigners. This was true after Mexico crashed in 1994—two of the country's leading economic policymakers insisted years later, against all the economic evidence, that "Mexico experienced a politically triggered speculative attack, not a crisis based on the misalignment of real phenomena."[44] The architect of Argentina's boom and bust between 1991 and 2001 insisted in its aftermath variously that the collapse was due to "excessive provincial spending" or to the fact that "Argentina's main trading partners were strongly devaluing their currencies" or by "the perception of important leaders that there was foreign support for liquidating all debts, including private debts."[45]

Policymakers may hope that their luck will carry them through, or they might engage in what could be called "rational procrastination." A collapse could happen, which would be a bad thing, but it might come well into the future—and far into the future for a politician usually means after the next election. Facing a trade-off between recession now versus recession later makes the choice easy: you're in office now, somebody else will be in office later.[46] Or the forecasts might be wrong, and a wonderful surprise—a drop in the price of oil, a rise in the price of an export commodity—might solve the problem. So you roll the dice: don't adjust, keep the boom alive, hope that the experts are wrong and the economy either stays healthy long enough for you to win the election or it gets bailed out by some happy coincidence. It's a long shot, but if the alternative is the end of your political career, it might be a gamble worth taking to try to resurrect your political fortunes.

And so perhaps the Republicans weren't simply ignoring the economic advice. Perhaps they were hoping that the decline would come late enough to allow them to win the 2008 election. Or perhaps they were hoping that something unexpected, and wonderful, would come along to salvage the economy. In the event, they were wrong on both counts, but maybe it was politically worth the risk. Anyway, it is not as though there were massive political pressures to rein in the expansion and impose economic restraint. But why weren't there? Certainly somebody other than academic observers had an interest in keeping the American economy from collapsing.

Who might have belled the cat?

The forces for American economic restraint were weak. They often are in boom times—but not always. There have been instances in which a bubbling economy that experts tag as unsustainable is brought down gradually. It doesn't happen that often, and it doesn't happen without cost. Nonetheless, if policymakers can decompress a booming economy before it turns into an irreversible bubble, they may be able to avoid a terrible crash.

This was, for example, the case of Brazil in the mid and late 1990s. Like Argentina a few years before, Brazil in 1994 fixed its currency to the dollar to bring inflation down. This worked, and by 1997 the economy was booming. But signs of stress were everywhere. Because inflation had come down gradually, the real exchange rate had been going up (appreciating): prices of nontradables had risen about 50 percent relative to tradables. As a result, millions of jobs were lost in the tradables sectors, especially manufacturing and agriculture, and the job growth in service sectors did not keep up with losses elsewhere. Soon economists began insisting that the government needed to delink the currency (called the "real") from the dollar and devalue. The Brazilian government delayed a bit, until the 1998 election was over and won. But in January 1999 the government did in fact devalue the real. The shock pushed the country into a very mild recession, from which the economy recovered quickly.[47] Meanwhile, it was increasingly clear that Argentina needed to do the same, devaluing its currency to avoid a crisis. Yet successive Argentine governments refused to act. By 2001, the long-delayed adjustment was forced on the country—leading to history's biggest default and Argentina's most severe economic collapse. But Brazil had avoided the worst, demonstrating that government action to avoid a collapse is not impossible. When does it happen?

Some things delay a constructive government response to an impending crisis, while others seem to permit or accelerate one.[48] It is no surprise that an impending election makes a government very reluctant to hit the economic brakes. So too does political weakness, as a fragile government is unlikely to be able to get support for harsh policies. By this standard, if the Argentine elections had been earlier, and the Argentine government had been more secure in office— like its Brazilian counterpart—it too might have engineered a more gradual decompression.

Another force for delay is debt. If governments, firms, and households in a booming economy have taken on large debts, slowing the economy is likely to increase the real burden of debt. In a boom, prices of assets like housing and stocks rise, so that loans taken out against them are lucrative. But if prices stop rising, or fall, the real debt burden grows. Again, this was the case in most of the financial and currency crises of the 1980s and 1990s: heavily indebted companies and governments needed the merry-go-round to continue.

Some economic and political forces—in particular, the influence of manufacturers and farmers—tend to rein in borrowing booms. The reason goes back to the impact of foreign borrowing on tradables and nontradables. Binges such as those experienced by borrowing countries raise domestic prices and wages. Local manufacturers and farmers eventually find themselves priced out of world markets. Since borrowing also leads to a surge of imports, often imports that compete with local products, the results can be disastrous for domestic industry and agriculture. One of the strongest predictors of government action to pop a currency or financial bubble before it

becomes unmanageable is the size of the manufacturing and farm-
ing sectors: the bigger they are, the more political power they have,
and the sooner the government acts.

In the American borrowing boom of the early and middle 1980s,
in fact, American farmers and manufacturers were vocal in their
concern. Between 1980 and 1985, that era's capital inflow led the
prices of services to rise twice as fast as those of manufactured goods,
while farm prices actually dropped. In this instance, the problem
was reflected in a very strong appreciation of the dollar, which farmers and manufacturers were desperate to limit or reverse. The strong
dollar, the president of Caterpillar said, was "the single most important trade issue facing the U.S."[49] Sympathetic members of Congress
introduced a flurry of protectionist trade bills, and manufacturers
tripled the number of protectionist complaints they filed with the
International Trade Commission.[50] This pressure was important in
encouraging the Reagan administration to work to restrain the dollar's value, eventually moderating and reversing the harm it was
doing to America's farmers and manufacturers.

But after 2001, there were few such expressions of concern. The
economy had changed fundamentally in less than twenty years, and
many of the manufacturing industries that had complained so bitterly in the 1980s had long since left the country. Where there had
been nearly 20 million manufacturing workers in America in 1980,
by 2006 there were barely 14 million; manufacturing had plummeted from employing more than one in five American workers to
just one in ten. Globalization had led many American industries to
outsource production to lower-wage locations, mainly in East Asia
and Latin America. Many of the industries that had not shifted production simply shrank or went out of business. Meanwhile, American farmers had become so reliant on government supports that their
market position was less relevant than their political backing. And a
worldwide increase in farm prices in 2007 stanched whatever agricultural concerns there might have been. So while the Bush boom
had effects of special concern to American manufacturers and farmers engaged in international competition—it led to a huge upsurge
in imports and raised the price of doing business in America—there
were now very few such manufacturers and farmers around. The

potential complainants had taken their factories elsewhere, gone out of business, or resigned themselves to relying on government handouts. There was almost nobody left to complain.

Staying out of trouble

Those who thought that the Bush boom between 2001 and 2007 was unique were wrong. The main features of the American trajectory were common to the United States, Spain, Ireland, and the United Kingdom—and to Iceland, Greece, to the Baltic states of Lithuania, Estonia, and Latvia, and to many other countries that became major debtors over the course of the decade. In these countries, as in dozens of others over hundreds of years, foreign borrowing fostered financial and housing booms, and trade deficits.[51] The United States after 2001 could not escape the macroeconomic realities of a borrowing nation.

But there is nothing inevitable about borrowers running into crises. Nor is it inevitable that the problems of borrowing countries will lead to crisis. This is true even if the problems are homemade, as they were in the United States, whose fiscal and monetary policies were central to the borrowing boom and eventual bubble.

The man who took over from Alan Greenspan at the helm of the Federal Reserve in 2006, Ben Bernanke, was intellectually well equipped to evaluate financial threats. Bernanke is an MIT-trained economist who was chair of the Princeton University Department of Economics until he joined the Fed's Board of Governors in 2002. Three years later, Bernanke took over the chairmanship of the Bush administration's Council of Economic Advisers, and after only a few months in that position he was appointed to succeed Greenspan at the Fed.

Bernanke was only the second Fed chair to have an academic background in economics (the first was Arthur Burns, who served in the 1970s).[52] Bernanke was indeed a prominent and respected academic economist long before assuming his post. Much of his scholarship, with titles such as "Permanent Income, Liquidity, and Expenditure on Automobiles," was of interest only to other scholars.[53] But Bernanke also had a major interest in financial crises, and his most famous scholarship looked at what happened to countries during the Great Depression. On the basis of detailed studies of the Depression experience, in the United States and elsewhere, Bernanke concluded that the scale of a country's collapse did not just depend on its macroeconomic conditions, or on its debt burden, or on how serious the shocks it faced were. What really pushed a country over the brink, from a recession to a full-fledged catastrophe, was a financial system prone to panics, one that could not withstand the series of monetary and other shocks to which it was subjected.[54]

Bernanke's conclusion, that financial strength could help protect against crisis, should have reassured Americans. Certainly it reassured Bernanke, who early in 2007 attempted to set minds at rest about the possibility that the growing difficulties in one segment of the mortgage market might portend more extensive problems: "the effect of the troubles in the subprime sector on the broader housing market will likely be limited, and we do not expect significant spillovers from the subprime market to the rest of the economy or to the financial system."[55]

So calm continued to reign among policymakers and the general public, even as the housing market began to slow in 2006 and 2007 and as problems developed in one segment of the mortgage market, that for subprime mortgages. For the American financial system was, by common agreement, one of the world's most stable. There had not been bank panics in the United States since the 1930s. There were dozens of state and federal regulatory agencies watching over the financial system. Macroeconomic imbalances might be the unavoidable result of the country's foreign borrowing, but strong banks and sober regulators were a guarantee against serious crisis.

Or so it seemed.

Risky Business Models

And so it seemed to Ken Guy, the finance director of King County, Washington, the county that includes Seattle. Guy was in charge of safeguarding the approximately $4 billion in investments of the county's libraries, fire departments, school districts, and other agencies. In the middle of September 2007, he woke up to a brutal reality: he might have lost the taxpayers of King County hundreds of millions of dollars by putting money into investments he thought were practically risk free.

Guy had invested $207 million of the county's money in firms called structured investment vehicles (SIVs). Banks and other financial institutions set up SIVs to issue commercial paper—short-term bonds with low interest rates—which they promoted as safe investments for risk-averse investors like the members of King County's asset pool. The SIVs then used the money raised from selling the commercial paper to make profitable investments. The difference between what the SIV paid to borrow on the commercial paper market and what it earned on its investments was the profit it— and the sponsoring bank or hedge fund—made. Prudent investors regarded lending to an SIV like this as secure, in part because the sponsoring financial institution stood behind the SIV.

The SIV that first alerted Ken Guy to the problem was called Rhinebridge. The name was apposite, as Rhinebridge was sponsored by IKB Deutsche Industriebank, a German bank based in Düsseldorf, on the river Rhine. The bank was partly owned by the German government, which seemed to make it that much safer. And in fact in June 2007, when Rhinebridge was set up and Guy invested King County's money in it, Moody's and Standard & Poor's gave it their highest rating. Merrill Lynch had assured Guy that buying SIV securities was safe: "They were all highly rated, AAA," he said.[1]

But within three months Rhinebridge was in trouble, and in October 2007 it announced it could not meet its obligations—including to King County. Rhinebridge and the other SIVs in which King County had invested had, like most SIVs, used the money they raised to buy bonds based on American home mortgages, which were earning high rates of return. But Rhinebridge could only honor the commercial paper it had issued, and King County had bought, if the investments Rhinebridge made paid off. As the American housing market slowed and began to drop, more and more American homeowners fell behind on their mortgage payments, and soon SIVs like Rhinebridge collapsed.

The Rhinebridge default was just part of a flood of SIV failures. Three weeks after Guy parked over $50 million in another SIV, Mainsail II, Moody's reduced its rating from the highest to junk. Within weeks, yet another SIV the county had invested in fell apart. The county's financial management had thought it was buying safe assets, sponsored by major banks and hedge funds and certified as extremely secure by the world's leading credit rating agencies. Yet King County ended up losing about half of its investment, and the members of the county's asset pool had to absorb major, unexpected losses—about $1.8 million for the library system, for example. Ill-fated German loans to American homeowners were depleting the coffers of Seattle libraries.

King County and its libraries were hardly alone. Springfield, Massachusetts, lost nearly $13 million of the $14 million it invested in another sort of security based on home mortgages (collateralized debt obligations, or CDOs). California's Orange County dropped tens of millions of dollars on its structured investment vehicles.[2] Indianapolis, Philadelphia, Miami, Oakland, California, and Snohomish County in Washington were blindsided by another financial asset. These municipalities entered into "interest rate swap" arrangements, which promised that they could pay lower interest rates to borrow than they were used to—as long as there were no big surprises. But the financial crisis was just such a surprise, and it triggered special provisions that drove up interest costs for these municipalities exactly when they could least afford it, in the middle of a recession.[3]

Why did the American financial system leave careful investors so unprotected? How did the world's best-developed financial market fail at its most basic functions? What led an apparently well-ordered financial system, set up to spread, monitor, and reduce risks to investors, so far astray? Who was to blame for King County's financial debacle, and those of so many others across the nation?

The great moderation, the conundrum, and the search for yield

The defining financial characteristic of the American borrowing boom was that bankers were desperate to raise their profits, and they searched continually for new ways to do so, for the country's financial institutions were finding it increasingly difficult to make money as the United States came out of the brief recession of 2001. The dot-com boom of the late 1990s had gone bust, eliminating one profit center. And by 2002 interest rates were very low and falling, a bad time for financial institutions.

The squeeze on the profits of banks and other financial institutions had several sources. First was the nation's ready access to a huge pool of foreign funds. As half a trillion to a trillion dollars a year flowed into the United States from abroad, the increased supply of funds put downward pressure on interest rates. This was the "global saving glut" much discussed at the time.[4] There was a more specific effect: much of the capital inflow came from governments in East Asia and the Persian Gulf, which were primarily interested in low-risk places to park their money. They turned mostly to U.S.

Treasury bonds and related U.S. government debt, driven more by a need for safety than by a desire for high returns. The money pouring into the market for U.S. government securities drove their interest rates down considerably, dramatically reducing the rate of return on these very safe investments. The second source of the squeeze on bank profits was the Federal Reserve's very low interest rate policy, which persisted for years after the 2001 recession ended.[5]

Another problem for the banks was something that Alan Greenspan called "the conundrum."[6] Typically, long-term interest rates are substantially higher than short-term rates. This is because holding long-term bonds exposes the investor to substantial losses if inflation and interest rates rise, and investors demand a premium to reward them for taking on this greater risk. This "spread" between short- and long-term interest rates is important to banks, because they generally make profits by borrowing short and lending long. They borrow from depositors (who can withdraw at will), or from short-term money markets, such as the market for commercial paper, and lend at the longer end of the term spectrum, to consumers, corporations, and homeowners. Unlike depositors and other short-term investors, banks are willing to take on longer-term lending, presumably because they specialize in gathering information about the nature of the long-term risks. And banks and other financial institutions get rewarded for this expertise: they profit from the spread between the cost of borrowing at the short end and the return from lending at the long end. The larger the spread, holding all else constant, the greater the profits.

Normally long-term and short-term interest rates move in tandem, so that when the Fed increases short-term interest rates, longer-term interest rates also rise. After the 2001 recession the Fed held interest rates at very low levels; however, when eventually in 2004 the Fed began to raise short-term interest rates, longer-term interest rates barely budged. In fact, in some cases long-term rates actually fell. The reason for this conundrum was much debated at the time. A major factor was, again, foreign central bank purchases of long-term Treasury securities, which drove their interest rates down; according to one estimate, these purchases accounted for at least half of the conundrum.[7] Another factor was the experience of twenty years of low inflation and stable growth—a phenomenon called "the Great Moderation." It was not clear whether to ascribe the Great Moderation to better macroeconomic management by policymakers, or to good luck (fewer bad surprises like the oil price increases of the 1970s), or to underlying changes that made the American economy more flexible.[8] In any event, the Great Moderation had made expectations for the future more stable, and so reduced the perceived risk in holding long-term assets. Whatever the reason, the conundrum— the unusually low interest rate spread between short-term and long-term interest rates—created a problem for financial institutions.

These interrelated pressures on bank profits—the foreign capital inflow, the Fed's low-interest-rate policy, the unusually narrow margin between short- and long-term rates—sparked a "search for yield" on the part of investors from 2002 onward. The search for yield drove financiers to try to find different sources of profits. There were several ways to do this.

Leveraging risk

One thing that the search for yield led financiers to do was to "leverage up," to borrow a lot more in order to lend a lot more. Leverage is the ratio of borrowed money to a firm's own money; a highly leveraged firm is one that has a great deal of debt compared to its equity (the value of its capital). For banks, leverage *is* the company's business: financial institutions do have their own capital, but the money they lend comes from money they borrow. They "intermediate," channeling money from people from whom they borrow (savers) to people to whom they lend (debtors). The more a financial institution borrows, the more it can lend.[9]

Banks use leverage to maximize profits. They borrow as much as possible at as low an interest rate as possible, and lend out as much of those borrowed funds as they can at as high an interest rate as possible. Ideally, a bank would like to have none of its own money at risk—to play entirely with other people's money. But banks do have their own capital in play, and they also have to hold some of the money they borrow in reserve in order to pay for the money they've borrowed, for example, to service commercial paper or to pay out depositors'

money when they want it. However, the greater the ratio of investments financed with borrowed money to the bank's own capital—the
higher the leverage—the more the bank can earn on its capital.

With the greater earnings of high leverage come high risks, on
both the asset and liability sides of the leverage ledger. First, the
firm's assets—what it has invested in, such as mortgage loans, or
assets backed by mortgage loans—can go bad. If the sum of the bad
assets exceeds the firm's capital, it could very well be bankrupt. The
more highly leveraged a financial institution is, the more exposed it
is to problems if some of the assets sour. Second, even if the assets
do retain their value, there can be problems with the firm's liabilities, what it owes to others. If commercial paper holders and other
short-term lenders to the bank get nervous and refuse to roll over
loans, or if depositors rush to take their money out of the bank, the
financial institution may simply run out of money and not be able to
honor its commitments. Again, the more highly leveraged the firm
is—the more it owes to others—the more exposed it is. Problems on
either the asset or the liability side, or both, are the typical causes
of bank failures.

In the 2002–2007 environment of ample supplies of foreign capital, low interest rates, and a small spread between short- and long-
term rates, financial institutions had great incentives to increase
their leverage, to borrow as much as they could in order to relend as
much as they could. And leverage in turn gave them strong incentives to make loans that were riskier than usual—such as writing
mortgages to less reliable borrowers than usual. Greater risks get
lenders additional return on each dollar's investment. Leverage
augmented this increased appetite for risk: owners of highly leveraged financial institutions have less of their own money at stake. If
something goes wrong and the firm goes under, its owners' down-
side losses are limited to their own capital. On the other hand, their
potential upside gains are enormous. The greater the leverage, and
the larger the risk undertaken, the greater the potential profits. The
economic environment induced leverage and greater risk taking,
and leverage itself induced even greater risk taking.

One innovation that allowed financiers to climb higher up the
risk ladder, making loans that were riskier and more profitable, was

the subprime mortgage. Subprime mortgages developed during the 1980s and were made possible by some of the deregulatory changes of that decade.[10] Their popularity exploded as housing prices rose. They typically were extended to people with relatively poor credit ratings and required little or no documentation and little down payment. Many of them also had a payment structure that was based on the assumption that housing prices would continue to rise. A typical subprime mortgage of this type started with a fixed, relatively low interest rate for the first two years. After the two-year "teaser" period ended, the mortgage would "reset" to a much higher variable rate for the next twenty-eight years. The idea was that by the time the teaser period ended, the house would now be worth a lot more money, which would allow the homeowner to refinance at more attractive terms. Such mortgages only made sense if house prices rose. If they did, loans would be refinanced, payments would be made, and the merry-go-round of borrowing and repaying could go on.

A typical subprime mortgage looked something like this mortgage written in early 2006.[11] The homeowner takes out a mortgage of $225,000—enough, with a small down payment, to buy a home with the country's median value in 2006 of $240,000. The mortgage is of a popular type: a 2/28 interest-only adjustable-rate mortgage (ARM). The interest-only option means that the borrower pays only interest for the first five years, after which he has to make both interest and principal payments. The 2/28 option means that for the first two years, the mortgage has a "teaser" interest rate, in this case 7.75 percent. After two years the rate becomes adjustable: it "resets" to an interest rate equal to the London Interbank Offered Rate (LIBOR, the rate banks charge each other in London) plus a margin of 6.13 percent; after that, it is adjusted every six months to equal LIBOR plus 6.13 percent. At the time, LIBOR was 5.31 percent. So—assuming LIBOR is steady—after two years the interest rate on the mortgage goes up to 11.44 percent (LIBOR at 5.31 percent plus the spread of 6.13 percent); a couple of years later, principal payments start to kick in.[12]

We can get a sense of what this means in terms of the homeowner's finances if we assume, as was typically the case, that the mortgage was designed so that original debt service payments were 40 percent of the mortgagor's gross income. This implies an income of about $42,000 in this case. For the first two years, the mortgage costs, as planned, 40 percent of income. After the reset, it rises to 58 percent of income; once principal payments start after five years, to over 62 percent of income. Since few, if any, homeowners are able to pay nearly two-thirds of their income in interest and principal, it is clear that both parties intended the mortgage to be refinanced quickly, and relied on housing prices to rise quickly. For if the house appreciated 15 percent a year in the first two years, by the time of the reset it would be worth almost $320,000, and the homeowner could certainly get a lower interest rate on a $225,000 mortgage for a $320,000 home.

Although they came to play a prominent part in the eventual crisis, subprime mortgages were only one of a wide variety of riskier loans that financial institutions made during the boom. Rising prices, after all, made borrowing attractive even for people buying houses using standard fixed-rate mortgages—even if, in more normal times, they could not have afforded the mortgage. Subprime mortgages were only an extreme manifestation of the borrowing binge. And while people with these mortgages were more likely to default than those with other mortgages, subprime mortgages never—even at the peak of the bubble in 2006—accounted for more than 20 percent of all new mortgages.[13] They were, nonetheless, emblematic of the continuing imaginative attempts of profit-seeking bankers to develop new ways to make money.

During the lending boom, financiers followed the simple principle that the easiest way to get higher returns is to make riskier investments. But there's a reason why risky investments pay higher interest rates—they're more likely to go bust. Bankers were well aware that they were playing a riskier financial game, whether with subprime mortgages or with other risky assets. They had, however, devised mechanisms that they thought made the risks more palatable, by spreading them around.

Spreading risk: securitization

Bankers in search of higher yields leveraged up and made dicier loans, and then they developed new methods that they argued would take the edge off the greater risks they were incurring. The principal financial innovation was "securitization," which distributes risk among a large number of investors, thus diluting it. Securitization is the process by which a financial institution takes a bundle of loans or other assets and repackages them as securities—bonds—which are then sold to investors. In its most common form, securitization was developed to package mortgages and to sell them off, as "mortgage-backed securities"; the process was also commonly used for credit card loans, auto loans, and student loans. In the case of mortgage-backed securities, the homeowners' interest and principal payments go, not to the banks that originated the mortgages, but to a pool created to service the bond made up of the bundle of mortgages.

Securitization gained prominence in the 1980s as a way to decentralize risk. It does so in several ways. First, it makes banks less subject to local business conditions. Before securitization, most local banks made loans to borrowers in their respective communities. When downturns struck the local economy, the banks got into trouble because the downturn affected many of the people or businesses that took out the loans from the banks. Now, a locally based bank could make loans, securitize them, then sell them to investors and remove them from the banks' books. Once the bank had sold off its risky loans, in principle it did not have to hold as much capital, which freed it to originate more mortgages. This raised the profit rate to the bank's shareholders and allowed the bank to make more loans. It also made any given bank less vulnerable to a local downturn. In turn, investors could invest in securities made up of mortgages from many different parts of the country, thereby diversifying their risks. In this sense, securitization allowed banks to offload the risk they took on, and allowed investors to earn relatively high returns on mortgage and other consumer debt to which they would otherwise not have access. Securitization was so successful that the original American method of mortgage lending—called "originate to hold" because banks originated the mortgages and then held onto them—was largely replaced by an "originate to distribute" model in which banks originated mortgages in order to securitize them and distribute them around the country.

To benefit from securitization, a bank would first set up a "special purpose entity" (SPE) whose special purpose was to buy up a set of mortgages, either from the sponsoring bank or from others. This entity would then issue bonds—the mortgage-backed securities—that would be bought by investors. The revenue from selling the bonds went to finance the purchase of the mortgages; the mortgages were the collateral that stood behind the bonds, with payments from the mortgages going to the bondholders.

Just as residential mortgages were packaged into bonds and the bonds sold, so too were commercial real estate mortgages, as well as auto loans, student loans, and credit card receivables. Throughout the borrowing boom, most of the action was in mortgage-backed securities, as can be seen in figure 3. The figure shows the explosion in this sort of securitization, also called "structured finance" because it is "engineered" to fit the needs of investors.

The development of the new structured finance owed a lot to the

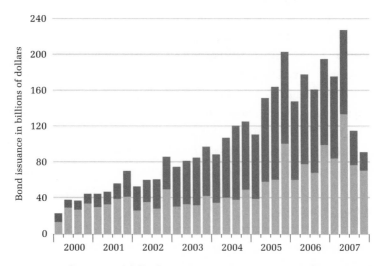

Figure 3. The rise and fall of securitization. Origination of structured finance, in billions of dollars per quarter, 2000–2007. Dark bars are residential mortgage-backed securities, and light bars are the sum of asset-based securities, collateralized debt obligations, commercial real estate–backed securities, and other asset-backed derivatives. Source: IMF, *World Economic Outlook* (Washington, DC: International Monetary Fund, April 2008), 15.

arrival on Wall Street of a new kind of financial expert: the quantitative analyst or "quant." Starting in the 1980s, financial institutions began hiring people with a background in math, physics, and statistics—but not in finance. Their job was to develop mathematical models to create and price assets that could be bought and sold on the ever deeper and more complicated international financial markets. By 2000, it was estimated that there were a thousand physicists working on Wall Street, along with similar numbers of people with graduate degrees in other highly mathematical—but not financial or economic—disciplines.[14]

The array of securitized products developed by the new financial engineers is enormous, and includes much more complex securities that are derived from the underlying assets, hence, the name "derivatives." Among these are CDOs, originally developed in 1987 by Drexel Burnham Lambert. CDOs, like mortgage-backed securities, turn some form of debt (such as corporate debt) into a bond that has as collateral the original debt.

An important structural feature of most structured finance was that it was typically divided into assets of different quality—different levels of risk and different, corresponding, rates of return. The securities were structured so that investors could buy different slices—individually called "tranches" (which in French means "slice"). The different tranches had different priority for payment, meaning that the most privileged, or "senior" tranches would be paid off first. Credit rating agencies, such as Moody's and Standard & Poor's, would often advise the bank on how to structure the securities so that as many of the bonds as possible would receive the highest, AAA, rating. Less senior tranches, that is, securities farther back in the line to receive interest and principal payments, would receive lower ratings. Investors who bought the senior, higher-rated tranches would not be in danger of losing money even if a few of the less senior tranches fell behind in payments, so they were protected from much of the risk. In this way, a bundle of mortgages could be combined into a mixture of "higher-quality" and "lower-quality" instruments. The sponsoring bank could sell the securities to investors of different types, so that those who wanted a safer investment

would get the tranches with a AAA rating, while those more willing to take risks would get the lower tranches, which paid a higher
interest rate but bore more risk.

Southern California–based New Century Financial, the country's
second largest originator of subprime mortgages, worked with Goldman Sachs to create a typical special purpose entity of this type in
June 2006.[15] New Century originated the mortgages—a total of 3949
subprime mortgages, for a total amount of $881 million—and sold
them to a Goldman Sachs subsidiary, which passed them along to
a conduit, a trust with the no-nonsense name of GSAMP TRUST
2006-NC2. The average mortgage in the pool was for $223,221, and
nine-tenths bore adjustable rates with a teaser. The mortgages were
then divided into seventeen tranches with different degrees of
seniority (priority for payment), and Moody's and Standard & Poor's
rated each tranche. Investors could buy securities representing each
tranche; the securities would pay an interest rate in line with the
tranche's riskiness. The most protected, senior, tranches would pay
an interest rate of LIBOR plus 0.07 percent; the least protected, a rate
of LIBOR plus 2.50 percent. As with all such asset-backed securities,
although there was a clear risk that some of the mortgages would go
bad, investors who bought the higher (senior) tranches felt they were
protected because the lower tranches would be hit first. Overall, the
average security issued by the trust paid LIBOR plus 0.23 percent;
LIBOR at the time was 5.32 percent, so the total average return was
5.55 percent. The average interest rate on mortgages in the pool was
about 8.30 percent, allowing the trust and its sponsors to make a
neat profit on the difference between what they were paying out and
what they were taking in.

Securitization relied in many ways on two important "government-sponsored enterprises" (GSEs), the Federal National Mortgage
Agency and the Federal Home Loan Mortgage Corporation, popu-
larly known as Fannie Mae and Freddie Mac, respectively. The federal government originally established Fannie Mae in 1938 during
the Great Depression, so that it could buy mortgages from banks and
repackage them to sell to investors. This was an early form of securitization with many of its advantages, especially that of allowing the
banks to make more mortgage loans, which was a crucial goal in the

late 1930s. The government privatized Fannie Mae in 1968 and set up Freddie Mac in 1970 to compete with it; the two GSEs had government charters that provided no explicit guarantee of government support. However, investors often behaved as if the firms would be bailed out if they encountered difficulties. Because of this implicit guarantee, they could borrow at very low rates even while maintaining lower capital ratios.[16]

Without these two GSEs, securitization would have been much more difficult. This is because without them, investors might believe that banks would spin off only the least creditworthy mortgages, holding the best for themselves. Given this, investors would have been wary to buy the securities. But because the GSEs were committed to buying all qualified mortgages, they vastly expanded the "secondary market" for mortgages, that is, the pool of mortgages that investors would be willing to buy and therefore the range of investors willing to participate. By making more money available to the mortgage market, this opened up more mortgage opportunities for homeowners. In addition, the fact that most investors assumed that Fannie Mae and Freddie Mac were implicitly backed by the government probably lowered the cost of borrowing for many homeowners. Without Fannie Mae and Freddie Mac, securitization would not have extended as far as it did, and the demand for housing would not have been so great.

Some observers have blamed Fannie Mae and Freddie Mac for the proliferation of subprime mortgages. However, the GSEs were constrained by law in their purchases of these mortgages. Private firms were much more engaged in securitizing subprime mortgages, particularly after 2006 when the GSEs' regulator imposed new restrictions on the types of mortgages they were allowed to securitize.[17] These "private label" mortgage-backed securities are the ones that proved so problematic, and they went bad at a much faster pace than those that had been securitized in earlier years.[18] Nonetheless, bankers were aware that even with securitization, extending more and more money to less and less creditworthy homeowners meant they were taking on greater risks. They had, however, developed even more imaginative ways to keep risky debt from contaminating their balance sheets.

Off-loading risk: the shadow banking system

As bankers leveraged up and took on more risk, they faced a problem: they were required to set aside more money to protect themselves against the greater risks. Regulators do not allow banks simply to lend out as much as they want; they have to have some of their own money at stake. This is a "capital charge" against a bank's operations, that is, a requirement that the bank has to have capital (typically, shareholder equity) equal to some fraction of its loans outstanding. The capital requirement is like a reserve requirement, and it limits a bank's ability to make profitable loans, constraining loans to be some multiple of the bank's capital.[19] Both more leverage and riskier loans require a larger capital charge, but this would have defeated their purpose, by pulling profits back down. The financial engineers came up with an innovation to deal with this too.

Banks were required to hold capital in reserve against their loans, but the independent companies the banks set up—special purpose entities, structured investment vehicles like Rhinebridge, conduits, whatever they might be called—did not. A bank could off-load its loans to a conduit of this sort and not have to increase its capital. And since the conduit was not bound by bank regulators, it did not have to hold any reserves either. This meant that a bank could make profitable loans, securitize them, spin them off to a conduit that it sponsored, and not have to increase its capital or other reserves.[20]

For example, in May 2004 the German bank Sachsen Landesbank set up a conduit based in Dublin called Ormond Quay, after a Dublin riverside street.[21] Ormond Quay borrowed about $12 billion on the commercial paper market, about two-thirds in euros. It then bought almost $12 billion of the asset-backed securities financial engineers had been designing. Four-fifths of the securities were backed by residential or commercial mortgages, mostly in the United States, the United Kingdom, Spain, and other borrowing countries. If the bank itself had made $12 billion in mortgage loans, it would have had a capital requirement that could have reached $1 billion. (The exact amount of the capital charge is hard to calculate, because there are different levels of capital requirements for different-quality loans; the requirement usually ranges from 2 to 8 percent.) But Ormond

Quay's equity capital was just $36 million, barely 0.3 percent of its assets and less than one-tenth of what the sponsoring bank would have needed. Ormond Quay, after all, was "off balance sheet," not on the books of the sponsoring bank, and not subject to the regulations governing the bank.

Investors were willing to buy Ormond Quay's commercial paper, lending to the conduit at low interest rates, because it was sponsored by Sachsen Landesbank, which guaranteed the conduit's debts. In this case the commercial paper was doubly safe, as the German sponsoring bank in turn had a guarantee from the government of the German state (Saxony) in which it was based. These guarantees led Moody's to give the conduit's commercial paper its highest rating.

This particular feat of financial engineering allowed the sponsoring bank, through Ormond Quay, to invest in nearly $12 billion in mortgages and other loans paying relatively high interest rates. They paid such high rates because they were risky, of course; but the bank and its conduit had to set aside only a trivial amount of money to offset the risk. There were two essential parts to the trick: first, the bank set up an off-balance-sheet conduit; second, the bank guaranteed the operations of the conduit. To be sure, the bank guarantee of the conduit incurred some risk—if the conduit collapsed, the bank would have to bail it out—but most bankers thought this was unlikely, and even if it did happen they expected governments to step in and help out.

By 2007, there were hundreds of conduits like Ormond Quay, with total assets of over $1.2 trillion.[22] And they were only a part of this new financial order, of what has been called a "shadow banking system." In the United States, more lending was now being done by this shadow system than by traditional commercial banks, savings and loans, and credit unions.[23] An ever greater share of finance was migrating to the shadow system, in large part to evade regulations that covered traditional banking. The major commercial banks were themselves using shadow banking to circumvent restrictions on their activities. By 2008, for example, Citibank had $1.1 trillion in assets that were not reflected on its balance sheet, compared to the $2.2 trillion reported on its books.[24]

The shadow banking system is composed of financial intermediaries that do much of what banks do: they borrow low and lend high, pocketing the spread as profit. The members of the shadow system include investment banks such as Goldman Sachs, hedge funds such as Bridgewater Associates, and private equity funds such as the Carlyle Group and the Blackstone Group, as well as the various legal entities that banks themselves set up to bypass regulations, such as SPEs, SIVs, and other conduits. The shadow financial system was particularly prominent in pushing the limits of financial innovation, in part because it attracted some of the more inventive entrepreneurs, in part because it was lightly regulated when it was regulated at all.

The new financial instruments increased continually in complexity. Securitization of mortgages to create mortgage-backed securities was only the beginning. The process could be repeated and repeated, in layer after layer of securitization. The financial engineers could repackage each round into new securities, structuring them to suit investors' needs. For there is, in principle, no limit to the number of levels of securitization. Financial engineers created CDOs, such as the tranched mortgage-backed securities backed (collateralized) by pools of mortgages organized by such SIVs as Rhinebridge and Ormond Quay. There was no reason to stop there. If mortgages could be pooled into securities, then these securities could themselves be pooled into other securities. Hence if there could be a CDO, there could be a CDO^2 (that is, a CDO-squared): a security backed by a pool of CDOs. This was simply another form of derivative—derived from the CDO just as the CDO had been derived from the mortgages—and investors could use CDO^2s to diversify their risks just as they could use the original CDO.[25]

Despite the inventiveness of the financial engineers and their clients, there were weaknesses in the shadow system. One problem was the galloping complexity of the financial instruments being created and traded. In the old days of originate-to-hold mortgage lending, local banks knew who owed them money and how likely they were to pay. Now, where thousands of mortgages were bundled, tranched, sliced and diced, sold and resold, it was virtually impossible for the ultimate owner of a mortgage—who was probably just one of a thousand owners of one-thousandth of the mortgage—to know much about the true nature of the asset. As complexity grew, transparency declined. With each additional layer of securitization, it became more and more difficult to figure out the real worth of a given security, and in particular how risky it might be.

The growing size and complexity of financial operations in the shadow banking system led its operators to develop ways to try to protect themselves. One was to devise a sort of insurance of its own. And so the financial engineers came up with yet another innovation, a derivative that could be used to protect investors from the risks of previous innovations: credit default swaps (CDSs). A CDS is a financial instrument tied to some underlying asset, such as a bond, that pays off if the bond goes bad. An investor who owns $100 million in bonds issued by General Electric, for example, can buy a CDS for $200,000 a year. If the GE bonds go bad, the issuer of the CDS has to pay out the full $100 million. CDSs are often thought of as insurance, since they protect investors from problems with their investments.[26]

Another way investors could try to protect themselves in the shadow financial system was to rely on credit rating agencies: Standard & Poor's, Moody's, and Fitch. These agencies were responsible for certifying the creditworthiness of the increasingly complicated financial assets being created. Many investors relied on credit ratings as guidance, and some financial institutions, such as money market mutual funds, were legally required to invest only in top-rated assets. Even the agreements that regulated the large international banks required that these ratings be used in determining how much capital these institutions had to hold.[27]

The credit rating agencies provided information, but they too were imperfect. For one thing, they had some perverse incentives. After all, they were hired by the firms that *created* the assets they were rating. So when Ormond Quay or Rhinebridge wanted to issue commercial paper to fund its operations, it went to Moody's or another credit rating agency and paid it to rate the commercial paper. Of course, if one rating agency didn't provide the desired rating, the firm could always "shop around" for a better rating. The credit rating agencies had strong reasons to provide the most positive possible assessments of securities they evaluated.[28] At some level, between opaque securitization and questionable credit ratings, the shadow banking system was magically turning financial dross into gold—but it might, in fact, be fool's gold.[29]

Questions about the solidity of the shadow financial system, and of the enormous edifice of interlocking financial connections it was creating, were not of concern only to those with money directly at stake. If the only parties injured by financial difficulties were the immediate borrowers and lenders, there would be little cause for concern on the part of society at large. But financial institutions—including those operating in the shadow banking system, with assets held off their balance sheets—provide the oil that lubricates the machinery of the modern economy. If a number of banks fail, especially a number of large banks, the collapse can have repercussions far beyond the directly involved parties. If the financial institutions are sufficiently large or sufficiently interconnected, their failure can threaten the entire economy. The hazards being created during the borrowing boom were reason enough for America's broad and deep system of financial regulators to mobilize for action.

But the shadow financial system's development, and concern about its safety, shone a spotlight on two key differences between traditional commercial banks and the new order. First, commercial banks were covered by deposit insurance. The purpose of deposit insurance is to limit or remove the incentive for depositors to engage in bank runs, which can have devastating effects not just on one bank but also on the economy as a whole. But firms in the shadow financial system did not borrow by taking deposits from the public. Investment banks, for instance, borrow on short-term credit markets. Hedge funds rely on individual investors. Special investment vehicles issue short-term debt in the commercial paper market. These firms were not covered by any sort of explicit insurance, which made them vulnerable. Second, commercial banks were supported by the Federal Reserve's commitment to act as a "lender of last resort," to lend to banks in trouble when they cannot obtain funds elsewhere. Like deposit insurance, this is meant to address short-term liquidity problems that could reverberate throughout the banking system. But there was no lender of last resort ready to jump in as needed to stabilize the shadow financial system. Without deposit insurance or a lender of last resort, all that stood between the shadow financial system and a system-wide crisis was the vigilance of government regulators.

Regulating risk?

Americans had learned the hard way how risky operations by financial markets could bring down the economy as a whole. For a century and more before 1929, the American banking system was intermittently rocked by panics and crises. Banks are fundamentally fragile. At their core there is a fundamental asymmetry called the "maturity mismatch," reflecting the divergence between the term of loans and debts, assets and liabilities. A bank borrows short and lends long; if the people to whom the bank owes money (depositors, holders of commercial paper) decide they want their money now, the bank cannot turn around and ask for immediate prepayment from the people who owe it money.

The maturity mismatch makes trust in a bank essential. Depositors who fear trouble will withdraw their deposits as soon as they can, even if a bank is fundamentally solvent.

Throughout the nineteenth and early part of the twentieth century, the government maintained a very light touch in managing financial crises. The absence of any substantial government backing to banks meant that it was largely up to depositors to keep track of how well banks were run. The attention paid by depositors exercised a certain discipline on banks, but an environment of imperfect information about bank activities was an invitation to instability, bank runs, and panics. When such problems materialized, it was usually banks themselves that mounted the major interventions necessary to stabilize markets, typically in the form of loans to bail out shaky banks. During the panic of 1907, J.P. Morgan and Company took the lead in cajoling other major New York banks into supporting their competitors who were on the verge of collapse.

This private approach to crisis management failed miserably after the stock market crash of 1929. As property and stock prices fell, the banking system collapsed. In the absence of deposit insurance, there were successive waves of bank runs, and nine thousand banks went out of business between 1930 and 1933. Banks were the key channel by which firms and households obtained loans, and the destruction of the banking system resulted in a steep decline in the real economy, contributing to the depth and breadth of the Depression.

When Franklin Roosevelt became president in March 1933, he was faced with a failing financial system and a devastated economy. A day after his inauguration, Roosevelt declared a week-long bank holiday during which the government took over and closed insolvent banks and enacted new legislation that in effect allowed the Federal Reserve to stand behind all bank deposits. Within weeks, confidence in the banking system had been restored, bank runs stopped, and the economy began to recover.[30]

The 1933 bank holiday, however, was a temporary measure. The underlying problem remained: nervous lenders always stood ready to withdraw deposits in times of stress, which would exacerbate the stress and magnify the nervousness. To reduce this fundamental instability, the Banking Act of 1933 established the Federal Deposit Insurance Corporation (FDIC) to provide deposit insurance for commercial banks. Deposit insurance removed the incentive for depositors to engage in a run on the banks. However, deposit insurance also had the problematic effect of reducing the discipline imposed by watchful depositors on bank behavior. Backed by deposit insurance, bankers had incentives to take on greater risks than desirable; after all, if they got into trouble, they would be bailed out by the FDIC. This tendency for the insured to take on greater risk—"moral hazard"—is an intrinsic problem with any insured activity.

The benefits of deposit insurance are counterbalanced by the excessive risk taking that insurance can induce. If the government provides deposit insurance, then it has to exercise rigorous supervision and oversight of the insured institutions to make sure that they do not take on undue risks. And so a comprehensive regulatory framework was put into place in 1933–1934, in large part to constrain the moral hazard created by deposit insurance. The new regulatory structure included an array of agencies. The Federal Reserve and either the FDIC, the Treasury's Office of the Comptroller of the Currency, or the relevant state bank regulator regulated commercial banks. The Federal Savings and Loans Insurance Corporation

(FSLIC), the Treasury's Office of Thrift Supervision, or the relevant state agency did the same for savings and loans. The Securities and Exchange Commission (SEC) regulated investment banks and the trading of stocks. Some financial institutions were combinations of commercial and investment banks, and many observers believed that mixing the two types of banking had been at the root of some of the financially questionable behavior of the financial system in the run-up to 1929. As a result, one section of the Banking Act of 1933, known as the Glass-Steagall Act, made it illegal for one firm to run both commercial and investment banks; the combined entities that existed had either to split up or to sell off one or the other business.

But American financial regulation was far more complicated than even this would suggest. Some banks were chartered by the states, and some by the federal government. In addition, the Federal Reserve was charged with regulating bank holding companies, corporate entities that control one or more banks. As a result, even commercial banks were regulated by a multitude of state and federal regulators. When one considers that there were many other types of financial institutions in the system—insurance companies, hedge funds—one can see why American financial regulation was often described as a patchwork quilt.

Despite its complexity, the American regulatory framework worked well for many decades. However, over the decades after World War II it became less and less effective. Financial institutions gradually learned how to evade the most onerous restrictions by relocating, setting up subsidiaries in low-regulation jurisdictions, or redefining themselves. Financiers, who were past masters at finding arbitrage opportunities that allowed them to buy low in one market and sell high in another, now became experts at "regulatory arbitrage," choosing corporate forms and locations that would limit the constraints of regulation, even playing one regulator off against another—including regulators in one country against those in other countries.[31] This is why so many American financial institutions conducted their more daring off-balance-sheet operations out of London, far removed from U.S. regulators. One example is the American International Group, the world's largest insurance company, which in 1987 set up its Financial Products division in London.

By the 1990s, it was clear that the regulatory structure needed some revision. Banks and other financial institutions had found ways to move many of their operations into unregulated or lightly regulated portions of the financial system. The intermingling of traditional banking with the complex investment vehicles in the shadow banking system meant that distinctions between commercial and investment banking were being eliminated in practice. Completely unregulated hedge funds were the fastest-growing segment of the financial market. In an attempt to make the regulatory structure more realistic, Congress passed the Financial Services Modernization Act of 1999. The act permitted more conglomeration and consolidation among financial institutions. Most prominently, it repealed the Glass-Steagall Act, breaking down barriers between investment banks, commercial banks, and insurance companies. By so doing, the act probably exposed financial institutions to greater competition, which put pressure on them to take on additional risks—something the legislation did not address.[32] However, the 1999 deregulation, including the repeal of Glass-Steagall, was more a recognition of the galloping evolution of financial activities than a cause of its acceleration.

Even with the regulatory revisions, there were plenty of opportunities for financial institutions to search out more forgiving regulators for their more questionable operations. In 2006, for example, Countrywide Financial, one of the largest players in the origination of residential mortgages, changed its status from a bank holding company to a savings and loan. The explicit purpose was to move the firm from the tougher supervision of the Federal Reserve to the more lax regulation of the Office of Thrift Supervision.[33]

There is little wonder Countrywide was happy to switch over to being a savings and loan as it shopped for a more sympathetic regulator. During the administration of George W. Bush in particular, the Office of Thrift Supervision prided itself on its opposition to stringent regulation. Bush's first appointee to head the agency, James Gilleran, was particularly enthusiastic. "At one press event in 2003," wrote the *Wall Street Journal*, "several bank regulators held gardening shears to represent their commitment to cut red tape for the industry. Mr. Gilleran brought a chain saw." Gilleran also oversaw a downsizing of the agency's workforce by 20 percent.[34]

After 2000, it was not just that regulators were finding it difficult to rein in the financial system; in the Bush administration, the regulators were often indifferent or even hostile to concerns that circumstances required more rigorous financial regulation. Yet both the new financial techniques and the flood of money into the country raised important issues that needed to be addressed. Foremost among these were the greater risks being taken on by financial institutions as they increased their leverage ratios dramatically. As figure 4 vividly illustrates, some financial institutions were extraordinarily exposed. The figure shows the leverage, measured as the ratio of assets to capital, for different segments of the financial sector. Banks were restricted by regulators; hedge funds and the GSEs were not, and so hedge funds had leverage ratios above 30, meaning that

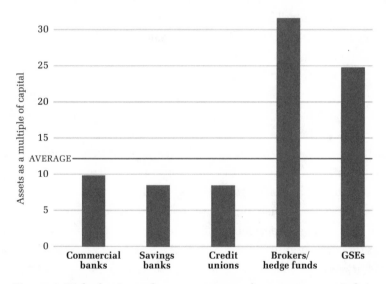

Figure 4. Risky business: leverage, measured as assets to capital, in the financial sector, July 2007–September 2007. The government-sponsored entities (GSEs) are Fannie Mae and Freddie Mac. Source: David Greenlaw, Jan Hatzius, Anil Kashyap, and Hyun S. Shin, "Leveraged losses: Lessons from the mortgage market meltdown," U.S. Monetary Policy Forum Report no. 2, February 2008.

total lending was 30 times equity. Of course, these numbers did not include all the conduits and other entities that had flooded into the shadow financial system.

As leverage ratios soared, financiers worked hard to make sure that regulatory restrictions did not limit their profits. The country's five big investment banks were particularly adamant, as they were more stringently regulated than some of their head-to-head competitors, such as hedge funds. Early in 2004, the investment banks— including Goldman Sachs and its head, Henry M. Paulson Jr. (who became Treasury secretary two years later)—went to their regulator, the SEC, to ask it to allow them to increase their leverage. Specifically, the investment banks wanted the SEC to relax constraints on how much capital the brokerage firms they controlled had to hold.

The investment banks argued that the regulators were misassessing the firms' activities as much riskier than they actually were. And they proposed, remarkably, that the regulators allow the investment banks *themselves* to evaluate and report on the risks associated with their investments. This self-regulation was justified, the investment banks claimed, because their sophisticated computer models were far better than anything the SEC used to measure risk. Furthermore, the firms and their managers had every reason to be prudent in their own risk management, so SEC involvement would be superfluous. The logical conclusion was that the investment banks should be allowed to determine how much capital they needed to hold, based on their own self-assessment.[35] As Lehman Brothers' lawyers put it, evaluations of risk "should be based upon a firm's internal estimates of annual default probabilities." And how would the firm estimate risk? It would use "default probabilities . . . derived from either actual historical experience or forward-looking market implied figures or some combination of the two."[36] Apart from the fact that the "historical experience" of many of these instruments went back at most a few years, the essence of the commitment was that the bank would look at previous experience, or at its models, and draw its own conclusions.

On April 28, 2004, the five commissioners of the SEC met in a basement room of the agency's headquarters to consider the investment banks' request. The discussion was led by Chairman William

H. Donaldson, a Wall Street fixture—founder of the investment bank Donaldson, Lufkin & Jenrette, former chairman of the New York Stock Exchange—who had been in office for a bit over a year. The commissioners debated the investment banks' plea for barely fifty-five minutes. Only one SEC commissioner voiced his doubts: Harvey Goldschmid, a professor of securities law at Columbia University, on leave at the commission. Goldschmid had been on the staff of Senator Paul Sarbanes (D-Md.) when the collapse of Enron had focused attention on the potential for corporations to abuse off-balance-sheet operations. The Enron scandal had, as a result, spurred new regulations requiring additional reporting of corporate accounts. The SEC staff assured Goldschmid that only big, sophisticated investment banks would be allowed to write their own capital requirements, and he observed, "We've said these are the big guys, but that means if anything goes wrong, it's going to be an awfully big mess."[37] The other commissioners laughed nervously. But after less than an hour, they decided unanimously to honor the investment banks' requests. The SEC loosened capital requirements and allowed investment banks to use their own risk management techniques to determine how much capital they needed to hold. The agency in charge of policing an important segment of the financial system had effectively decided to allow the financiers to police themselves.[38]

The SEC was not alone in responding to the capital inflow and financial boom by loosening restrictions. Some regulators were concerned about the safety of the commercial banks' off-the-book operations. For even if the conduits were off the banks' balance sheets, the sponsoring banks remained responsible for the activities of their special purpose entities, and they were not holding any additional capital in reserve to protect against eventual problems. In 2003, the SEC's designated arbiter of accounting standards ruled that commercial banks had to reel in the conduits they guaranteed, which would have required them to set aside much more capital. But almost immediately, the country's main bank regulators—the FDIC, the Fed, the Office of Thrift Supervision, the Office of the Comptroller of the Currency—collectively reversed this decision, decreeing that the all-important conduits issuing asset-backed commercial paper would not be bound by this requirement. This effectively meant that the commercial banks were off the hook for their principal off-book operations in the shadow financial system.[39]

Ignoring risk?

As financial institutions made ever riskier loans and investments, and raised leverage to unprecedented levels, the regulatory response was weak at best. There had been deregulation in the 1980s and 1990s, much of it addressing the new financial realities of electronic banking and trading. But after 2000 deregulation turned to nonregulation. This was especially true of the shadow financial system, which was growing quickly and becoming more important to the smooth running of the economy. The regulators should have enforced adequate capital requirements to ensure that this system could withstand shocks. However, like the SEC, the country's financial regulators decided explicitly either to leave the shadow financial system alone or to leave the management of its risks to the financial institutions themselves.

The same was true for CDSs, which were proliferating like financial kudzu. The Commodity Futures Modernization Act of 2000 had exempted CDSs from regulation, permitting investors to buy and sell CDSs over the counter, that is, in private, direct transactions rather than on organized markets. This practice was surprising since CDSs were both derivatives and securities, which normally would have required them to be traded on central exchanges subject to clear rules about information, disclosure, and prudence. Other derivatives, such as interest-rate futures and options on the S&P 500, were traded openly on central exchanges such as the Chicago Mercantile Exchange and the New York Mercantile Exchange. But CDSs were not subject to either derivative or securities regulations, and because they were traded in private there was no real way to know exactly which firms were or were not protected in the event of difficulties. Nor were those issuing CDSs required to hold reserves, even though it was clear that inasmuch as these securities effectively operated as insurance, it might be necessary for the issuers to pay off the purchasers in case the credits they were meant to insure went bad.

The opacity of the CDSs helped mask the dangers building up in the shadow financial system. Many investors felt that CDSs protected them against the risks they were taking, but it turned out the risk was only being camouflaged.

Financial regulators might have been expected to attempt to restrain some of these activities. All of the boom-era developments—shadow markets full of new and untested financial instruments, financial innovations that left investors in the dark about the nature of their investments, financial institutions whose profits depended on avoiding provisions against potential losses—put the financial system as a whole, and the economy as a whole, at risk.[40]

But the atmosphere in Washington at this time was dominated by a powerful predisposition to keep regulatory hands off the financial system. Fed Chairman Alan Greenspan was a key spokesman for that hands-off approach. He insisted in 2005 that "private regulation generally has proved far better at constraining excessive risk-taking than has government regulation."[41] While there were good reasons to question Greenspan's assertion both theoretically and empirically, when the top financial regulator argues so strongly for a hands-off approach, others follow his lead.

And so there was little or no attempt to rein in the financial excesses. It was not just ideology that protected the bankers from intrusive regulators and politicians. Finance, as an industry, was politically powerful. America's financial institutions have long had close ties to the country's economic policymakers, and in the heady years of financial expansion they used their power to protect their profits from potential regulatory oversight.

Financiers, of course, had a lot at stake. By the middle of the decade, financial activities were accounting for an unprecedented 8 percent of GDP, over $400 billion in 2005.[42] And the participants in this financial boom were richly rewarded; a third of all corporate profits were accounted for by finance.[43] At every level, and especially at the top, compensation was pushed up—at least a third of the salary differential between workers in the financial sector and elsewhere was attributable to profits that financiers were simply extracting from the rest of the economy, rather than to any economic value they were creating.[44]

The special role of finance in the modern American political economy was certainly evident during the borrowing boom between 2001 and 2007. The inventory of Wall Streeters involved in making crucial policy decisions before, during, and after the Bush boom is virtually endless. Indeed, a reporter investigating the influential associations of just one of the principal investment banks of the era, Goldman Sachs, remarked that trying to keep track of them was "like trying to make a list of everything."[45] Robert Rubin, former co-chairman of Goldman Sachs, served as Treasury secretary for most of Bill Clinton's time in office, and was succeeded by his protégé, Lawrence Summers; they were central to important regulatory decisions that made the Bush boom in finance possible. Henry Paulson, former CEO of Goldman Sachs, was Treasury secretary for the crucial last years of the Bush administration, starting in the spring of 2006; Bush's chief of staff, Joshua Bolten, was another Goldman alumnus. "The heads of the Canadian and Italian national banks are Goldman alums," the list-making journalist continued, "as is the head of the World Bank, the head of the New York Stock Exchange, the last two heads of the Federal Reserve Bank of New York—which, incidentally, is now in charge of overseeing Goldman."[46]

Wall Street's impact on Washington goes deeper than just the personal relations between financiers and policymakers; there was a deep and mutual dependence from 2001 to 2007. The government depended on access to domestic and international finance to underwrite its own borrowing as deficits grew; the private sector's vibrancy similarly depended on a continued flow of funds from and through the world's financial institutions. The influence of financial markets on government policy stems largely from finance's central position in the contemporary American economy—a reality that led Democratic strategist James Carville to remark that if there is reincarnation, "I want to come back as the bond market. You can intimidate everybody."[47] None of this rules out the possibility of purposive manipulation of the political process by self-interested bankers— there is a long history of that—but even in the absence of anything conspiratorial, the American political economy was increasingly centered around the financial services, insurance, and real estate complex.[48]

All this made the American financial system ever more volatile. Capital inflows provided the fuel; leverage and greater risk taking supplied the oxygen and ensured a ready supply of sparks; financial regulators ignored the dangers and even deactivated some of their alarms; and financiers with great political influence prevailed on policymakers to let them continue to do business as usual even as flames began to break out, acting as if there were no smoke, let alone fire. All the ingredients for a massive conflagration were in place.

"We're all subprime now"

Despite the proliferation of warnings, key policymakers continued to view the boom in housing prices with equanimity.[49] They attributed rising housing prices to economic dynamism: as productivity and wages rose, with interest rates very low, the prices of housing and other assets were going to rise. Some pointed to demographic trends and to such local factors as regional land-use restrictions and tax policy, since the boom was concentrated in coastal regions.

During the summer of 2006, there were growing indications that housing prices had stopped rising, and that some of the regional housing price indices had even turned down. The optimists argued that the problems in the housing market were containable. They pointed out that the early declines were limited to some parts of the country; that residential construction was not a particularly large share of the economy; even at its peak, it didn't account for more than 5 percent of total GDP. Moreover, the Fed had been increasing interest rates after 2004 to cool off the housing market, so perhaps the central bank had simply been successful.

The situation virtually demanded optimism, for the viability of the new financial system depended on continually rising housing prices. So long as one assumed that housing prices would continue to rise, then the new mortgages were safe—including those to subprime borrowers. If the new mortgages were safe, so were the financial assets they backed, and the ones based on those assets, and the contracts that insured the other assets, and the rest of the components of the new financial system. But if there were a nationwide decline in home prices, the entire financial edifice would be at risk, and trouble would jump from asset to asset, floor to floor, until the financial structure as a whole was in flames.

Policymakers were about to be reminded of one of the central lessons of the Great Depression: the financial system intermittently experiences booms and busts, and the busts can be disastrous not just for bankers but for the entire economy. When a major building in the middle of a city catches fire, it endangers all the others—which is the justification for fire codes to ensure that building owners take into account the impact of their behavior on others as well as on themselves. Like fire prevention, financial stability is a public good, something that cannot be provided effectively only by the private sector but that requires government involvement. This is the reason for comprehensive government regulation of finance; without it, the banking system, the entire financial system, and the economy as a whole could be subjected to periodic panics and crashes. The financial expansion of 2001–2007, driven in large part by a continual increase in housing prices, was vulnerable to a turnaround and consequent panic. Optimists in the financial community, and their supporters in government, argued that such a turnaround was unthinkable, that there could not be a deep, nationwide decline in housing prices. In 2007, the unthinkable began.

The Death Spiral

CHAPTER FOUR

On the evening of Thursday, September 18, 2008, as the world's financial system seemed to grind to a halt, America's principal economic policymakers and the leaders of Congress gathered around a conference table in the office of Speaker of the House Nancy Pelosi (D-Calif.). Treasury Secretary Henry Paulson, with Securities and Exchange Commission Chairman Christopher Cox at his side, called the meeting to order. Paulson immediately turned the proceedings over to Federal Reserve Chairman Ben Bernanke.

"We are facing a financial crisis on multiple fronts," Bernanke said. "Despite our actions over the past several months, investors are still losing confidence. There's a run on the money-market funds. The last two big investment banks are under siege. The situation is severe . . . and the Fed is out of tools." Something needed to be done, and quickly: "We are headed for the worst financial crisis in the nation's history. . . . We're talking about a matter of days."

The presentation was intended to impress on the senators and members of Congress who were present the need for immediate action. It had the desired effect. Senator Charles Schumer (D-N.Y.)

reported, "When you listened to them describe it, you gulped. . . . History was sort of hanging over it, like this was a moment." According to Senator Christopher J. Dodd (D-Conn.), "We have never heard language like this."[1]

The capital flow cycle had ended with a bang, and the economic future seemed to hang in the balance. How did it come to this? What turned the end of a borrowing binge into a financial collapse that threatened the very fabric of the American, and the world, economy?

Mis-estimating risk

For seven years, as we have seen, foreign capital flooded into the United States, helping to fuel an explosion in housing finance and in home prices. There was nothing particularly surprising about this, as most large-scale capital inflows are associated with dramatic financial and real estate expansions. The eventual emergence of a bubble in housing, and in housing finance, was similarly unremarkable: expansions often grow into booms, then into bubbles. Nor was it unusual that the upswing eventually came to an end. Bubbles feed on themselves as they continue, but in time they burst. In the final stages of a bubble, all it takes is a reversal in sentiment to pull investors out of the market, for the first rule for investors as a bubble bursts is that the sooner you get out, the better. And so it was inevitable that something in the American housing market would give, and that housing prices would cease rising at a rate of 10 to 15 percent a year. There were special features of this particular bubble, though, such that when it popped, the entire financial system crashed.

The most commonly watched measure of housing prices, the Case-Shiller index of twenty major metropolitan areas, tracked the end of the bubble. From the middle of 2006 until the middle of 2007, housing prices drifted downward by about 3 percent. During the summer of 2007, the index began to fall precipitously, by 10 percent over the next six months. Over the course of 2008, prices dropped by nearly 20 percent. In one year, Americans saw their homes lose over $3.3 trillion in value. As 2009 began, American housing prices were one-third below where they had been at the height of the boom in early 2006, and were headed still lower.[2] By then, one in six American homeowners with a mortgage was in a house worth less than the mortgage—putting the mortgage "underwater," in the parlance of the industry—and more than one-fifth of all homes sold had been in foreclosure.

The overall decline in housing prices masked much greater collapses in certain parts of the country, and with especially vulnerable homeowners. Where the boom had been particularly pronounced, the collapse was particularly devastating; among lower-income homeowners, it was doubly devastating. In the Los Angeles, Miami, and San Diego areas, prices of the lower tier of houses peaked in early 2007 at 3 to 3.5 times their 2000 levels; over the course of the next two years, their prices dropped by between 50 and 60 percent. Las Vegas was even harder hit: after rising to a 2007 peak at 2.4 times 2000 prices, lower-tier home prices fell nearly two-thirds, and by mid-2009 they were 15 percent *below* their 2000 levels. In places like this, half to two-thirds of all mortgages were underwater, and half of all house sales were of foreclosed properties.[3] And the recession that began in December 2007 hit hardest precisely those regions and the people who were already having the most trouble meeting their payments.

As prices dropped, the feedback loop that had fed the bubble took hold in reverse, with a vengeance. Homeowners with mortgages worth more—sometimes much more—than their homes had good reasons simply to give up and turn the house over to the bank. As foreclosures mounted and creditors tried to unload the houses they had been stuck with, prices were forced down further. Even many of those who wanted to try to keep up payments were done in by the financial innovations that had previously made their mortgages attractive. When home prices were rising, it was easy to refinance at attractive rates; as they fell, it became impossible to refinance. This was especially a problem for the millions of homeowners with two- or three-year teaser rates who had planned to refinance before the loan reset to a higher interest rate. For many of these homeowners, the reset made it simply impossible to pay the mortgage. Just as the ready availability of mortgages before 2007 depended on constantly rising home prices, the price decline virtually dried up the supply of loans, including refinancings, to all but the most creditworthy of borrowers.

The subprime segment of the mortgage market was the first to go, for several reasons. Because most subprime mortgages did not require a big down payment, even a small decline in house prices could wipe out any equity the mortgage holder had in the house and put the mortgage underwater, with a strong incentive to default. In addition, the teaser/reset structure of most subprime mortgages was extreme, with the rise in interest rates particularly large. This made the viability of subprime mortgages especially reliant on rising home prices, and meant that it was particularly likely that a decline in the value of the home would confront the homeowner with an interest rate well beyond his means.[4] In addition, many of the subprime mortgages were on properties in areas that had experienced the biggest bubbles and were now going through the biggest busts, and the homeowners were typically on weak financial footing to start with. By early 2008, one-fourth of all homeowners with subprime mortgages were at least three months behind on their payments, and subprime mortgages accounted for about half of all foreclosures, even though they represented only one-fifteenth of mortgages outstanding.[5]

The subprime market was simply the canary in the coal mine for the rest of the housing sector. Unsustainable borrowing and adjustable interest rates were not restricted to the subprime market. Nor were expectations of rising house prices specific to subprime mortgages. The housing finance sector's merry ride upward had been self-reinforcing: people bought houses in anticipation of appreciation, and bankers financed these purchases because they shared this anticipation. In that environment, low down payments, resets, and adjustable interest rates were not a problem. But the process also worked in reverse. As home prices fell, defaults proliferated, the demand for housing collapsed, the number of foreclosures multiplied—and each of these things accelerated the others. As one close observer of the housing market concluded early in 2008, "We're all subprime now."[6]

The continued decline in housing prices began to cause concern even among policymakers in the Bush administration. Nonetheless, in March 2007, Chairman Bernanke assured Congress's Joint Economic Committee that "the problems in the subprime market seem likely to be contained."[7] Bernanke and others did not yet appreciate that sliding housing prices were reverberating through the structure of housing finance that had built up over the decade. But how could a decline in home prices implicate the entire American financial system? Where were the flaws in the business models financiers had been using that left them so exposed?

The first step in turning the housing crisis into a financial crisis was to savage the assumptions on which structured financial instruments had been constructed. The financial engineers and the quantitative analysts who worked with them had developed sophisticated models to assess the risks associated with various assets, and innovative securities to reduce the impact of what risk there was.[8] When housing prices stopped rising, began falling, and continued to fall, the financial engineers and their customers were quick to argue that what was happening was an incredibly rare, hard-to-predict series of events—a "black swan," in the phrase of Nasim Nicholas Taleb.[9] David Viniar, Goldman Sachs' chief financial officer, said of the movement of asset prices in response to the housing crisis, "We were seeing things that were 25-standard deviation moves, several days in a row."[10] This is nonsense: a standard deviation is the measure of how variable movements are, and a 25-standard-deviation move occurs once every several thousand years, while the models were based on data collected over just a few years. It was also ingenuous, as the forecasting errors were a clear result of the financiers' unjustified assumption of a continual rise in housing prices, and of their denial of the possibility of a nationwide downturn, even though such a downturn has happened several times over the past century.[11] Moreover, most of the instruments whose future was being predicted had been around only for a decade at most, which was far too short a period to make accurate estimates of their riskiness.[12]

The possibility of a decline in housing prices was not the only thing the financial engineers had missed. Securitization with the pooling of mortgages was supposed to reduce risk dramatically, because it would include mortgages from many regions whose housing prices would not, investors were assured, move together. But the 2007–2009 housing downturn was largely synchronized across the country. While the prices in some regions started to decline before those in others, and some regional prices fell more than others, by 2009 virtually the entire country had experienced declining house prices. The diversification benefit from pooled mortgage-backed securities dissipated, for the shocks to the underlying assets—home prices and the fate of associated mortgages—were correlated, rather than uncorrelated.

But to turn a housing crisis into a financial breakdown required more than just bad predictions: it required an explicit reliance of financial markets on the bad predictions. In fact, the collapse in housing prices called into question the assets that underpinned the shadow financial system, and with it the entire structure of American finance. All of this rested on expectations built into the innovative financial instruments developed over the previous decade, expectations that were now being proved wrong. The delicate architecture of structured finance that had been engineered with the housing boom as its foundation was beginning to sway dangerously.

Compounding risk

The business model driving America's financial system, traditional and shadow, was now based on mortgage-related securities. Virtually every financial institution—commercial banks and their conduits, investment banks, hedge funds—relied heavily on investments in securities related to home mortgages. If the mortgages were bad, the securities based on them were just as bad, or worse, or much worse. The more flawed were the predictions embodied in the mortgage-related securities, the more disastrous would be the results for the securities, and for the business model that had come to dominate the American financial system.

One of the main reasons for the popularity of the collateralized debt (or mortgage) obligations (CDOs or CMOs) was precisely that they were backed by collateral, the mortgaged houses. Even if a $200,000 mortgage on a $250,000 house wasn't serviced, the bank (or other servicing agent) could foreclose on the house. This was cumbersome and costly, but at least it more or less guaranteed that investors would get their money back. However, this calculus depended on the value of the house rising, or at least not falling. For if the house was now worth $150,000—a decline in line with that seen around the country—then a foreclosure still meant a massive loss to the investor. As the value of the collateral dropped, so did the value of the mortgage, and then the value of the security based on the mortgage, and with it the value of the investment. The safety that collateral was supposed to provide was gone.

The structured finance that had become the mainstay of American finance was seriously exposed. It was not only that mortgage-backed securities were losing their collateral backing, but also that as homeowners fell behind with their payments, the value of the mortgages declined, and so did the value of any securities based on these mortgages. If the trouble were with one homeowner, or a scattered few, the problem might be dissipated through diversified mortgage pools. But now over ten million homeowners were seriously behind on their payments, and one in five mortgages was underwater.

The complex financial instruments that dominated markets turned out to be exquisitely vulnerable. The tranche construction was engineered to protect investors in the senior (more creditworthy) tranches from problems that might arise with less reliable mortgages. If the mortgage pool ran into difficulties, investors in the upper tranches were supposed to be protected from whatever endangered the lower-rated tranches. However, as problems proliferated much faster than the engineers had expected, trouble crept upward toward the top-rated tranches. The more house prices declined, the faster delinquency rates and foreclosures for subprime mortgages skyrocketed, the more tranches of the securities were corrupted. The idea had been to set up a structure that would quarantine healthy securities from infection by mediocre mortgages, but instead the tranche structure was allowing mortgages gone bad—toxic assets— to poison higher and higher tranches, assets that were supposed to be practically riskless.

Problems with assets in the lower tranches were soon affecting the upper tranches at an accelerating rate, as the rot proved contagious. The implications were brought home to Robert Rodriguez and his colleagues at First Pacific Advisors when they spoke to analysts at Fitch, the credit rating agency, in March 2007 to try to see how bad things could get. The Fitch analysts told one of Rodriguez's associates that their ratings relied on an expected home price appreciation (HPA) of several percentage points a year. Rodriguez recalled, "My associate then asked, 'What if HPA was flat for an extended period of time?' They responded that their model would start to break down. He then asked, 'What if HPA were to decline 1% to 2% for an extended period of time?' They responded that their models would break down completely. He then asked, 'With 2% depreciation, how far up the rating's scale would it harm?' They responded that it might go as high as the AA or AAA tranches."[13] The point was clear: a 2 percent decline in housing prices could turn top-rated assets into junk. And prices were in the process of declining more than 10 percent in six months.

As the crisis gathered, investors and others uncovered further flaws in the financial structure erected over the previous decade. One was that the financial engineering had made it very difficult for investors to figure out what was happening with their investments. The difficulties caused by complicated connections between ultimate investors and the original mortgage debtors were illustrated by a *New Yorker* cartoon that showed two bewildered gangsters in an office complaining, "With these credit default swaps, I never know whose legs I'm supposed to break."[14] In adding layer on layer of securitization, of increasing degrees of complexity, the financial engineers had reduced the transparency of the overall financial system. This meant that as concerns grew, they would not be restricted to particular mortgages or mortgage pools, or to particular mortgage lenders, or to particular investors in mortgage-backed securities. These opaque operations were piled on top of each other in ways that almost nobody understood, which created massive uncertainties and scared investors everywhere.

Another problem that emerged as the mortgage market spiraled downward was that the predominance of the originate-to-distribute model of mortgage finance had reduced the incentive for banks to assess carefully the risk attributes of borrowers, and to monitor what the borrowers did with the loans. If the bank could off-load the loans, then it was not really concerned if the borrowers defaulted after a couple of years. By then, it would be someone else's problem.

As investors came to realize that the mortgage originators had, in many cases, been exceedingly cavalier with lending standards, their concerns about the underlying value of their investments only grew.

There were also suspicions that many of the subprime mortgages were questionable, even fraudulent. The FBI in fact found that mortgage fraud had become increasingly common. Typically, industry insiders would collude with borrowers to falsify income statements, inflate home appraisals, or otherwise deceive the ultimate investors into thinking they were getting a more valuable asset than was in fact the case.[15] Some of the financial institutions involved have even been accused of purposely loading up securities with bad mortgages, so that they and their customers could bet against the securities. On April 16, 2010, the SEC charged Goldman Sachs with working together with hedge fund manager John Paulson to create securities designed to fail if the housing market declined, so that Paulson could bet against them. Goldman Sachs then sold those securities to its clients, including the German bank IKB Deutsche Industriebank, without disclosing that the securities were in fact expected to fail. These were among the securities that Ken Guy bought on behalf of the King County investment pool. As events unfolded, Paulson made nearly $1 billion by betting against these securities, Goldman made $15 million in fees, while IKB lost most of its $150 million investment.[16] These losses were then passed on to other investors in the securities, including King County.

The complex architecture of American finance made it easier to mask fraud, abuse, and misuse. As home prices plummeted and the weaknesses were revealed, floor after floor of the financial house of cards gave way.

Marking to market when there is no market

Housing finance difficulties grew over the course of 2007. It was apparent that housing prices had stopped rising, and even started falling, but the lack of transparency of the structured financial instruments made it hard to gauge the extent of the problem. As one asset manager put it, "No one knows what subprime securities are really worth."[17] This failing was rectified by yet another financial innovation. In January 2006, a firm called Markit launched an asset-backed securities index called ABX, which tracked the value of securities backed by subprime mortgages. The index was compiled from a group of securities based on subprime mortgages and sponsored by major investment banks; there were different indices for securities with different credit ratings. Whereas previously investors had had only relatively imprecise ways to evaluate the CDOs they were considering buying, or they owned, the new index reflected the market's valuation of CDOs with different ratings. For its first year, the index was stable. But early in 2007, as intimations of disaster began to circulate, it gave clear warnings.

In February 2007, the credit rating agencies were beginning to downgrade some of the lower-rated tranches of mortgage-backed securities, and the ABX index began to fall. By the end of the month, the index for the lowest tranches of subprime mortgage–backed securities was down almost 40 percent. Some investors took comfort in the fact that these drops were concentrated in the lower-rated indices, and even these stabilized during the spring. But in July, another decline in the lower tranches began, and this time the decline hit even the higher-rated, supposedly safer, indices. By the end of August 2007, the lower tranches were worth barely thirty-five cents on the original dollar, while the AA index, the second highest, was down more than 30 percent, and even the AAA index was down by 10 percent.[18] Meanwhile, Moody's was rapidly downgrading thousands of tranches of structured finance securities, and *one-third* of the securities being downgraded had been in Moody's highest-rated, AAA, category—a class that was supposed to be practically risk free. This meant that the trillions of dollars' worth of securities backed by subprime mortgages were now worth only a fraction of their original value—and the fraction was shrinking continually.[19] The subprime segment of the housing finance market was in something close to free fall.

Even accounting standards were playing a role. Financial institutions are required, by generally accepted accounting principles, to make sure that their assets are "marked to market." This means that they have to record the value of assets on their books at the price at which the market evaluates them at that moment, not at the price purchased or at some other figure. A bank might hold a mortgage-backed security, like a CDO, for which it paid $1 million, at a time when all the mortgages that backed the security were up-to-date. But as homeowners fell behind on payments or defaulted on many of the underlying mortgages, the value of the CDO dropped. The bank then had to revalue the security at the market price, which was now substantially less than $1 million.

The principle of marking to market makes sense in normal times, when markets provide accurate signals of the true value of assets. But in times of turmoil, markets can be buffeted by forces that affect their ability to evaluate assets, and that can send prices gyrating in ways unrelated to economic fundamentals. As more mortgages defaulted at the same time, the market price of the securities they backed fell; this left banks with less valuable assets on their books. But they still had the same liabilities, and the same reserve and capital requirements from the regulators. This forced the banks to sell off some assets, such as the falling CDOs, to stay solvent. These "fire sales" themselves put more downward pressure on CDO prices, so that the remaining assets in the banks' portfolios were worth even less, which forced the banks to sell more assets, which caused yet more CDO price declines. The reasonable accounting principle of marking to market added yet another component to the massive adverse feedback loop, and made movements in asset prices more extreme, pushing them inordinately lower in the downswing just as it pushed them inordinately higher in the upturn.[20]

Clever financial engineering continued to exacerbate the difficulties. Just as successive layers of securities had allowed financial institutions to leverage up the scale of their investments, the layering compounded problems at one level by infecting other levels. The CDO^2s in particular were extremely sensitive to a deterioration in the mortgage market. They had been constructed on the assumption that mortgage problems around the country would not be synchronized. But with a nationwide decline in housing prices, correlations soon rose above what was anticipated, and the securities lost value *very* quickly. This turned out to be true even for the most highly rated CDO^2s. A subprime-backed CDO^2 with a AAA rating could be made into junk simply if it turned out that mortgage defaults were somewhat more correlated with one another than had originally been assumed.

The CDO^{2}s were even more sensitive to rising mortgage default rates. A typical CDO^2 tranche with a top, AAA, rating might assume a default probability of 5 percent. If the actual default rate went to 10 percent, the tranche would be junk, worth at best fifty cents on the dollar. And by early 2007, the probability that a subprime mortgage written in 2005 or 2006, at the height of the boom, would be in default was about 20 percent.[21]

As more and more of the mortgage-backed securities became toxic, the financially engineered quasi-insurance represented by credit default swaps (CDSs) also turned out to be largely illusory. In theory, CDSs could allow investors to protect themselves against risks. But in practice, their primary market was among investors who used them as tools of speculative finance, that is, as a way of betting against other assets.[22] By 2007 the actual value of the underlying contracts on which the CDSs were based was about $2 trillion, but there were at that point more than $50 trillion in CDSs outstanding, most of them bought with borrowed money for purely speculative purposes.[23] With this proliferation, there was a good chance that there was not enough money standing behind the contracts to make good on them if things went wrong. Now that it seemed increasingly plausible that the "insurance" would be called upon, it became clear that it would be impossible for the holders to honor all of the protection contracts. The problem was compounded by the fact that CDSs were traded over the counter, that is, just between the two involved parties, so that nobody could form a broader view of how exposed the financial system as a whole might be.[24]

With mortgage-backed assets distributed throughout the financial system, the crisis quickly spread throughout the economy. Only a third of the mortgage-backed assets were held by FDIC-insured commercial banks; the rest were held by investment banks, life insurance companies, pension funds, foreign investors, and state and municipal government funds—like Ken Guy's King County fund in Washington.[25]

The downward slide revealed a key irony. Securitization and mortgage-backed derivatives had as one goal the dispersion of region-specific risk across the country and around the world. In doing that, housing catastrophes in South Florida and Southern California were now felt everywhere. The counterpart to the dispersion of risk was that securitization had increased risk to the system as a whole. The country's most important financial institutions had invested in assets that were protected from isolated regional real estate downturns, but that were all massively exposed to a broad national housing price decline. So the American financial system was practically defenseless against the system-wide shock it was experiencing. Entire classes of investments that had become central to the nation's finances were disintegrating and were bringing the financial system down with them.[26]

In 2003, Warren Buffett warned the shareholders of his Berkshire Hathaway holding company about opaque and complex financial innovations. America's most famous investor said, "Derivatives are financial weapons of mass destruction, carrying dangers that, while now latent, are potentially lethal."[27] Buffett's warning seemed particularly apt now, as housing-based derivatives had become toxic assets, poisoning previously healthy investments. As investors everywhere rapidly lost confidence in the financial system, it spiraled down toward a traditional bank run. But how could there be a bank run if the nation's finances were no longer dominated by banks, but by derivatives markets? The world was about to find out.

Counterparty risk

The modern financial system could experience a bank run even without banks, for it turned out that investors could engage in a run on the shadow banking system that was just as devastating as an old-fashioned bank run. In a traditional bank run, depositors in a bank are worried that the bank will fail, and they pull their money out. The depositors, who have lent the bank money, typically fear that the bank's own investments have gone bad. In accounting terms, the bank has liabilities—owes money—to depositors, and has assets from—is owed money by—its debtors (and its other investments). If the bank's debtors cannot pay the bank, or the bank's investments lose money, the bank cannot pay its depositors: the bank's assets are inadequate to cover its liabilities. Bank runs can lead to broader panics, which can freeze the entire financial system, and with it the entire economy—as they did in the early 1930s, before deposit insurance and extensive regulatory supervision existed in the United States.

A similar pattern emerged in the shadow banking system when people lost confidence in hedge funds, investment banks, special purpose entities, and derivatives. Investment banks, for example, borrow money in the short-term money market in order to be able to make investments. This means that they have to continually "roll over" their short-term borrowing to match their assets—just as commercial banks have to convince depositors to keep their money in the bank. Many of these loans are on extremely short terms, often overnight. At the height of the boom, even the country's smallest investment bank, Bear Stearns, with assets of about $400 billion, had to roll over between $50 and $60 billion every day.[28] The more highly leveraged a financial institution is, the more it relies on borrowing in the short-term markets and the more it depends on being able to continue that borrowing.[29] If those who have been lending to the investment bank are worried that the bank's assets are going bad, they will refuse to roll over their short-term loans. If the investment bank can't borrow, it has to sell off some of its assets to pay off its debts. If all investment banks are having increasing trouble borrowing—perhaps because there are widespread fears about the whole range of investments they've made—then they will all try to sell off assets at once, driving prices down.

A loss of confidence can start a "death spiral." Worries about mortgage-backed securities, for example, lead short-term lenders to reduce lending to investment banks; the investment banks have to sell off their mortgage-backed securities to meet their obligations; the price of mortgage-backed securities falls further, leading short-term lenders to withdraw even more loans from the investment banks; and so on.

Hedge funds, special purpose entities, and other components of the shadow financial system faced similar problems. Conduits such as Rhinebridge and Ormond Quay issued short-term asset-backed commercial paper to raise money, which they then invested in mort-gage-related securities such as CDOs. The lenders to Ormond Quay were willing to buy its commercial paper because these short-term bonds were backed by the CDOs that Ormond Quay bought (it was, after all, *asset-backed* commercial paper). Early in 2007, before the crisis hit, $10 billion in Ormond Quay's assets, investments in CDOs and other securities, might serve as collateral for $9.8 billion in com-mercial paper.

But borrowing by a conduit depended on the collateral it could provide, and the collateral depended on the performance of the con-duit's investments. In 2007, as the value of the mortgages backing the CDOs fell, the value of the CDOs fell with them, and as the value of the CDOs fell, their worth as collateral declined. By September 2007, with the value of even highly rated CDOs falling, only $10 bil-lion in CDOs would be accepted as collateral for $9 billion in com-mercial paper borrowing. Ormond Quay would have to sell off $800 million in assets to pay back the commercial paper it could not roll over. Of course, this forced sell-off contributed to a further decline in CDO prices, as the death spiral proceeded. By the end of 2007, $10 billion in the most highly rated CDOs would only allow $8 bil-lion in commercial paper issues, so Ormond Quay would have to sell another billion dollars' worth of assets. And this was for the most highly rated mortgage-backed securities: the lower-ranked CDOs were dropping in value at least twice as fast, and by early 2008 they were not even being accepted as collateral. Their decline brought down higher-ranked CDOs as well, so that by the middle of 2008 even AA-rated CDOs were no good as collateral.[30]

Short-term lenders to financial institutions increasingly came to believe that the institutions had made bad investments and were at risk of failing. Investors refused to make the short-term loans, such as with short-term commercial paper, that investment banks, hedge funds, conduits, and other nonbank institutions relied on.[31]

The buzzword of this run on the markets was "counterparty risk," the risk that one party to a contract would not fulfill its obligations. The most common counterparty risk was that a debtor would default on its debts. As the subprime crisis evolved into a broader financial crisis, investors who had previously been happy to lend to commercial banks, investment banks, hedge funds, special purpose entities, and conduits were more and more concerned that these financial institutions were saddled with some very bad investments, and that they might not be able to service their debts. This hit the market for the commercial paper used for such purposes particularly hard. In the middle of 2007 many investors simply stopped buying asset-backed commercial paper. There was a panic-stricken flight away from these short-term loans, with all the effects of a bank run.

Another indication of how short-term financing had dried up for the masters of the shadow financial system was a previously little-known indicator, the "TED spread." This is the difference between the interest rate on three-month Treasury bills (hence "T") and the three-month London Interbank Offered Rate (LIBOR; originally the euro dollar rate, hence "ED"). The "T" in TED is what a bank or other financial institution would get for parking money in riskless three-month Treasuries; the "ED" is what the bank would get for lending money on the three-month London interbank market. Since loans from one bank to another are practically risk free in normal times, the TED spread is usually about 0.3 percent—that is, the three-month LIBOR is 0.3 percent higher than the rate on three-month Treasury bills. But in the summer of 2007 this spread began to rise, as counterparty risk made banks and others wary of lending money even to the very largest international banks. In August 2007, the TED spread went above 2 percent, some seven times its normal level: it was increasingly hard for even the world's biggest banks to borrow money. This was the ultimate in counterparty risk: Citibank would not lend to Goldman Sachs, and vice versa, because they feared they would not be repaid.

The death spiral had begun. And it seemed that there might be one big difference between a run on commercial banks and a run on shadow finance. The commercial banking system could avoid the death spiral either with deposit insurance, so that depositors had no reason to withdraw funds, or with a lender of last resort, to make emergency loans to stop the spiral. With neither deposit insurance nor a lender of last resort, the shadow financial system entered the death spiral and soon faced the prospect of death.

The collapse

In June and July 2007, as rating agencies downgraded tranche after tranche of previously trustworthy CDOs, hedge funds came under increasing pressure. Investors in the funds withdrew more and more of their money. This came on top of demands that the hedge funds pony up more cash due to the falling value of the collateral they had provided their lenders. Soon two hedge funds associated with Bear Stearns could not provide enough backing. One of the fund's creditors claimed $850 million in CDOs that had been put up as collateral, but they could find buyers for only $100 million of the securities. This put Bear Stearns over a barrel: even though the parent company had staked only about $40 million on the funds, they were so highly leveraged that the attempt to rescue them required Bear Stearns to pour $3.2 billion of its own money into the two funds in June 2007.[32] Even with this massive assistance, the two funds were bankrupt by the end of July. At much the same time, the German bank IKB, which had sponsored the Rhinebridge conduit, failed, brought down by the collapse of the conduit itself; Ken Guy and municipal funds everywhere were starting to feel the effects. The next few weeks saw further bank failures in the United States and Europe.

Some of Goldman Sachs' flagship in-house hedge funds were next to feel the heat. One of them, GEO (Global Equities Opportunity), lost one-third of its value in two weeks in early August 2007. Goldman Sachs, the fund's sponsor, had to sink $2 billion into the fund to build up its capital. Two other Goldman Sachs funds—North American Equity Opportunities (NEO) and Global Alpha—also hit the skids. Over the course of the next several months, the assets of these three funds plummeted from $16 billion to less than $4 billion, and NEO had to be closed down.[33] As fear spread to Europe, the Fed and the European Central Bank injected about $150 billion into the overnight market, allowing banks to borrow more freely from one another.

As problems spread, the Fed responded by loosening monetary policy at a breakneck pace. In September 2007, the central bank reduced interest rates (the Federal Funds rate) from 6.25 percent to

5.75 percent, then later to 5.50 percent, then again to 5.25 percent in December. Still the rot spread. On January 22, 2008, the Fed dropped the Federal Funds rate an unprecedented 75 basis points (that is, 0.75 percent), with another 50-basis-point reduction just over a week later. Within three months, the Fed had reduced interest rates by 2.25 percentage points. Policymakers were starting to take the problems seriously. But as long as house prices continued to deteriorate, their options were limited.[34]

The central bank's principal remaining tool was to lend to troubled financial institutions that were having difficulties borrowing elsewhere. In normal times, the Fed lends to commercial banks that need liquidity—ready money—through the "discount window." This is a facility for the Fed to make loans relatively cheaply, requiring that the bank post collateral, usually Treasury bills or other high-grade securities. By late 2007, many of the banks most in need of money did not have enough eligible securities to post. In addition, banks that used the discount window were perceived to be in trouble, which could exacerbate the run on them. For these reasons, in December 2007 the Fed instituted the Term Auction Facility (TAF) for commercial banks. Under its terms, the Fed could accept many other assets as collateral, including mortgage-backed securities, so long as they were rated AAA. In addition, use of the facility would be anonymous so that the banks could avoid any potential stigma.

But the central bank could not do much to affect the continuing decline in home prices, which was the fundamental cause of the financial storm that was gathering. The assets underlying much of the financial system—the mortgages behind the asset-backed securities—were going sour at an accelerating pace. Rates of delinquency and default were rising in other categories of mortgages, in addition to the subprime, and all over the country. And as the prices of mortgage-related securities, CDOs, and other derivatives continued to fall, suspicions grew apace about the general health of financial firms. Investors even began to worry about the risks associated with debt owed by Fannie Mae and Freddie Mac, the two government-sponsored enterprises that were major issuers of mortgage-backed securities.

As fear cascaded through the financial system, it began to threaten the more vulnerable institutions. Bear Stearns, the smallest of the major investment banks, had expanded very aggressively during the boom. This put the firm on particularly shaky footing. Bear Stearns had relied unusually heavily on borrowing short term in order to finance its holdings: it had almost $400 billion in assets but barely $11 billion in capital, for a leverage ratio of more than 35:1.[35] This left it highly vulnerable to liquidity risk—the possibility that it could not roll over its debt day by day. Bear Stearns was also particularly heavily exposed to CDOs and other mortgage-backed securities, including a lot of the increasingly doubtful Fannie Mae and Freddie Mac debt. And in March 2008 it emerged that Bear Stearns was owed substantial amounts by Carlyle Capital, a conduit whose mortgage-backed securities investments had gone bad and which was in the process of defaulting on over $16 billion in obligations, including to Bear Stearns.

Bear Stearns' investments were failing and nobody would lend to it; its demise seemed inevitable. Officials at the Fed and the Treasury worried that the failure of one of the country's major investment banks would further disrupt markets. The firm had 150 million active trades, with counterparty commitments all over the world; untangling them would be extraordinarily difficult, and any intimation that they might not be honored would throw markets into white-knuckle panic. The Federal Reserve Board argued that "given the fragile condition of the financial markets at the time, the prominent position of Bear Stearns in those markets, and the expected contagion that would result from the immediate failure of Bear Stearns, the best alternative available was to provide temporary emergency financing to Bear Stearns through an arrangement with JPMorgan Chase & Co."[36]

And so on March 16, 2008, the government arranged for JPMorgan Chase to take over Bear Stearns at a share price of $10, which was 95 percent below the share price a year and a half earlier. In order to persuade JPMorgan Chase to take the deal, even at these bargain-basement prices, the Fed had to effectively guarantee $30 billion worth of Bear Stearns' mortgage-backed investments.

The problems of Bear Stearns were not so different from those afflicting other financial institutions. As fear spread, economic policymakers searched for more ways to try to stabilize the markets. The central bank dropped the Federal Funds rate down to 2 percent, and set up a new Term Securities Lending Facility (TSLF). This, for the first time, allowed the Fed to lend to investment banks, using asset-backed securities as collateral.

And still the bad news continued. The nation's biggest mortgage lender, Countrywide Financial, responsible for nearly one-fifth of America's mortgages, had been in difficulties since the middle of 2007. In January 2008 Countrywide began negotiations to be taken over by Bank of America. As negotiations dragged on, it became clear that the institution was in deep trouble. Eventually Bank of America closed the deal in June 2008, paying one-sixth of Country-wide's market value a year earlier. Meanwhile, the states of Illinois and California were suing Countrywide for deceptive lending prac-tices, with clear prospects for many more such court battles involv-ing mortgage lenders.[37]

A few weeks later, on Monday, July 14, hundreds of people lined up before dawn outside the doors of the Pasadena headquarters of the IndyMac Bank. This Countrywide spinoff had become a major mortgage lender in California, with $32 billion in assets. The pre-vious Friday, after a run on the bank began, the FDIC stepped in to take over IndyMac, but nonetheless depositors were anxious to get their money out as quickly as possible.[38] Rumors of major bank runs were circulating widely, and there was no shortage of troubled banks to fuel the rumors.

The death spiral continued and began to affect the very biggest players in the mortgage market, Fannie Mae and Freddie Mac. As private mortgage markets froze, the two government-sponsored enterprises had been left holding practically the entire mortgage securitization business solely in their hands: almost half of the coun-try's $12 trillion in mortgages was owned or guaranteed by Fannie Mae or Freddie Mac. But this had become a business hardly worth monopolizing. The two enterprises had over $5 trillion in obliga-tions from mortgage-backed securities—money it owed to investors around the world, or had effectively guaranteed. As the mortgage business skidded, so did Fannie Mae and Freddie Mac's stock prices, with Freddie's dropping by almost half in the first week of July.

Investors had always assumed that the U.S. government implicitly stood behind the two giants—despite legislative changes intended to sever the relationship—and they turned out to be correct. Rather than see the American mortgage system crumble, on July 13 Treasury Secretary Henry Paulson announced that the government would do what was necessary to keep Fannie and Freddie afloat. The Fed would give the government-sponsored enterprises access to the discount window, and the Treasury would inject billions into the companies. Paulson's justification was simple: "Fannie Mae and Freddie Mac play a central role in our housing finance system. . . . Their support for the housing market is particularly important as we work through the current housing correction."[39]

But the government's explicit commitment to Fannie and Freddie could not be accomplished without congressional approval. This was achieved by the passage and signing of the American Housing Rescue and Foreclosure Prevention Act at the end of July, although not without controversy. While all but three congressional Democrats voted for the bill, more than three-fourths of the Republican members voted against it, despite the fact that it was effectively a bill requested by the Republican administration. Not surprisingly, the one-fourth of Republicans who did vote for the bill came disproportionately from districts with particularly high mortgage default rates, which had the most to gain from the relief that the bill promised to provide for the distressed housing finance system.[40] Both the administration and Congress—at least a majority of it—were now committed to intervening to try to stop the death spiral.

Black September

But home prices were declining by 20 percent over the course of 2008, and nothing could paper over the effects of this skid. After trying for two months to keep Fannie Mae and Freddie Mac afloat and independent, on September 7 the federal government had little choice but to take over the two enterprises. This turned them from private companies with an implicit (now explicit) government guarantee, into fully government-owned enterprises. Shareholders lost everything, and the federal government was now directly responsible for whatever losses the enterprises realized. The government committed to providing up to $200 billion in capital to make up for the losses, and over the next two years spent $150 billion.

The next twist of the spiral involved another major investment bank, Lehman Brothers. Lehman had a massive presence on Wall Street, with assets of over $600 billion and 2007 profits of $4.2 billion. But the firm had been in trouble for most of the year—following the unwinding of Bear Stearns, Lehman Brothers' stock plummeted to half its value in one morning. While the firm's management continued to express confidence, it could not hide the fact that it had lost $2.8 billion in the second quarter of 2008.

Lehman began to look for merger partners, but its losses were accumulating at the rate of more than $40 million a day. There were few offers, and none that Lehman management was willing to accept. The Treasury and the Fed worked desperately to help find a buyer for Lehman over the weekend of September 13–14, 2008, even as another huge investment bank in trouble, Merrill Lynch, was snapped up by Bank of America. At one point, it appeared that the British bank Barclays might purchase Lehman, but British regulators refused to approve the deal at a time when their own banking system was at risk.[41] On Monday, September 15, Lehman Brothers filed for bankruptcy.

Despite repeated government attempts to salvage collapsing financial institutions and failing financial markets, this time the government stepped back and let Lehman go under. Barney Frank (D-Mass.), the chair of the House Financial Services Committee, opened the committee's next hearing by calling for a resolution to declare September 15 "Free Market Day." Frank joked, "The national commitment to the free market lasted one day. It was Monday."[42]

Unlike for Bear Stearns, and eventually many other firms to come, the Treasury and the Fed did not offer financial backing for a potential Lehman takeover. There were two reasons for this. The first was concern about moral hazard: if the government stood ready to bail out all large financial institutions in trouble, the financiers would have no reason to find their own ways out of the swamps they'd driven into. The second, related, reason was the sense that Lehman had been trying to game the system, attempting to force the federal government to step in and save it. As Phillip Swagel, then Treasury assistant secretary for economic affairs, put it, "The feeling at Treasury . . . was that Lehman's management had been given abundant warning that no federal assistance was in the offing, and market participants were aware of this and had time to prepare. It was almost as if Lehman management was in a game of chicken and determined not to swerve."[43]

The Lehman bankruptcy was followed immediately by another, even larger, swing down the death spiral. The American International Group (AIG) was founded in 1919 in Shanghai, but after the 1949 Chinese Revolution it moved its headquarters to New York City. It had since become one of the world's largest insurance companies, with over $1 trillion in assets; in the United States alone, it had 375 million policies with a face value of $19 trillion.[44]

AIG appeared to be an unlikely threat to the stability of the international financial order. It was a long-established and profitable company whose core businesses were automobile and property insurance, life insurance, and related retirement services. The staid company's principal stint in the public eye was in 2005, when the SEC and other regulators accused AIG of fraud and accounting abuses; the scandal forced Hank Greenberg, the principal architect of the firm's expansion, to resign after nearly forty years at the helm of the company. But those troubles seemed behind AIG, which continued to grow in size and profitability, and which appeared to be a well-run, basic, insurance conglomerate. However, one small segment of the corporate giant had become a major player in issuing CDSs for CDOs.

AIG began to pursue the corporate market aggressively in the 1960s, and in 1987 it set up a London subsidiary—AIG Financial Products (AIGFP)—to enter the derivatives business. The financial services arm grew rapidly, earning $3.26 billion in profits in 2005—nearly one-fifth of all of AIG's profits. This remarkable feat was accomplished by a subsidiary with 377 people, less than 0.5 percent of AIG's 116,000 overall employee base. The London employees were richly compensated for their success, averaging annual compensation of more than $1 million a person.[45]

One of AIGFP's most profitable strategies was to take advantage of the parent company's sterling reputation to deal in CDSs that required no collateral, only AIG's good name as backing. This meant that the London office was writing something like insurance without being required to hold reserves against the possibility that it would have to pay out on the insurance—and without being regulated by insurance supervisors. By the end of 2007, AIGFP had over $500 billion in these insurance-like contracts outstanding. Many were for corporate or other prime loans and were extremely secure; but over $60 billion was in CDSs that were meant to protect CDOs based on subprime mortgages. If the mortgages went bad, the CDOs would go bad, and AIG would have to pay out to the protected holders of the contracts. Even as housing prices declined, the head of AIGFP, Joseph J. Cassano, was supremely confident about the strategy. In August 2007 he assured doubters: "It is hard for us, without being flippant, to even see a scenario within any kind of realm of reason that would see us losing one dollar in any of those transactions."[46]

As housing prices dropped and mortgage defaults proliferated, however, many of the securities that AIGFP's CDSs were supposed to protect did in fact default. The London office started losing money on its portfolio of CDSs, starting with a few billion dollars in the middle of 2007 and eventually surpassing $25 billion by September 2008. Even worse, as the mortgage crisis continued and the market value of the CDOs that were supposed to be protected by AIGFP's CDSs dropped, the parent company that stood behind the London office was now forced to put up collateral to back its protection. In July and August 2008, these demands for collateral totaled $6 billion. AIG simply did not have the money to stand behind its subsidiary's obligations. The extraordinary profitability of the London office's derivatives-based operation had turned into extraordinary losses, and had bankrupted the entire company.

Over the same weekend during which they decided not to rescue Lehman, Treasury Secretary Paulson and Fed Chair Bernanke were confronted with the imminent failure of one of the world's largest insurance companies. This prospect scared them more than Lehman's bankruptcy. AIG was so interconnected with so many major financial institutions—it had so many outstanding counterparty obligations—that its failure might have begun a chain reaction of bankruptcies throughout the financial system. Bernanke said of AIG, "Its failure could have resulted in a 1930s-style global financial and economic meltdown, with catastrophic implications for production, income, and jobs."[47]

And so, on the evening of September 16—the day after Barney Frank's "Free Market Day"—the Fed announced that it was organizing an $85 billion bailout of AIG, in return for which it would receive 80 percent of the company's equity. The goal was to wind up AIG's Financial Products division, gradually delivering on the billions of dollars in obligations it had accumulated. Doing so meant making up the losses the subsidiary had dug itself into, and as the scale of AIG's losses became clear—over $99 billion in 2008—the Treasury was forced to allocate more funds to the bailout. Within a couple of years the rescue cost the federal government more than $180 billion.[48] While the AIG bailout headed off immediate financial catastrophe, one analyst noted that it also showed that "the U.S. Treasury is still all that stands between the current market environment and the ongoing threat of systemic financial meltdown."[49]

For despite the AIG rescue, the financial system was continuing its downward spiral. The Lehman bankruptcy had grabbed the attention of the markets, and not in a good way. As prominent investment manager Mohamed El-Erian put it a couple of months after the bankruptcy, as its effects continued to work their way through the financial system, "Virtually every indicator of economic and financial relationships exhibits characteristics of cardiac arrest. The situation will get worse before it gets better." And in fact the situation did get worse.[50]

"Armageddon is coming"

As government officials worked their way toward letting Lehman go broke, the firm's lawyer warned them, "Armageddon is coming. You don't know what the consequences will be."[51] But the federal government's "Free Market Day" with respect to Lehman was motivated in large part by the belief that the financial system could absorb the shock of a Lehman failure—that, unlike AIG, the investment bank was not so tightly interconnected with other financial institutions as to create broader problems. This turned out to be a mistake; Lehman was more interconnected than the Treasury Department and the Fed had anticipated. As soon as Lehman announced its bankruptcy, its transactions were frozen. This meant that investors, including other financial institutions, that were owed money by Lehman could not get it back. And since, in the complicated international financial markets, almost every financial institution is owed money by almost every other financial institution, this meant that no institution was safe. Any firm that needed the money Lehman owed it to operate was out of luck.

The Lehman shock immediately hit institutions that had generally been seen as nearly invulnerable, the money market mutual funds. These funds offered investors what was supposed to be an absolutely safe place to store their money. They acted like checking accounts, giving investors shares worth one dollar apiece, so that investors "redeemed" a share by writing a check for the dollar amount, knowing that each share would be worth a dollar. The $3.6 trillion in the money market mutual funds was invested in short-term assets that were regarded as almost without risk, in particular in very highly rated commercial paper. Investors, fund managers, and almost everyone else regarded commercial paper as supremely safe, able to be sold at will, at a moment's notice, if they needed ready cash.

When Lehman declared bankruptcy, it ceased payment on its debts, including its commercial paper. The effects were felt immediately. The earliest impact was on the Reserve Primary Fund, the oldest money market mutual fund. This fund, which had over $62 billion in assets, was still run by Bruce Bent, the man who invented money market mutual funds themselves. Among its assets, the Reserve Primary Fund held $785 million in Lehman commercial paper, which the bankruptcy made impossible to sell. On that Monday, September 15, within hours of the Lehman bankruptcy, as word of the implications spread, Reserve Primary's clients demanded $18 billion in redemptions, more than one-fourth of the fund's assets. By the middle of the next day, redemptions had risen to nearly $40 billion. There was no way the fund could meet these demands. It was forced to "break the buck," to reduce a share's price to ninety-seven cents. This was like a bank telling people with checking accounts that their accounts were now worth only ninety-seven cents on the dollar—it was tantamount to bankruptcy. And that in turn meant that depositors might be stuck, unable to get their money out. This was no small matter even for large corporations: Visa had $1 billion tied up in the Reserve Primary Fund, Wal-Mart $250 million. This was money the corporations needed to pay suppliers and make payroll, money they had thought of as being completely secure and instantly available.[52]

The idea that a major financial institution's commercial paper might be worthless, and that depositors in a money market mutual fund might not be able to get their money out, sparked a near panic. And this was not all. Financial institutions, such as hedge funds, that were Lehman customers, and that therefore had money parked with Lehman, now found that they could not get their money back either. As uncertainty spread, the market for commercial paper dried up, banks refused to lend to each other, and investors everywhere took their money out of stocks, bonds, and money market funds, putting them instead into cash and Treasury securities.

A classic bank run—in this case, a run both on banks and on financial markets more generally—was underway. Mohamed El-Erian was worried enough that the entire financial system was breaking down that he called his wife and told her to go to the ATM and take out plenty of cash. "She said, 'Why?' I said, 'I don't know whether the banks are going to open tomorrow.' The system was freezing in front of our eyes."[53] The ripples were felt immediately around the world. Mervyn King, the governor of the Bank of England, was clear: "Not since the beginning of the first world war has our banking system been so close to collapse."[54]

A TARP for the problem

This is what led Treasury Secretary Paulson, SEC Chairman Cox, and Fed Chair Bernanke to go to Capitol Hill to meet with the leaders of Congress on the evening of Thursday, September 18, the meeting at which Bernanke told the senators and members of Congress, "The situation is severe . . . and the Fed is out of tools." The global financial system stood on the brink of a meltdown, characterized by

Ben Bernanke as "Depression 2.0."[55] Lending around the world was at a standstill. A machinery of immense size and scope, which had powered the world economy for decades, was grinding to a halt, its gears frozen by distrust. No financial institution could be sure that the party it was lending to would still be in business in the future—or even tomorrow. In the United States, investors put their trust only in the government, the only entity able to print money if it needed to.

The fundamental economic news was getting worse by the week. Housing prices kept falling, mortgages soured at an increasing rate, and bank balance sheets continued to deteriorate. The number of ratings downgrades was above 10,000 and rising. Of the asset-backed CDOs issued between the middle of 2006 and the middle of 2007, at the height of the CDO frenzy, more than two-thirds were in or headed to default.[56]

As the implications for financial institutions became ever clearer, more bank runs began. Major financial institutions' difficulties could no longer be ascribed simply to cash-flow problems; if their underlying investments were suspect, they were likely to go out of business altogether. Within hours of the Lehman bankruptcy, a run began on Washington Mutual, the nation's largest savings and loan with over 40,000 employees and $300 billion in assets—most of this, unfortunately, in home loans. Soon depositors were pulling out their money at the rate of nearly $2 billion a day. By September 25 the bank had been closed by the regulators and sold to JPMorgan Chase for a pittance. Meanwhile, depositors also began to withdraw their money from the nation's fourth-largest bank, Wachovia, which had lost nearly $9 billion in the second quarter of the year; under pressure from federal regulators, it was sold to Wells Fargo.

The terrible economic news was compounded by confusion over the government's response. On Monday, September 15, the federal economic authorities had allowed Lehman to fail; the next day, they had rescued AIG. Some banks were being closed, others told to merge. For months, Bernanke and Paulson had insisted that the problems were manageable, but now they seemed incapable of managing them.

The government had to do more, but this required further congressional action. Hence the meeting with congressional leaders on

September 18, to sell them on the need for action—and for money. Unfortunately for the administration, one could hardly imagine a worse salesman than Treasury Secretary Paulson. After a stint in the Nixon White House, Paulson had spent his entire career in the world of investment banking, at Goldman Sachs. He rose from the ranks to lead the country's premier investment bank, first as chief operating officer from 1994 to 1998, and then as chairman from 1998 to 2006. He had been at the helm of Goldman Sachs in 2004 when the firm, along with other investment banks, had convinced the federal regulators to let them regulate their risk management themselves, as they best saw fit. Now a populace already angry about a potential taxpayer bailout of wealthy financiers was going to see a wealthy financier who happened to be Treasury secretary shepherding the bailout through Congress.

But Paulson and Bernanke had little choice: they needed congressional agreement to allocate $700 billion in funds to save the country's financial system. The general idea behind the proposal was straightforward. In any circumstances, a major decline in housing prices would have harmed the economy, but the financial innovations of the previous decade, in particular the engineering of structured financial instruments that layered mortgages and their derivatives on top of one another, magnified the financial impact of the underlying problem. The financial system was crashing because some of its foundations had turned out to be fatally weak; if the weakest foundations could be strengthened, the panic could be reversed.

The $700 billion would be used to purchase the securities whose inclusion in structured financial instruments had had such disastrous domino effects. Hence the core of the plan was the Troubled Assets Relief Program, or TARP, euphemistically calling the "toxic assets" merely "troubled." TARP would use the $700 billion to buy toxic assets, especially those based on the largely defaulted subprime mortgages, from the financial institutions being poisoned by them. This would allow banks to off-load the toxic assets, either directly from their balance sheets or from the conduits they had sponsored. It would also, by using a complicated auction system, help establish prices for assets for which the market had nearly disappeared. This last effect was very important, as part of the panic arose from a fog of uncertainty about how much the securities were worth, and thus whether banks and other financial institutions were in fact solvent.

Whatever its intentions, the Bush administration continued to flounder clumsily through the political process. Apart from the name of the program—it hardly seemed prudent to cover toxic assets with a tarp—all that Treasury Secretary Paulson sent Congress was a three-page document, in essence asking for a blank check in the amount of $700 billion. To make matters worse, the proposal specified that "decisions by the Secretary pursuant to the authority of this Act . . . may not be reviewed by any court of law or any administrative agency."[57] A Yale law professor characterized this as telling the House and Senate, "I'm not going to fire you; you can still be called Congress. But you don't have any power."[58] While there was some justification for asking for wide discretion—it was not really clear what Treasury would need to do—Paulson was calling on taxpayers simply to trust him, and the bankers he was working with, to spend the $700 billion wisely.

The Paulson plan, quickly dubbed "cash for trash," was met with a firestorm of condemnation. There was outrage at the spectacle of the former head of Goldman Sachs asking taxpayers to pay his fellow financiers $700 billion for securities widely regarded as worthless. Criticism came from all sides of the political spectrum. Conservative Republican Newt Gingrich wrote, "Watching Washington rush to throw taxpayer money at Wall Street has been sobering and a little frightening."[59] Liberal Democratic stalwart Robert Reich echoed the thought: "Never before in the history of American capitalism has so much been asked of so many for . . . so few."[60] And most Americans seemed to agree: a *USA Today*/Gallup Poll conducted on September 24 indicated that only 22 percent of the public supported the Paulson plan, with 56 percent wanting an alternative and another 11 percent in favor of no action.[61] Nonetheless, the proposal was critical for the financial services industry, which lobbied hard for its adoption.

Yet on September 29, the Emergency Economic Stabilization Act was defeated in the House of Representatives, by a vote of 228 to 205. Two-thirds of the Republican members of Congress voted against the administration's bill, along with more than a third of the Democrats.[62] Some opponents complained that the administration and congressional leaders had not given a satisfactory explanation of the need for the bailout. Others were skeptical that the affected firms would use the federal money to resume lending. There were concerns about the lack of oversight, and about the lack of restrictions on Treasury action. Again, protests came from both Left and Right. Liberal commentator Robert Kuttner wrote, "Paulson is treating the U.S. Treasury as a branch office of Wall Street."[63] Jim Bunning, Republican senator from Kentucky, railed, "This massive bailout is not the solution, it is financial socialism, and it is un-American."[64]

The principal reason for the bill's defeat was the popular revulsion at what appeared to be a gift to Wall Street. A general election was five weeks away, and the lame-duck Bush administration was extraordinarily unpopular, so much so that even many Republicans were running against it, often on a quasi-populist platform. Even though the leaders of both parties, and both parties' presidential candidates, supported the bill, popular anger was a powerful force. "When calls are 1,000 to one against something," observed one lobbyist with close ties to the Republicans, "that's a tough thing to overcome."[65]

Main Street may have exulted in the news from Washington, but Wall Street was terrified. By the end of the day of the vote, the Dow Jones had dropped over 770 points, its largest ever one-day drop in points—wiping out about $1.2 trillion worth of stock value.[66] Financial markets were equally spooked. The TED spread—a faithful indicator of confidence in the short-term money markets—had come down after the spikes in the summer and fall of 2007, and was hovering around 1.00 percent. But the day after the House vote, the TED spread rocketed above 3.00 percent, and it kept going, to an unprecedented maximum of 3.87 percent. Other short-term rates soared, and the commercial paper market effectively shut down. A credit freeze—the counterpart to a bank run, in which financial institutions will not lend to each other, or to anyone else, for fear of a wave of imminent bankruptcies—was on.

As Americans focused on the drama on Capitol Hill, the rest of the world was sliding rapidly into similar financial turmoil. One reason was that so many foreign banks had lent so much to the United States, especially to the U.S. housing market. European financial institutions in particular were so heavily invested in

American mortgages, and in securities derived from them, that they were crashing down every bit as emphatically as their American counterparts. The underlying default crisis was compounded by the evaporation of reliable relationships among financial counterparties, which was a global phenomenon. As interbank lending ceased, commercial paper was not rolled over, and bank runs proliferated, Europe was sucked into the whirlwind.

Markets and depositors soon began a run on Fortis, a conglomerate based in the Netherlands and Belgium that had grown to be one of the world's largest financial services firms and the twentieth biggest company in the world. On September 28, the governments of Belgium, the Netherlands, and Luxembourg took over the bank with an €11 billion bailout. The next day the market ran Dexia, a major Franco-Belgian financial institution, and forced a €6 billion bailout by the governments of France, Belgium, and Luxembourg. The same day, the freeze hit Hypo Real Estate, one of Germany's principal real estate lenders, with €400 billion in assets; the German government was pulled into a €50 billion bailout. Also that Monday, the British government nationalized Bradford & Bingley, a major bank involved in the home mortgage business. Meanwhile, the panic went public, and retail depositors began pulling billions out of consumer deposits. A traditional bank run began in Ireland, but quickly spread to the rest of the continent. A Europe-wide run on the financial system was underway.

As dread spread through the international financial system, and the American stock market continued its free fall—the Dow Jones Industrial Average fell 1786 points between September 29 and October 9—Congress continued to spar with the administration over the TARP legislation. A variety of new provisions were added, including raising the ceiling on FDIC-insured deposits from $100,000 to $250,000 and a series of tax cuts. Of more direct relevance to the cash-for-trash deals, the revised law mandated that the firms that were bailed out had to be willing to give the government a stake in their businesses, so that taxpayers could share in any benefits reaped from the rescue. In addition, Congress insisted on restrictions on executive pay for the assisted financial institutions, and on some other provisions intended to protect taxpayers. Congress also set up a series of watchdogs to oversee Treasury's management of the program, and required the administration to return to Congress for reauthorization of the second half of the bailout money.[67]

On October 3, 2008, the House took up the modified legislation. The desperate straits of the financial system had become clearer, as had the desperation of financiers themselves. Faced with the prospect of further financial catastrophe, about sixty members of Congress who had opposed the bill five days ago now changed their votes, half Democrats and half Republicans. The Emergency Economic Stabilization Act passed, 263 to 171, and President Bush signed it later in the day. In the end, support for the bill was particularly strong among members of Congress who received large campaign contributions from the financial industry and whose districts included many workers in finance,[68] for it was apparent that the government rescue operation was all that stood between the American financial system and generalized bankruptcy. However, the life preserver had only been designed; it remained to be seen how it would be built and deployed. Meanwhile, the American and international financial systems, and the American and world economies, were sinking fast.

Bailout

CHAPTER FIVE

At three o'clock in the afternoon of Monday, October 13, 2008—
the day Columbus Day was celebrated—the heads of America's nine
largest banks filed into a conference room at the Treasury Department. They had been summoned over that holiday weekend by
Treasury Secretary Paulson, who met them together with Fed Chair
Bernanke, FDIC head Sheila Bair, and the president of the Federal
Reserve Bank of New York, Timothy Geithner. The executives present ran financial institutions that together controlled roughly half
of the assets and deposits of the American banking system. Looking down on the conclave was a painting of Salmon P. Chase, the
secretary of the Treasury who crafted the National Banking Act of
1863 and so established the country's modern banking structure.
Chase's portrait was about to witness the most momentous single
act in modern American banking history: the government was forc-
ibly going to take partial ownership of the country's biggest banks.

Secretary Paulson spoke from talking points that began, "The
United States needs to take strong and decisive action to arrest the
stress in our financial system. . . . You must be central to any solu-

tion." Each of the nine bank executives was given a one-page form, that started, "In support of the US financial system and the broader US economy, the [name of QFI] agrees to . . ." where "QFI" was Qualifying Financial Institution. Each QFI was agreeing to sell preferred stock to the U.S. government, in amounts that varied with the size of the bank: $25 billion each for Citi, JPMorgan Chase, and Wells Fargo; $15 billion for Bank of America; $10 billion each for Goldman Sachs, Merrill Lynch, and Morgan Stanley; and $3 and $2 billion, respectively, for Bank of New York Mellon and State Street. The stock purchases averaged a bit less than one-fifth of the total equity in the firms. Each executive was to fill in the name of his bank, the amount (dictated by the Treasury), and sign and date the form.[1]

There was little choice in the matter. "Your firms need to agree," continued Paulson. And then, the muscle: "If a capital infusion is not appealing, you should be aware that your regulator will require it in any circumstance." And there was little doubt that the regulators had the power to do so. "It was," in other words, said one person privy to the details of the meeting, "a take it or take it offer. Everyone knew there was only one answer."[2]

It was an offer the bankers could not refuse, not only because they had no choice, but also because it was extraordinarily attractive. The shares would pay dividends of 5 percent; this would rise to 9 percent after five years, so that the banks had incentives to buy back the shares eventually—but not before they were in a healthier condition. The government would also get warrants, an opportunity to buy common (voting) stock in the future. These conditions were much more favorable for the banks than private investors would have demanded. In fact, just a couple of weeks earlier, Goldman Sachs had had to give Warren Buffett a far better deal for a $5 billion injection of capital, paying 10 percent dividends and giving him much more attractive warrants. Now Goldman Sachs was getting $10 billion in capital and had to pay only 5 percent dividends, with less costly warrants. The government's preferred shares in each bank were nonvoting, although if no dividends were paid for eighteen months, the government could appoint two directors.

There were other components of the offer that made it a good deal for the banks. The government would insure $0.5 trillion of otherwise uninsured deposits, and guarantee $1.5 trillion of new borrowing by the financial institutions. These would go a very long way toward easing pressure on the banks and allowing them to continue in business. The equity shares were probably most important, as they added $125 billion in capital to these nine banks (another $125 billion would be invested in other, smaller financial institutions over the following few weeks).[3] For financial institutions that were stretched extraordinarily thin—in some cases, perhaps beyond their capacity to survive—this was crucial. The infusion of new money would dramatically expand their capital, the core of any financial enterprise and the final line of defense against bankruptcy.

Some of the bankers resisted for a while. Kenneth Lewis of Bank of America and Richard Kovacevich of Wells Fargo insisted that their banks did not need the support, but Paulson and his colleagues were adamant that the program had to be applied to all the big banks. Otherwise, the institutions singled out for a capital infusion would be tainted as weak, which would invite bank runs at further cost to the government. Eventually, even Lewis relented: "I don't think we need to be talking about this a whole lot more," he said as the meeting wound down. "We all know that we are going to sign."[4] By 6:30 in the evening, all the bankers had filled out, dated, and signed their commitment forms. America's principal financial institutions were now wards of the state.

What had happened? The Emergency Economic Stabilization Act (EESA), passed just ten days earlier, directed the Treasury to buy questionable assets from troubled banks; this had now turned into the U.S. government's taking partial ownership of the country's most important financial institutions. What led Paulson, who had been one of the nation's leading investment bankers, to force his former colleagues, the country's most powerful bankers, to accept effective government control of their banks? And would it work?

Out of cash or out of business?

The passage and signing of EESA on October 3 had not calmed markets; in fact, in the subsequent week, the Dow Jones Industrial Average had dropped a staggering 1874 points, some 18 percent. The

TED spread, that barometer of panic on the short-term money markets, had rocketed to 3.87 when the House voted down the original TARP proposal, which was interpreted as evidence for the financial markets' desperate desire for TARP to be enacted. But after the bill eventually passed, the TED spread continued to rise, hitting a peak of 4.64 percent on October 10. The credit freeze had grown and spread, and the world was now in the throes of a full-blown financial panic.

That Friday, October 10, the finance ministers of the Group of Seven industrial countries met in the Treasury building in Washington. They produced a predictable call for "urgent and exceptional action," replete with references to "all available tools" and "all necessary steps," but nothing concrete came of it. The next day, the finance ministers met with President Bush across the street, at the White House. Bush, too, mouthed the expected platitudes—"We will do what it takes to resolve this crisis"—but did nothing beyond that.[5]

Even as the finance ministers met and produced rhetoric and little else, one of their governments was pushing forward with an aggressive new strategy. On Wednesday, October 8, British Prime Minister Gordon Brown announced a £500 billion ($800 billion) rescue program, the centerpiece of which was that the British government would take £50 billion in equity stakes in the country's largest banks, in effect partially nationalizing them. This would provide the banks with new capital, which was what they needed most. The public-sector stake would allow the government to keep close tabs on the banks, to try to make sure that the banks receiving an infusion of public money would not hoard it, but would instead use it as a basis on which to begin lending.

The British planners were cognizant of how a bank bailout in Japan, nearly twenty years earlier, had gone wrong. Japan's banks had simply used government money to paper over their problems without addressing them—and, more important, without resuming customary financial operations. The result had been ten years and more of stagnation—Japan's lost decade. Earlier in the week, a parliamentary committee had flown to Japan to find out what the Japanese had learned from their woeful experience. The deputy chairman of the committee reported back, "The Japanese told us that we will have to nationalise not just a few banks—that would be just the first step. They told us that we would have to nationalise the entire banking system."[6] While so drastic a move hardly seemed necessary or feasible, the general point was brought home: simply shoveling money at the banks was not enough; there had to be direct government engagement to ensure that they restarted lending to their customers. So the Brown plan gave the British government partial control over the country's major banks, and an enhanced ability to monitor and affect their behavior. In return, the banks were saved from almost certain failure.

Over the next few days, other European governments rolled out a €1.3 trillion ($1.8 trillion) plan that followed many of the particulars of the Brown plan. American Treasury officials were meanwhile developing their own variant of the British rescue operation, for they had decided to abandon the TARP scheme as originally developed. The administration was about to do a stunning about-face. Two weeks earlier, it had asked Congress for funds to buy toxic (or troubled) assets; now, it was using that money to buy up stakes in the nation's leading banks. What had changed?

Events of the weeks during and after the passage of the TARP legislation had revealed a chilling fact: the American financial system was effectively bankrupt. Originally, policymakers believed that the problem the banks faced was one of "liquidity," that is, access to ready cash. This is common in a bank run: a financial institution that is fundamentally sound can find itself unable to operate because it is illiquid. A solvent bank that is illiquid faces a temporary problem, one that can and should be dealt with so as to keep the bank in business. Other banks, including the central bank, might lend it money to help it weather the storm. Other banks, or public agencies, might buy the bank's assets to provide it with the liquid cash it needs.

But a bank in trouble might not just be illiquid; it might also be insolvent—in other words, broke. If the value of the bank's assets (what it has lent) is lower than the value of its liabilities (what it has borrowed), it is bankrupt. No amount of liquidity will paper over the fundamental fact that even if every debtor paid the bank back tomorrow, it would still not have enough money to pay back all of its creditors. A bank that is facing liquidity problems is out of ready cash; a bank that is insolvent is out of business.

When American and then international financial markets froze up over the summer and fall of 2008, the original diagnosis was that the major financial institutions were in a liquidity crisis. Certainly there was a bank run, as well as its more modern equivalent, a run on short-term financial markets. Policymakers responded by making it possible for banks to meet their immediate needs for cash, in particular by massive lending from the central bank to the banks facing liquidity constraints.

The original TARP focused on a particularly important part of the liquidity crisis that developed over the course of 2007 and 2008, the run on short-term money markets. Treasury and Fed policymakers saw that it had become nearly impossible for banks (or anyone else) to sell some of the complex financial assets. There was so much uncertainty about the true value of the collateralized debt obligations (CDOs), CDO^{2}s, and other mortgage-related securities that almost nobody would buy them. Banks had assets, but they could not sell (liquidate) them, hence, the liquidity crisis. Under the TARP legislation, the Treasury would buy many of the troubled assets, and it would create an auction system that would establish a price for the assets, which would give investors more confidence about buying them. This way, the market for the assets could be restored. The market would then reveal the securities' prices, and banks and investors would no longer have to rely on guesswork. Each financial institution would now know with some certainty how much its assets were worth, and how strong its balance sheet was. Banks would know whether their financial counterparties were reliable or not. The fatal uncertainty would be dispelled, lending could resume, and liquidity would be restored.

But as time went on, investors and policymakers looked more closely at the actual assets that banks were holding. And the closer they looked, the more concerned they got about their true value. By late 2008 the scale of the housing collapse was evident, with housing prices down 25 percent from their peak, delinquencies soaring, and foreclosures proliferating. Analysts were beginning to see clearly the direct impact of the housing collapse on the value of trillions of dollars in securities owned by, or through, major financial institutions. Simply put, many of these investments were now worthless.

In October 2008, the International Monetary Fund issued one of its periodic reports on global financial stability, including calculations of the losses American financial institutions would suffer from bad investments in mortgages and mortgage-related securities. The estimate was a staggering $1.4 trillion, half a trillion dollars more than the International Monetary Fund had announced six months earlier. By April 2009, the estimate had ballooned to $2.7 trillion, and losses in the rest of the world were estimated at an additional $1.4 trillion. For the American financial system, the implications were relatively simple. The nation's financial institutions were, in the aggregate, bankrupt. There was not enough capital in them to cover the expected losses. And to restore a reasonable leverage ratio—for example, to return the country's financial system to where it had been in the middle 1990s—would require additional equity of $500 billion, a virtually unimaginable sum. Europe's banks were if anything in worse condition: to get their leverage ratios down to a reasonable level would require $1.2 trillion in additional equity capital.[7]

The problem, then, was no longer one of liquidity, but one of solvency—or rather, insolvency. Vast segments of the American and international financial system were broke. If a financial system facing a liquidity crisis can be compared to a car that has run out of gas and needs to be refueled, a financial system that is insolvent is akin to a car whose wheels have fallen off and needs fundamental repair before it can move again. Given that many financial firms were close to insolvency, merely providing liquidity was no longer enough—somehow, the solvency of the big financial players had to be clarified. If the private sector couldn't do it, the government would have to, even if this meant putting taxpayer money at risk.

To carry out this fundamental repair to the American banking system, the Treasury envisioned using the revised TARP to provide new capital to the troubled banks. This would actually provide them with an enhanced cushion against further losses. The other measures were important too: the $0.5 trillion in insurance for uninsured deposits would avoid a further run, and the $1.5 trillion in guarantees to bank borrowing would allow the financial institutions to return to normal operations. But the capital injections—the government's purchases of equity—were the centerpiece of the revised program.

Treasury officials realized early on that losses were mounting up so rapidly in the financial system that using TARP money to buy toxic assets might not be enough; this is why they had included the possibility of equity purchases in the EESA legislation. But, as Phillip Swagel, the assistant secretary for economic policy, put it, "Secretary Paulson never would have gotten legislative authority if he had proposed from the start to inject capital into banks." Although Paulson apparently truly believed in the toxic assets purchase plan, he and his staff knew that they might have to move to the next level. But, Swagel said, "Secretary Paulson would have gotten zero votes from Republican members of the House of Representatives for a proposal that would have been portrayed as having the government nationalize the banking system. And Democratic House members would not have voted for the proposal without the bipartisan cover of votes from Republicans. This is simply a political reality."[8]

In the event, the Treasury used EESA primarily to buy shares of American banks: $125 billion for the big nine, then another $125 billion for a variety of smaller banks. These capital injections quelled some anxieties about counterparty risk; the TED spread started to decline the day after the new TARP policy was announced. While the country's financial system had been stabilized, concerns remained about the state of the banks. By mid-November, it was increasingly clear that Citibank (and its parent Citigroup) was insolvent. The company was hit by a massive stock sell-off that saw the total value of the firm drop to barely $20 billion, as compared to $244 billion just two years earlier. The government mobilized once more, providing another $20 billion in equity and agreeing to pick up about 90 percent of the costs of losses Citigroup realized on over $300 billion in toxic assets.[9] Even this was not enough, and in February 2009 the government converted its preference shares into common (voting) stock and took a controlling 36 percent interest in Citigroup. America's largest bank had been nationalized.

As 2008 turned into 2009, financial markets gradually calmed.

The capital injections had also injected a bit of confidence into expectations. This was not necessarily confidence that the banks were healthy, but rather that the government—and now the new administration of Barack Obama—would do what was necessary to stand behind the country's banking system. This perception was reinforced after the new administration carried out a series of "stress tests" in the spring of 2009, to see if the major financial institutions could withstand further pressures. Nine of the nineteen tested banks passed with no need for new capital, while the other ten were ordered to increase their capital by a total of $70 billion. The relatively positive results of the stress test, along with the government's promise to commit capital to banks too weak to pass the stress test, further reassured the market that the financial system was finally safe.[10]

By the end of April 2009, the U.S. government had spent about $2.5 trillion directly in bailing out, shoring up, and rebuilding the nation's financial system. This did not include the various commitments to guarantee or otherwise support assets, which amounted to more than $12 trillion.[11] The amounts were almost unimaginable. But the massive government intervention had averted full-blown panic and restored some semblance of order to the financial system. Not everything had gone as hoped. Renewed confidence in the banks did not, despite some promises to the contrary, lead to greater lending that would help counteract the growing recession. Given how much money they had lost, banks desperately needed to reduce their risk, which in turn meant less lending. Nonetheless, a systemic financial collapse had been avoided.

The hazardous morality of a bailout

But was the cost of the bailout worth it? Most Americans were unconvinced. As Congress debated the TARP legislation, polls typically showed that those opposed to the bailout outnumbered those in favor. One of the more reliable polls, taken in early October 2008, found fewer than one-third in favor, 45 percent opposed, and 25 percent undecided. There was little disagreement about who the bailouts would help the most: two-thirds of Americans thought that Wall Street would benefit more than the rest of the country. As the crisis unfolded, opposition stiffened. By February 2009, fully 56 percent of those surveyed opposed the additional bailout measures being put in place at that point.[12]

Politicians and activists on both the Right and the Left were blistering in their criticism of the bailout. Representative Marilyn Musgrave (R-Colo.) expressed a common view in the Bush administration's own party in opposing the original TARP proposal: "I simply cannot stomach transferring that kind of money from the middle class families to a bunch of Wall Street bankers whose avarice and greed put us in this situation in the first place. It's interesting that, when working families were being crushed by soaring energy prices this summer, Congress went on vacation. Yet, when Wall Street faced the consequences of its actions, we worked around the clock to help them. We should place the same priority on helping Main Street that we place on helping Wall Street."[13] At the same time, in the *Nation* magazine iconoclastic economist and Nobel laureate Joseph Stiglitz wrote that "Paulson's proposal looks like another of those shell games that Wall Street has honed to a fine art" and charged that the banks were getting "a free ride at taxpayers' expense."[14] Paul Krugman, another Nobel laureate who was highly critical of both the Bush and the Obama administration's handling of the crisis, used his *New York Times* column to attack "the new voodoo, which claims . . . that elaborate financial rituals can reanimate dead banks. Unfortunately, the price of this retreat into superstition may be high. . . . I suspect that taxpayers are about to get another raw deal—and that we're about to get another financial rescue plan that fails to do the job."[15]

Even those who believed that some form of government involvement was necessary to avoid a complete economic meltdown suggested that there were better ways to respond to the financial disaster. The most common alternative was outright, temporary, nationalization of the banks. Krugman was probably the most prominent advocate of this path, of an "explicit, though temporary, government takeover" of the banks that were essentially insolvent.[16] To some extent what the Bush administration had ended up doing under the revised Paulson plan was a nationalization: the government's equity stake was large enough to control the banks, should it be converted to common (voting) shares, and even without this the banks were by now so reliant on the Treasury, the Fed, and the regulators that they had little real independence. But to engage in outright nationalization would have been politically difficult, and more pragmatically, it might have exposed the government to even greater losses in the event that the banks turned out to be in worse shape than anticipated.

Another commonly expressed concern was that the bailout would ratchet upward the already grave problems of moral hazard. Any government commitment to insure or otherwise back risky behavior creates the possibility of moral hazard; in fact, private insurance has the same effect. A firm or individual that is even partially insulated from the consequences of its actions is likely to act less carefully. In the case of the troubled banks, everyone could see that moral hazard had been part of the problem: the financial institutions did not bear the full costs of their bad judgments and irresponsible risk taking, at least in part because they anticipated a government bailout. Making this expectation a reality would simply encourage subsequent risk taking, and perhaps an even bigger collapse in the future. While there are strong arguments for government backing to keep financial markets functioning, there are equally strong arguments that such backing has to be tempered with punishments for those who take advantage of them.

But by the time the economy was in full-fledged crisis, the question of how to minimize moral hazard was moot—the irresponsible risks had been taken, the bad bets had been made. To take a stand against a bailout of any sort in the midst of the worst financial crisis in seventy-five years would mean letting the economy slide into the abyss, in exchange for the faint possibility of greater market discipline in the future. As Jeffrey Frankel, a top Clinton administration official observed, "They say there are no atheists in a foxhole. Well, there are no libertarians in a financial crisis, either."[17] Fixing the moral hazard problem would have to wait until after disintegration of the international financial order was no longer an imminent threat.

There are times when, in order to protect the innocent, society has to bail out the guilty, and this crisis was one of those times. Certainly it is galling that most of the financiers whose recklessness had made the disaster so severe were well treated throughout the crisis. Certainly there is little doubt that the principal direct beneficiaries of the bailouts were the bankers themselves. Certainly it defies any sense of reason or equity to privatize profits and socialize losses. And yet by the time the government stepped in, the principal alternative to a bailout would have been an even greater economic catastrophe. By the time the crisis hit, it was too late to avoid an outcome that was repugnant to most Americans.

Trapped by ZIRP

While policymakers struggled to stabilize the financial system, they also had to worry about general economic conditions. At the end of November 2008, the National Bureau for Economic Research committee that determines the state of the U.S. economy made it official: a recession had started in December 2007. And the financial collapse was certain to aggravate the general economic weakness. Policymakers turned their attention to trying to keep the macroeconomy from collapsing along with the financial system.

The first line of defense was monetary policy. The Federal Reserve had moved aggressively as soon as economic problems arose, using all of its traditional tools. The principal goal of Fed policy was to stimulate the economy. It went about this in the usual manner of monetary policy: by reducing interest rates and putting more money into circulation. The Fed affects short-term interest rates by conducting open market operations, buying and selling short-term Treasury securities. When the Fed buys a Treasury security from a commercial bank, it credits the bank with funds that the bank can then lend out.[18] Greater lending spurs business borrowing, investment, and hiring, and leads the economy upward. When the Fed announces a change in the Federal Funds rate (the interest rate banks charge each other), it is declaring how it expects these open market operations to affect monetary conditions. And as interest rates come down, economic activity should increase.

The Fed had been pushing interest rates down since the financial trouble began. Between September 2007 and September 2008, the central bank had reduced the Federal Funds rate from 5.25 percent to 2.00 percent. Over the course of October 2008, as financial markets broke down following the Lehman bankruptcy, the Fed dropped the overnight rate still further, to just 1.00 percent. And yet the American economy continued its free fall, shrinking by 5.4 percent in the last quarter of 2008. In December the Fed reached rock bottom: on December 16, it set the target Federal Funds rate at an unprecedented 0 to 0.25 percent. The country was in the uncharted territory of a "zero interest rate policy," or ZIRP.

With interest rates at zero, the central bank has reached the end of its traditional road. The main tool of monetary policy is the interest rate, and the main way monetary policymakers try to stimulate an economy in recession is by lowering interest rates. But they cannot lower interest rates below zero; that would mean giving out free money, or even paying people to borrow. As the United States entered ZIRP territory, one analyst calculated that the Taylor rule for appropriate monetary policy indicated that the Fed should be setting interest rates at -6 percent, which is impossible, of course, but indicative of how limited the scope for normal monetary policy was.[19]

ZIRP is reminiscent of the "liquidity trap," one of the principal explanations John Maynard Keynes put forth for the depth and breadth of the Great Depression of the 1930s. With interest rates right around zero in the early 1930s, freezing any effective monetary policy, Keynes insisted on the need for aggressive, expansionary, fiscal policy—deficit spending—to help lift the economy out of the Depression. The arrival at ZIRP suggested as much to modern followers of Keynes, such as Paul Krugman, who wrote in his *New York Times* blog, "When monetary policy is up against the zero bound, the optimal fiscal policy is to expand government purchases enough to maintain full employment."[20]

America's entry into ZIRP territory was also strongly suggestive of Japan's lost decade. In fact, Japan had hit the zero interest rate bound a decade earlier, and had been a macroeconomic basket case ever since consigned to apparently intractable stagnation. As Krugman put it, "America has turned Japanese. . . . Seriously, we are in deep trouble."[21] American policymakers were desperate to avoid this fate. If ZIRP marked the end of the road for traditional monetary policy, the United States needed to find a new path.

The Fed had started implementing some decidedly unconventional monetary policies even before interest rates hit zero. It expanded its lender-of-last-resort function, its role as provider of emergency loans to banks facing serious liquidity problems. The Fed had already made short-term loans at low interest rates to just about any bank that was illiquid, and to many that were probably insolvent, but the impact was limited because the commercial banks for which the Fed was responsible were only part of the problem.

The Fed now invoked an obscure provision of the Federal Reserve Act that authorized lending to almost any firm in "unusual and exigent circumstances."[22] The American central bank drew on these emergency powers to make money available to financial institutions other than commercial banks. Early in the crisis, these facilities included the Primary Dealer Credit Facility and the Term Securities Lending Facility. As all sorts of credit markets froze up in the aftermath of the Lehman and AIG failures, the Federal Reserve added a bewildering array of facilities, each aimed at unfreezing a different segment of the financial markets. These included the Asset Backed Commercial Paper Money Market Mutual Fund Liquidity Facility, the Commercial Paper Funding Facility, the Money Market Investor Funding Facility, and the Term Asset-Backed Securities Loan Facility.

The Fed used these facilities to try to get financial institutions back in the business of lending, by providing cash for assets they owned whose value was in question. The Fed stepped into the troubled markets as a sort of "customer of last resort." It committed itself to lend to firms using as collateral the assets that the firms were having trouble selling or even pricing elsewhere.

The Fed lent out nearly $2 trillion, using as collateral a variety of assets that their owners, and the markets, regarded as highly suspect. The aim was twofold: The first was to restore a normal state of affairs to financial markets so that the value of these assets would be more accurately, and highly, priced. The second justification was that, as with lender-of-last-resort facilities in a bank panic, the Fed was stepping in to help markets return to their proper functional role. If both expectations were borne out, the Fed would eventually get its money back, and the economy would be on its way to recovery.

Over the course of 2009, the Fed gradually wound down most of the emergency loan programs and began buying up the troubled assets outright. Prior to the crisis, the Fed restricted itself almost entirely to owning short-term Treasury securities and assets derived from them. But as the crisis dragged on and the Fed looked for new ways to rekindle the economy, it began buying up long-term Treasury securities, the debt of Fannie Mae and Freddie Mac (so-called Agency debt), and eventually such other troubled assets as mortgage-backed securities. The aim here was also to reset the impaired markets for these assets, which were so weighting down the balance sheets of the country's financial institutions that normal lending was not resuming. It is estimated that Fed purchases of about $1.7 trillion in long-term Treasuries, Agency debt, and mortgage-backed assets reduced ten-year interest rates by between a third and a half of a percentage point—enough to matter, but not to revive lending on its own.[23]

Behind these exceptional policy moves lurked a terrible fear that the economy might fall into a deflationary spiral, in which prices and wages decline for a substantial period. Theory and experience have shown that deflation creates real dangers for a modern economy. Major deflation beginning in 1929 was almost certainly an important cause of the Great Depression of the 1930s. Japan's lost decade has been the most prominent deflationary episode in recent history, and nobody wanted to replicate that experience.

Deflation is dangerous for several reasons. First, it increases the real burden of existing debt: wages and prices fall, but debts stay the same. This puts even greater pressure on firms and households that are already highly indebted. Second, falling prices can start a downward spiral in which businesses and consumers postpone spending as they wait for prices to go lower still. This weakens the economy still further, putting another round of downward pressure on prices, and so on. Finally, deflation makes it more expensive to borrow in real terms—even if lenders charged 0 percent interest, the true burden of the debt would be the rate of deflation. And since the Federal Funds rate is already at zero, there is nothing the central bank can do to affect borrowing costs directly. The unattractiveness of borrowing would further impair consumer spending, the housing market, and business investment.

Fed Chair Bernanke has long been concerned about deflation, in part due to his scholarship on the 1930s. In 2002, when he was a member of the Fed's Board of Governors, Bernanke spoke to the National Economists Club in Washington, D.C., about the subject. He made clear the seriousness of the problem in general: "Sustained deflation can be highly destructive to a modern economy." But he also expressed confidence that the United States could avoid deflation: "A particularly important protective factor," he said, was "the strength of our financial system. . . . Our banking system remains healthy and well-regulated, and firm and household balance sheets are for the most part in good shape."[24]

Bernanke's discussion was almost entirely theoretical and hypothetical, with the exception of a brief mention of Japan. By 2009, the threat of deflation was a live policy issue: the banking system had collapsed, and balance sheets were in shambles. Over the course of 2009 and 2010, prices barely rose at all, and the possibility of eventual deflation could not be ruled out. In the middle of 2010, St. Louis Fed President James Bullard warned, "The U.S. is closer to a Japanese-style outcome today than at any time in recent history." The origin of the warning was notable, coming as it did from somebody with a reputation for great concern for *inflationary* threats; Bullard was one of the more "hawkish" members of the Fed's monetary policy decision-making group, the Federal Open Market Committee.[25] Similar fears were voiced by two other Fed bank presidents, Eric S. Rosengren of Boston and William C. Dudley of New York.[26]

Bernanke had spoken back in 2002 about what to do when deflation threatened too. He noted that the Fed had more tools in its arsenal than most supposed, and anticipated many of the policies that were eventually adopted after 2007. But he concluded that monetary policy was unlikely to be enough: "The effectiveness of anti-deflation policy could be significantly enhanced by cooperation between the monetary and fiscal authorities." Fiscal policies to combat deflation would include "tax cuts or increases in transfers," and "the government could increase spending on current goods and services or even acquire existing real or financial assets."[27] And in fact, as monetary policy, even of the nontraditional variety, seemed inadequate to the task of getting the American economy going again, policymakers turned to fiscal policy.

Stimulus

Long before the scale of the crisis was clear, the Bush administration attempted to counteract it with a fiscal stimulus. In February 2008, Congress passed and President Bush signed into law a $168 billion tax rebate plan. But at that point it was not obvious that the economy was weak enough to warrant much more. Phil Gramm, principal economic adviser to presidential candidate John McCain, argued that the downbeat mood was simply a "mental recession."[28] As late as a few days before Lehman's collapse, one commentator insisted that we "just stick to facts. We are not in a recession."[29] But by mid-October, the facts were undeniable. Credit markets had frozen, and industrial production dropped precipitously in September while job losses soared. As consumer sentiment crumbled, unemployment rose rapidly, and the stock market fell, something had to be done.[30]

The presidential election of November 2008 determined who would be responsible for doing something. The new Obama administration inherited an economy all of whose indicators were flashing red, with financial markets still in deep freeze. At the end of November President-elect Obama announced his principal economic policymakers: Timothy Geithner as secretary of the Treasury, Larry Summers as director of the National Economic Council, and Christina Romer as chair of the Council of Economic Advisers. All were known quantities, well within the economic-policy mainstream. Geithner had been deeply involved in managing the crisis, in his position as president of the Federal Reserve Bank of New York. Summers had been Treasury secretary under President Bill Clinton, and Romer was a respected macroeconomist at the University of California, Berkeley. The new policymakers in the incoming Obama White House and the Democratic Congress moved quickly to craft a stimulus package, including tax cuts and spending increases, to combat the economic decline. In this they followed traditional guidelines for fiscal policy in a recession.

The standard macroeconomic view is that in recessionary conditions, incremental government spending and tax cuts can stimulate the economy. If the government spends an additional million dollars to build a bridge, that spending directly adds to GDP. But that is only the beginning: the spending on materials and labor is income to suppliers, contractors, and workers, and some of this income will be spent on consumer goods and services, which then further increases GDP. This in turn becomes income for other workers, who similarly increase their spending, again adding to GDP. This process suggests a "fiscal multiplier," typically associated with Keynesian macroeconomics, such that every one-dollar increase in government spending results in a greater-than-one-dollar increase in GDP. Especially when the economy is stuck at ZIRP, so that private borrowing and spending are particularly weak, the multiplier can be large. Scholars have estimated that in these conditions a dollar in new government spending can lead to a two-dollar, three-dollar, or even greater increase in GDP.[31] Tax cuts have an analogous impact, albeit less directly. A tax cut raises the disposable income of households, so that they can spend more on goods and services, thus increasing GDP—and with a similar multiplier effect.

Even before the new administration took office, its economic team had been considering a fiscal stimulus. Romer's evaluation indicated that a $1.2 trillion package was needed. However, President-elect Obama's political advisers insisted that this was not feasible, and the numbers were shaved. Once in office, President Obama proposed a $675–$775 billion package to stimulate the economy.[32]

The stimulus proposal turned out to be politically contentious. The issue was not really about deficits themselves. It was generally understood that a severe recession would cause large deficits almost automatically through declines in tax revenues and increases in government spending on unemployment benefits, food stamps, and other social programs tied to income. Over the course of the three years starting in October 2008 the federal government was already going to be in deficit by about $1 trillion. The federal government was going to lose about $840 billion in revenue due to the recession, and it was going to have to make about $160 billion in additional automatic payments triggered by the downturn. The question was whether the government should do anything else, and if so, what.[33]

Some policymakers and economists believed that any government intervention, even in so troubled an economy, was unjustified. Congressman Ron Paul (R-Tex.) complained that "the US government just won't allow the correction the economy needs." He invoked the recession of 1921, which was deep but short, in Paul's view, because the government permitted insolvent companies to fail. "No one remembers that one," he averred. "They'll remember this one, because it will last 15 years."[34] Paul's view was reminiscent of the position of the "liquidationists" of the early 1930s, who were led by Treasury Secretary Andrew Mellon. Mellon's advice to President Herbert Hoover was typical: "Liquidate labor, liquidate stocks, liquidate the farmers, liquidate real estate . . . purge the rottenness out of the system."[35] The idea was almost moralistic: bad loans, bad debts, bad businesses, and bad deals had to be exorcised before the economy could right itself. Satisfying as such a scorched-earth policy might be (at least to those not caught in its path), few serious economists or policymakers ever considered it.[36]

Some theoretical objections to an active fiscal stimulus were based on the view that government spending would inevitably be wasteful, providing no real benefit to the population. Others emphasized the expectation that increased government spending would be counteracted by an offsetting reduction in private spending. The budget deficits that would result from tax cuts or more government spending would drive interest rates higher and reduce, or "crowd out," private investment and spending. The economists who held these positions were generally hostile to traditional Keynesian views, especially because of the Keynesian inclination to assume that there were market failures that government could correct. The antistimulus economists tended instead to hew to the "New Classical" position that unfettered markets always deliver the best-possible outcome. This outlook has generally been associated with macroeconomic theorists based at the Universities of Chicago and Minnesota, which has led other economists to dub them "fresh-water macroeconomists."[37]

But among most economists, there was a general consensus on the desirability of some form of active fiscal policy. In a February 2009

Wall Street Journal poll of economists, 68 percent said that the proposed stimulus package was about the right size or too small. Only 31 percent said that it was too large. Most economists in the policy and business circles viewed a stimulus package as something that could soften the blows of a deep downturn and hasten the arrival of a recovery.[38]

Even many conservative economists tended to agree. Harvard professor Martin Feldstein, who had headed Ronald Reagan's Council of Economic Advisers, stated categorically, "There is no alternative to fiscal policy if we want to reverse the current downturn." He came to this view based especially on the relative ineffectiveness of monetary policy, with credit markets frozen and ZIRP in place: "I support the use of fiscal stimulus in the US, because the current recession is much deeper than and different from previous downturns. Even with successful countercyclical policy, this recession is likely to last longer and be more damaging than any since the depression of the 1930's." Feldstein was clear that the deficits that would ensue were troubling: "The resulting increase in the national debt is the price that we and future generations will pay for the mistakes that created the current economic situation."[39] But he, and most of his fellow economists, believed the price was worth paying. Because the more consensual view was particularly strongly held in major universities in the Northeast and California, its proponents were sometimes dubbed "salt-water macroeconomists."

Even among supporters of a stimulus, there was disagreement over its character and size. Some, especially more conservative economists, viewed tax cuts as the ideal way to proceed. Others, primarily among liberals, preferred government spending on infrastructure, services, and transfers to the states. Tax cuts and rebates had the advantage of being quick (cutting a check is faster than planning and building a bridge). Most Keynesian analysts favored government spending, because they believed its multiplier effect gave it a bigger impact than corresponding tax cuts. By early 2009, in any event, the timing advantage of tax cuts seemed irrelevant: while most recent recessions had been short enough that time was of the essence, this crisis promised to be much deeper and more prolonged. The Obama administration and Congress opted for a spending-oriented stimulus package, although the package also included substantial tax cuts.

Consensus among economists did not translate into easy political times for the new administration. There was powerful partisan opposition from the Republicans in the House and Senate, who fought the proposal. Apart from the general desire to deny the new administration an easy victory, there was an economic-interest basis to the opposition. While the economy as a whole was suffering, and it was hoped that the economy as a whole would benefit from the stimulus, there was little doubt that some would benefit—and others would pay—more than others. Much of the benefit was likely to go to poorer and working-class Americans, closer to the traditional Democratic constituencies. And although paying for the stimulus was far in the future, eventually it would have to be paid, and the resulting taxes were likely to fall primarily on upper-middle-class Americans, closer to the core constituencies of the Republicans.

Against the backdrop of partisan wrangling and intellectual debate, on February 14, 2009, Congress passed the American Recovery and Reinvestment Act of 2009 (ARRA), a $787 billion multiyear stimulus bill—without a single Republican vote of support in the House of Representatives.[40] The spending was spread over three years—in federal government terms, fiscal years 2009, 2010, and 2011, which stretch from October 1, 2008, through September 30, 2011. The $787 billion stimulus on average accounted for a bit less than 2 percentage points of GDP in each of those three years. Commentators such as Joseph Stiglitz and Paul Krugman argued that the stimulus was far too small.[41]

The fiscal stimulus had its most concentrated impact on state governments. The crisis hit the states very hard: as with the federal government, their revenues dropped and expenditures grew, but unlike the federal government their ability to borrow was limited. Over the course of the three 2009–2011 fiscal years, the states faced a budgetary shortfall of almost $0.5 trillion, averaging about one-fifth of their total budgets over the three years. To help counteract the effects of this gap, about $140 billion in ARRA money was transferred to the states, which made up about one-third of their shortfall. This money had immediate effect, inasmuch as it allowed states to avoid laying off public employees, especially in the public safety and education fields.[42] Even still, by one estimate all of the federal stimulus spending in 2009 barely made up for the countervailing collapse in state finances.[43]

The largest single component of the fiscal stimulus was in tax cuts of about $300 billion. After that, more than $100 billion went to individuals in the form of enhanced unemployment insurance, food stamps, and other transfers. Another $100 billion was targeted at infrastructure development. Between TARP, the ARRA, and other related programs, the fiscal response to the crisis amounted to over $1.76 trillion.

What was the impact of the stimulus and of other government spending measures? On ARRA, the nonpartisan Congressional Budget Office estimated that the bill's programs had raised the level of real GDP by between 1.7 percent and 4.5 percent, and lowered the unemployment rate by between 0.7 and 1.8 percentage points by the first quarter of 2010.[44] Two prominent economists, Alan Blinder and Mark Zandi, looked at all of the fiscal, financial, and monetary measures introduced in response to the crisis and concluded that if none of them had been implemented, the country's GDP in 2010 would have been about 11.5 percent lower, with over eight million fewer jobs, and the country would have been in the throes of deflation. The biggest effects were from the financial and monetary policies, but the various fiscal stimulus efforts had helped. According to Blinder and Zandi, the fiscal stimulus made real GDP about $460 billion greater by 2010 (that's about 3.4 percent of GDP), created 2.7 million more jobs, and pushed the unemployment rate almost 1.5 percentage points lower.[45]

And yet there was little to celebrate. By some lights, developments bore out misgivings about the inadequate size of the stimulus. Long after the recession began, output remained far below normal levels, and unemployment remained stubbornly stuck above 9 percent. Nonetheless, Obama's political advisers were almost certainly correct that any attempt to pass a larger stimulus bill in 2009, let alone later in the electoral cycle, would have failed. Fiscal policy had done just about as much as it could do politically, even if it might have been able to do more economically if given the chance. It was not just the U.S. government whose response to the crisis was facing political obstacles, though.

The global picture

America had company in its misery: all over the world, financial markets were in disarray and economies were heading downward. The policy response varied. In the advanced industrial countries, the monetary policy trajectory was very similar to that taken by the United States. In Europe, as soon as financial markets froze in the aftermath of Lehman Brothers' collapse, the European Central Bank moved quickly to drop interest rates (see figure 5). Just as in the United States, they soon reached a few tenths of a single percentage point, essentially at the 0 interest rate floor (Japan was already there), and embarked on extraordinary measures to attempt to rekindle bank lending.

Central bankers in the United States and Europe worked closely together as they tried to counteract the decline. They coordinated their monetary policies and lent to each other as necessary. This

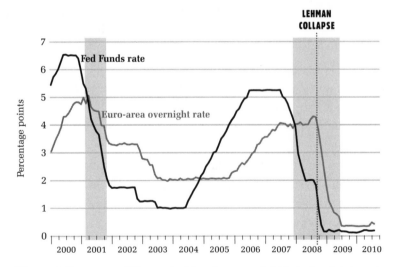

Figure 5. Response of the central banks: overnight interbank interest rates in the United States and euro area, 2000–2010. U.S. recession dates shaded gray. Source: Federal Reserve Board and International Monetary Fund, International Financial Statistics.

was particularly helpful because the integration of global financial markets meant that European banks were as likely to need dollars as they were euros, and the European Central Bank and Bank of England did not have anything like the necessary supply at hand. The Federal Reserve stepped in to loan dollars to other central banks, swapping dollars for euros, or dollars for pounds, allowing the partner central banks to provide the funds in dollars their own banks needed. By December 2008, these lending arrangements between the Fed and other central banks had reached nearly $600 billion.[46]

European attempts to cope with their own banking crises were less well coordinated and more varied. Some provided retroactive deposit insurance; others established bailout funds; still others bought up shares in troubled banks.[47] The politics of banking is thicker with special interests than is monetary policy, and as national special interests kicked in, national variety showed itself. France and Germany guaranteed private deposits. The United Kingdom, Sweden, and Switzerland set up funds to recapitalize the banking systems. The Italian government stated that no bank would be allowed to fail, and no depositors would lose money.[48] Although the approaches varied, each government had similar goals: to stem panic and to rescue its insolvent, or nearly insolvent, banks.

Fiscal policy was, as in the United States, fraught with even more disagreement and diversity. Late in 2008, the IMF and World Bank recommended a fiscal stimulus amounting to around 2 percentage points of GDP. Nonetheless, there was very wide variation in discretionary fiscal policy measures in 2009–2010 among the member countries of the Group of Twenty.[49]

Many European countries resisted the level of stimulus the Americans had adopted. At the outset, Europeans often felt that the economic crisis was a problem made in America, and that the recession might bypass Europe. European governments also undertook quite a bit more fiscal stimulus by way of automatic stabilizers than did the United States, by virtue of their more generous social policies. There were also greater fears in much of Europe than in the United States about the long-term effects of further government borrowing, especially among the Germans and other northern Europeans who had traditionally been more deficit averse than Americans.[50]

Whatever the validity of the disagreements, the different paths caused considerable friction within Europe, and between Europe and the United States. This friction was aggravated by the realization that international trade was also declining sharply. The suspicion was that in addition to going their own ways with fiscal policy, the major economies were turning away from their trading partners. American foreign trade declined nearly one-third from the middle of 2008 to the middle of 2009, the sharpest decline recorded in postwar history.[51] Overall, the volume of international trade was declining at a faster rate than it had even in the first few years after 1929.[52] The global crisis seemed to be threatening globalization itself.

As world trade shut down, countries that had staked their fortunes on exports were forced inward. Foremost among these was China. As China's export markets dried up, the Chinese government enacted one of the most impressive domestic stimulus packages in the world. The government increased direct spending on infrastructure and health care. More important, it used its great regulatory and administrative power to push banks to increase lending massively—which they did, expanding credit by an astounding 50 percent in the first half of 2009 alone. Chinese policy was quite successful: while economic growth had slowed to 6 percent in early 2009, by the middle of 2010 it had bounced back to more traditional levels of nearly 10 percent.[53] What was good for China was probably good for the world: with the rest of the international economy in the doldrums, what little growth there was in 2009 came largely from China.

As the Great Recession ran its course, economies around the world began to recover. In the United States, as in Europe and Japan, short-term macroeconomic fixes helped their economies get through the most difficult times in eighty years. The monetary authorities had done what they could; the fiscal authorities had done as much as politics would allow. Nonetheless, the recovery was sluggish at best in most of the industrialized world. The recovery was not going to restore these economies to long-term health. This was true of Japan and Europe, and it was certainly true of the United States.

The problems facing the American economy are more severe than can be solved with looser monetary and fiscal policy. The country's banking system is damaged; the national debt burden is soaring; the country's role in the world economy is in question; the underlying imbalances of the American economy have not been tackled. These weaknesses, and the political difficulty of addressing them constructively, threaten to consign the country to continued stagnation.

Economy in Shock

As the Latin American debt crisis of the 1980s reached its darkest days, one of the region's military leaders lectured his subjects about the need to tighten their belts. "The party is over," he insisted somberly. The next day, mass demonstrations filled the streets, led by banners reading, "The party is over, and we weren't even invited."[1]

When Latin America's borrowing party ended in 1982, it threw the region's economies, societies, and politics into disarray. The region suffered through the first lost decade of the modern era, as economies stagnated and even regressed, while unemployment soared and inflation went above 1000 percent in many nations. The "lost decade" epithet was misleading, for it actually took Latin America fifteen years to climb back to the 1981 level of per capita GDP. The collapse erased generations of economic advance. If the Latin American economies had grown as much during the fifteen years of their lost decade as they had in the previous fifteen years, the continent would be roughly twice as rich as it is today.[2]

The collapse of the Latin American borrowing boom had equally striking political effects. Popular anger exploded at the governments that had borrowed their way into an indebted hole, and eventually the anger spread to include many in the middle and business classes. The storm of protest overwhelmed the region's governments, and virtually all of them were thrown out of office. Most of the debtors had been dictatorships, as in 1980 only two countries in South America were civilian democracies (Colombia and Venezuela). Popular and elite protests cast aside all of the autocrats, even Alfredo Stroessner of Paraguay, who had ruled for thirty-five years, and Augusto Pinochet, whose dictatorship had governed Chile with an iron fist for fifteen years. Ironically, one of the principal results of the debt crisis was a wave of democratization.

The crisis also ended a half-century of Latin American economic organization. Since the 1930s, the region had focused its efforts on industrializing for the local market. Country after country used borrowed billions to build up domestic industries for domestic consumption. But the collapse of the borrowing binge ended this phase of Latin American economic history. The region spent its lost decade and a half plagued with inflation, soaring unemployment, and growing poverty, all of which discredited the strategies in place. By the early 1990s, desperate to find a new way to grow, all of the region's countries had rejected their previous policies and turned toward world markets, toward globalization.

Japan descended into the second lost decade of the modern era after its housing bubble collapsed in 1991. The failure was not quite so complete as in Latin America, but still a country used to growing rapidly and continually went through more than ten years of stagnation. In the eleven years of 1992–2002, the Japanese economy grew less than it had in the two years before the crisis hit.[3] As in Latin America, the political fallout was immediate. In 1993, voters rejected the ruling Liberal Democratic Party, which had been in power for nearly forty years; popular anger even brought the Japanese Socialist Party into government. Politicians were forced into a major reform of the political system, and the country embarked on years of soul searching about its social, political, and economic organization.

The United States now faces the third lost decade of the modern era—or, more accurately, the nation has survived one and is headed for another. While borrowing pumped up the economy for much of the first decade of the twenty-first century, the eventual collapse erased most of the gains. The U.S. economy's growth rate over the decade was barely one-fourth that of the 1990s (6 percent as opposed to 24 percent).[4]

More troubling, the United States emerges from the immediate crisis confronting the prospects of another decade lost. Americans will have to sacrifice in order to restore balance to the U.S. economy and to create the basis for future sustained growth. The country largely wasted one decade in a frenzy of rash policies and foolish borrowing, and will spend much of another repairing the economic wreckage. The long-term impact of the crisis has only started to be felt. It will occupy center stage in the nation's economic and political life for years to come.

Hard times ahead

In 2007, America's party ended. The debt-fed bubble burst and forced austerity on most of the country, as firms, households, and state and local governments scrambled to stay afloat. Financial markets froze, companies failed, stock and housing prices crumpled, and a brutal recession began.

The Great Recession was deep and broad enough to affect almost everyone in the United States. The corporate and financial failures hurt executives of the companies that had previously been flying so high. But economic crises always hit middle-class and working-class Americans particularly hard, and the Great Recession was no exception.[5]

In the middle of 2010, the U.S. unemployment rate hovered just under 10 percent, but there were striking differences in its distribution among Americans. The poorest one-third of the country's workers, from households earning less than $40,000, suffered an unemployment rate of 18 percent (among the poorest tenth, it was over 25 percent). This did not include the underemployed (people who were working less than they would have liked) or those who would have liked to work but had given up looking. If these two groups are counted, the rate rises to 35 percent (among the poorest tenth, 45 percent). On the other hand, for the richest third of the country's workers the unemployment rate was barely 4 percent—double what it had been two years earlier, true, but hardly a catastrophe. Among this group, of people whose household income was above $75,000, another 5 percent were underemployed or no longer looking. One in eleven of the country's best-off people was out of a job, or on reduced hours, or had given up looking for work, which in itself indicated serious problems. But this pales next to the fact that unemployment, underemployment, and discouragement had hit more than one-third of the country's 50 million or so poorer workers.[6]

The collapse in housing prices and in the stock market had very broad effects as well. More than two-thirds of Americans are homeowners, and home prices nationally dropped by about a third during the crisis. Many Americans also have some stake in financial markets either directly or indirectly, through their retirement savings and pension funds. Between housing and savings, in the first two years of the crisis, household wealth dropped by more than $15 trillion, wiping out nearly one-fourth of Americans' assets.

As of the middle of 2010, almost one-fourth of all American home mortgages were still "underwater"—that is, homeowners owed more on their mortgages than their homes were worth.[7] This helps explain why one in seven mortgage holders were behind on payments,[8] and one-fifth of all home sales were of foreclosed units. The picture was even bleaker in some areas, such as Las Vegas, where housing prices had dropped by more than one-half, where two-thirds of home mortgages were underwater, and two-thirds of all sales were of foreclosed properties.[9]

The immediate impact of the crisis was severe; its longer-term effects will be even more serious. American households will see this directly, as they work to clean up their own finances. Many Americans were hit by a double or triple whammy: their houses slumped in value, their retirement savings dropped, and they may have lost their job or had their hours reduced.

The collapse of asset values ate up the personal wealth of American households, which in turn forced them to cut back on their spending in order to rebuild. The bust in housing prices made it impossible for many Americans to borrow against their homes, including refinancing to reduce mortgage payments. Reversing the pattern during the boom, declining house prices forced consumption down as people found it harder to borrow.

In the past the stock market bust might have hit almost exclusively at better-off investors, but today many stock holdings are directly or indirectly part of the retirement savings of working Americans. And retirement savings have been savaged: in the first year of the crisis alone, an estimated $4 trillion in savings was lost. Americans who are expecting to retire with some savings will have to save more to get back to their target retirement income.

Take the example of a couple in their early fifties who represented, in 2006, median values on three crucial fronts: a household income at the national median of $50,000, a home at the national median price of $240,000, and household savings at the national median of $180,000, largely for retirement. A retirement adviser would, with realistic projections, have recommended that they save $3500 a year for their retirement. After 2007, as asset values collapsed, they would have seen the value of their home drop by $70,000, to $170,000—a development that, depending on how they had financed it and whether they planned to sell it, would certainly affect their plans.[10] Their savings would have gone down to $135,000 if they were like the average retirement saver. At this point, the retirement planner would recommend that they save *twice as much* every year—$7000 a year, 14 percent of their income before taxes. This means cutting back by about as much as this average household usually spends on food at home every year. This dire scenario doesn't even take into account the possibility that a member of the family might be the one in six in this income bracket to be unemployed or underemployed for some or all of the crisis. Over the first three years of the Great Recession, American workers lost tens of billions of work-hours, and trillions of dollars in wages and salaries, due to unemployment. But even the lucky employed will have to reduce consumption and increase their savings.

Americans with pension plans with defined benefits—that is, who are promised a specific benefit payment upon retirement— might think they are safe. But many of the employers responsible for funding these pension plans will have trouble keeping them afloat. The crisis drove the average plan from being fully funded to being 25 percent short of what is needed to meet its pension obligations. The corporations responsible for the pensions have to add as much as $150 billion a year to bring the plans back to balance, an amount equivalent to what they would need to hire three million workers at $50,000 a year. There is a public enterprise that insures the pensions of 44 million Americans, the Pension Benefit Guaranty Corporation, but it also is underfunded.[11] And this does not include pension plans for state government employees, which are at least a trillion dollars short of what they will need to meet their obligations.[12] In what was expected to be the first in a long series of cases, in August 2010 the Securities and Exchange Commission charged the State of New Jersey with fraudulently misstating the condition of the state's pension funds.[13]

State and local governments faced some of the most serious fallout of the crisis, for they have less ability to borrow than the federal government, and they cannot print money. As revenues plummeted, the country's states and cities were forced into large-scale cutbacks and layoffs. Even as recovery began, the budgetary problems were so severe that many local governments were resorting to drastic measures. In March 2010, Detroit announced plans to close more than one-fourth of its public schools; in the same month, the Kansas City, Missouri, school board announced that it would close half of the city's schools.[14] State and local governments were driven to equally desperate actions to increase revenues. The City of Chicago, for example, sold 36,000 metered parking spaces to a group of private investors for $1.16 billion; the investors will pocket the profits from the parking meters for the next seventy-five years. As state budget deficits shot above $80 billion in 2011, there were even fears of municipal and state defaults, a prospect that had largely faded after the Great Depression of the 1930s.[15]

The burden of debt and the collapse in asset prices will require a fundamental reorientation of the American economy. This reorientation will demand sacrifices of large portions of the population in order to redress the blunders of a small minority of financiers, policymakers, and others. The United States must restore balance to its economic position. The government comes out of the crisis with debts well in excess of $10 trillion. Much of this is owed to foreigners. To service this debt it will have to spend less or tax more, or both. Private American citizens accumulated enormous debts too, and they will have to generate the resources to service them—by consuming less, producing more, and saving more. The country has to import less and export more. This means that real wages have to decline, or labor productivity has to rise, in order to make American products more competitive.

The result will be a reduction in the real living standard of many Americans, an adjustment necessary to restore macroeconomic balance. Such adjustments, familiar to those who have lived through other debt crises, are never pleasant. And they often lead to political upheaval with both national and international repercussions, as those who fear losing from the adjustment, and those who hope to win from it, square off in the political arena. History provides some instructive examples.

Global crises and national politics past

When the international economy crashed after 1929, it took many of the world's economic elites with it. For seventy years, the world's nations had been closely linked by an integrated world economy. These links were facilitated by the fact that very few governments were democratic, and even those that were in theory did not enfranchise much of the population in practice. This meant that when a national government had to impose sacrifices on its population to maintain the nation's position in the world economy, it did so. But with the spread of democracy in the early part of the twentieth century, by 1929 governments could no longer ignore the demands of the middle classes, farmers, and the working classes.[16] However, rulers could not come up with a response to the crisis that both satisfied the newly enfranchised masses and sustained economic ties with the rest of the world.

The result was a stunning rejection of the integrated world economy that had reigned for generations. Governments in Eastern and Central Europe, in Russia, in Japan, in the developing world, rejected globalization and erected high walls around their own economies. New nationalist interests did their best to undermine what was left of an integrated international economy. The remaining democratic capitalist governments in Western Europe and North America also turned away from global economic relations in order to address economic and social problems at home. Labor movements and their Socialist parties were brought into government. Conservative elements of the business community were displaced by new business leaders—in America, such "corporate liberals" as Edward Stettinius Jr. of General Motors and Gerard Swope of General Electric—who crafted compromises between labor, capital, farmers, and the middle classes, setting the stage for the modern welfare state.[17]

Not every crisis leads to a turn away from the world economy. The debt crisis of the 1980s in Latin America, for example, had much the opposite effect, forcing the region's economies to reorient themselves. The national markets they had built up were sheltered from the rest of the world and exported little. After the crisis, they could no longer rely on foreigners to fund industries and governments, and had to earn the money they needed to service their debts. Their currencies collapsed, their domestic markets shriveled, and their governments had to cut back drastically.

The surviving industries and farms turned toward foreign markets, taking advantage of new opportunities to export their way into the ranks of the world's leading corporations. Soon Mexican beer, Colombian clothing, and Brazilian aircraft were major international products, and their producers were heavily committed to global markets. These new exporters led the way in encouraging such regional trade agreements as the North American Free Trade Agreement (NAFTA) and the Southern Common Market (Mercosur) of Argentina, Brazil, Uruguay, and Paraguay. The economic adjustment of the Latin American debtors in the 1980s built up powerful *internationalist* interests rather than nationalist ones. In part this was because world markets were growing in the 1980s, unlike in the 1930s, so that there were economic opportunities to take advantage of. But it was also because the adjustments reoriented the Latin American economies away from reliance on borrowed foreign capital and toward stronger exports. The United States faces a similar need to wean itself from foreign lenders and increase its ability to compete in world markets. But there are major political obstacles to overcome before the country's economy is restructured in line with the new reality. Change will be costly to some, and beneficial to others; and the victims and beneficiaries are hardly going to be passive observers of debates over their fate.

Concentrated wealth, concentrated blame

The United States faces a decade of economic austerity and slow growth. Deep recessions combined with financial crises exact a heavy toll; output takes years to recover to the precrisis trend.[18] When associated with high levels of government debt, the outlook is even more dire. Advanced industrialized countries with a debt-to-GDP ratio as large as the United States now has usually stagnate for years after a financial crisis.[19]

Hardship and stagnation will compound the widespread anger over the crisis and its effects, and this anger will be intensified by resentment over the increasing gap between rich and poor in the United States. The country has become more unequal, almost without pause, since the early 1970s. There have been two clear phases of the process. In the first, from the early 1970s until the late 1980s, the earnings of unskilled and semi-skilled American workers collapsed. In the early 1970s, young men with a high school degree earned over $14 an hour (in today's dollars); by the early 1990s, they were earning less than $11 an hour, a decline of over one-fifth. Overall, the poorest one-fourth to one-third of the American population grew worse off over the course of those fifteen or twenty years—not just relative to the rest of the country, but in absolute terms.

The second phase in the rise of American inequality hit the middle class. From the early 1990s onward, the income gap between average Americans and the wealthy got larger and larger. In 1980, the richest 10 percent of American households earned one-third of the country's income; by 2007, they earned fully half. The trend was even more striking at the very top. The share of the country's income that went to the richest 1 percent of Americans, which had declined continually since the 1930s, began to rise after 1980 (see figure 6).

After 1980, this wealthiest 1 percent saw their share of the country's income go from 10 percent in 1980 to 23.5 percent in 2007. One of the most visible indications of the increasing disparity of wealth and income came from evidence of galloping pay increases among corporate executives. In 1980, the country's 100 best-paid executives made 100 times the national average wage; by 2007, they made 770 times the average wage.[20]

The gap between rich and poor grew wider during the boom years between 2002 and 2007. While the effects of debt-financed growth were felt almost everywhere, they were particularly favorable to the very wealthy. Over the course of the Bush expansion, two-thirds of the country's income growth went to the top 1 percent of the population. These very rich families, each earning more than $400,000 a year, saw their incomes rise by more than 60 percent between 2002 and 2007, while the income of the rest of the nation's families rose by 6 percent. Americans could hardly help but notice the extraordinary explosion in the prosperity of the rich and the super-rich.

The general feeling that the financial frenzy was leaving the

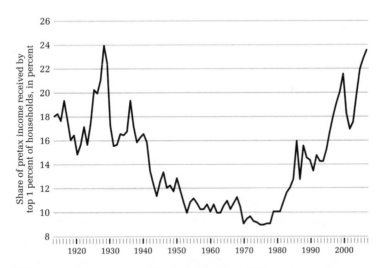

Figure 6. The very wealthy get even wealthier: share of pretax income received by top 1 percent of households, excluding capital gains, 1913–2007. Source: Anthony Atkinson, Thomas Piketty, and Emmanuel Saez, "Top incomes in the long run of history," *Journal of Economic History* (forthcoming).

middle class behind bubbled up into fury once the crisis hit. Even before the crash, many Americans were put off by the enormous salaries and bonuses bankers were paying themselves. Now it seemed that even as the financiers profited handsomely from the boom, their machinations had brought down the entire American economy. Outrage grew apace, as the government threw hundreds of billions of dollars of taxpayer money into bailing out some of those most responsible for the crisis, while the culprits continued to pay themselves huge bonuses.

Merrill Lynch lost $27.6 billion in 2008, collapsed spectacularly, had to be bought by Bank of America, and was rescued with $10 billion in federal money; yet at the end of that disastrous year, its management approved bonuses of $3.6 billion. Insurance giant AIG's London financial products group had created the most toxic of the toxic derivatives, which bankrupted the company and nearly brought down the global financial system; yet the firm paid $450 million in bonuses to the very group that had played the greatest role in causing the corporate collapse.[21] Joseph Cassano, the AIG executive who led the London group, left the firm with a $69 million golden handshake. In 2009, after trillions in federal money had been used to shore up the financial system, banks and brokers paid out $145 billion in bonuses—even more than they had in 2007, the previous record year.[22]

One influential statement of outrage at financial excess came from an unusual source. Simon Johnson, who advised the Securities and Exchange Commission in 2000–2001, taught students at MIT's Sloan School of Management, and then served as chief economist of the International Monetary Fund in 2007 and 2008, blamed financiers themselves for using their economic and political power to their own benefit, to the detriment of the nation and the world. Johnson had a unique vantage point on the crisis; at the IMF he served at the pinnacle of the world's leading international financial institution as the crisis gathered. In looking back, Johnson railed at how "a whole generation of policy makers has been mesmerized by Wall Street, always and utterly convinced that whatever the banks said was true." The result was to put the United States on a disastrous course: "lightweight regulation, cheap money, the unwritten Chinese-

American economic alliance, the promotion of homeownership . . . *all* benefited the financial sector. Policy changes that might have forestalled the crisis but would have limited the financial sector's profits . . . were ignored or swept aside." Johnson concluded bitterly, "Financiers played a central role in creating the crisis, making ever-larger gambles, with the implicit backing of the government, until the inevitable collapse."[23]

Current conditions are reminiscent of British debates in the 1920s over how to alleviate the country's chronic unemployment and stagnation. In that context, Winston Churchill said, "I would rather see Finance less proud and Industry more content."[24] Today, it would take a bold—perhaps reckless, even foolish—politician not to wish finance less proud. After all, the country's financiers have little to be proud about. Their job as intermediaries was to manage the capital inflow and its consequences, and instead they dealt with it recklessly.

Satisfying as it may be to punish the bankers for their misdeeds, vibrant banks are needed if the economy is to regain its footing. For even as the U.S. economy began to recover, the country's financial system was still seriously impaired. Bank profits had risen back toward precrisis levels, but bank lending had not. It was still relatively hard to get consumer credit, or to issue mortgage-backed securities, or for small businesses to get bank loans. Part of the problem was that banks were still carrying hundreds of billions of dollars in bad loans on their books. The IMF estimated that American financial institutions were going to have to write off about $885 billion in losses, but as late as the middle of 2010, three years after the losses began to accumulate, they had still failed to write off about $200 billion.[25] Banks with balance sheets heavy with bad investments were naturally reluctant to take on new risks, and so they didn't. And if normal channels of bank lending were not operating, the economy would continue to languish. The U.S. government had to find a way to restore a normally functioning financial system.

Zombie bank alert

American policymakers may have been unsure about the path to take to resolve the financial sluggishness, but they certainly knew which path to avoid. The Japanese experience in the aftermath of a similar banking crisis has become the lodestar from which to steer away. In Japan, the aftermath of a borrowing boom and bust led to a decade and more of economic stagnation from which the country has still not fully recovered.

Japan's experience began, like America's, with an economic boom. During the 1980s much of the world looked on Japanese growth rates with envy, and the bookshelves were full of titles like *Japan as Number One*.[26] The real estate market expanded along with the rest of the economy, eventually outpacing it. Very loose monetary policy pushed up property prices, and real estate loans seemed a sure bet. The Japanese government deregulated many segments of the financial markets, which allowed banks to take on greater risks.[27] Between low interest rates, deregulation, and easy bank credit, Japan steamed into what was called "the bubble economy." The bubble was unsustainable, and eventually real estate prices peaked, then fell.

The real estate collapse made many Japanese banks insolvent. However, neither the banks nor the Japanese government were willing to recognize reality and confront the massive insolvency. The banks themselves refused to recognize the losses on their books, and did not declare borrowers in default, because they did not want to expose the precariousness of their financial position. For its part, the government was concerned that recognizing the depth of the problem would cause a depositor panic and would so impair confidence that it would lead to a very deep recession.

Japanese politicians realized that bailing out the banks with taxpayer money would be extremely unpopular. Instead, the Japanese government attempted to postpone matters with what is called "regulatory forbearance," in which the regulators effectively ignore some of the problem loans on the banks' balance sheets—in essence, retouching the patient's X-rays. When it finally got around to injecting capital into the banking system, the government did so only half-heartedly. It set up a series of private, semi-public, and public enterprises to buy bad loans from the banks in order to get them off the bank balance sheets. But the government never committed enough money to bring the banks back to health or to provide them with sufficient new capital. Powerful financial interests insisted that the government keep the banks standing rather than recognize their bankruptcy; voters insisted that the government not throw good money after bad. As a result, the Japanese government allowed a dysfunctional financial system to grind along without resolving its problems.

The country's financial system was in the hands of "zombie banks," financial institutions that were effectively insolvent and thus incapable of acting like normal financial institutions, but were kept on their feet by tolerant regulators: not quite living, not quite dead. In their uncertain state, the banks did as little new lending as possible. And when the zombie banks did lend, they tended to lend to precisely the firms that had gotten themselves, and their lenders, into trouble. The banks struggled to keep their bad debtors alive because massive bankruptcies on the part of the banks' corporate customers would have exposed the insolvency of the banks themselves. To avoid this, the zombie banks lent to "zombie firms" to keep them going halfway between life and death.

Zombie banks lent to zombie companies, which denied healthy firms access to credit and drained scarce capital from the rest of the economy.[28] The Japanese government attempted to stimulate the economy with expansionary fiscal policy, but throughout the 1990s these attempts were stymied by the damaged banking system. The result was Japan's first lost decade, with stagnant growth and bouts of deflation. In the decade before 1990, Japan's per capita GDP had grown by an average of 4.1 percent a year. In the first of Japan's lost decades, the 1990s, growth declined to 0.9 percent. The unemployment rate, while low by international standards, doubled from 2 percent to 4 percent.

Eventually, after 2001, the new government of Junichiro Koizumi changed course. It injected large amounts of capital into the banks, bought up most of the bad loans, and restructured or closed up the problem debtors.[29] The new policies helped, as did buoyant growth in the world economy, but the enduring problems continued to be a drag on the national economy. In the decade beginning in 2000, Japan managed only a slight recovery, to an annual growth rate of 1.2 percent—and that was before the recession of 2009. Massive fiscal stimulus programs helped a little, as the government ran budget deficits averaging 5.9 percent of GDP from 2000 until 2008.[30]

But the result was government debt equal to nearly twice the size of the country's GDP.[31]

Japan's lost decades were unnecessary. Policymakers understood what they needed to do: acknowledge the bad loans, force the banks to take their losses, recapitalize the banks as necessary, and restructure the economy away from the declining, often insolvent, industries to more dynamic sectors. But powerful interest groups stymied action at every turn. The country's bankers resisted admitting to losses that might put them out of business. The indebted companies insisted on being kept alive, or at least half-alive. Japan's politicians avoided a bank recapitalization that would have been unpopular with taxpayers. Decades were lost in the process.

As American policymakers looked for a better model to follow, their own experience with the savings and loan crisis was a bit more attractive than the Japanese fiasco—but not by much. When the savings and loan crisis began in 1985 (see chapter 1), it was clear that much of the industry was insolvent and would have to be wound up. But the banks used their substantial political clout to avoid being shut down. Congress and the executive branch were unwilling to force all of the insolvent banks to close, and they were equally reluctant to fund the bailout necessary to recapitalize the viable portion of the industry. As in Japan, the government resorted to regulatory forbearance. Regulators looked the other way, pretending along with their charges that the banks' assets were worth more than they actually were.

But regulatory forbearance only postponed the inevitable, and in fact it aggravated the problem. The bad loans festered until a resolution could no longer be deferred. In 1989 Congress instituted a new regulatory regime that swept the slate clean. Insolvent banks were closed down or merged into stronger banks. A newly created entity called the Resolution Thrift Corporation (RTC) bought bad assets from the remaining banks, then pooled them and sold them to the highest bidder. The new policies eventually cleaned up the industry, and in the long run the Resolution Thrift Corporation actually made money. But five years of delay, resistance, and special-interest pleading were expensive: by the time the savings and loan crisis was finally resolved, ten years after it began, it had cost the taxpayers $150 billion.[32]

There was a far better example available to American, and other, policymakers: that of Sweden in the early 1990s. The background was familiar. A substantial financial deregulation allowed the previously tightly regulated banks to charge higher interest rates and move into new areas of lending with which they were unfamiliar. The financial boom was fueled by large-scale foreign borrowing of nearly $30 billion between 1989 and 1993, averaging 3 percent of GDP. The economy boomed and a housing bubble developed, with home prices doubling in five years.

A European recession eventually brought the bubble to an end, leaving most of the country's banks insolvent. The Swedish government turned out to be much less beholden to financial interests than the Japanese or American governments. It effectively nationalized much of the banking system and set up two separate government agencies. The Swedish regulators handed over to the new agencies the bad assets that had been weighing down the balance sheets of the banks; some called these agencies "bad banks." What remained of the financial institutions after the bad assets were given to the bad banks was fundamentally sound. The banks were cleansed of bad loans, and the financial system resumed normal operations— taking deposits, making loans, and buying assets. Within four years, the bad banks had sold off the bad assets. Although complete cost accounting is difficult, the Swedish government's aggressive response might have ended up costing it virtually nothing.[33]

As with prior experiences, the initial American response to the American crisis was engulfed in a political firestorm, with banks and their critics pushing the government in conflicting directions. Unlike the Japanese banks in the 1990s, American banks quickly wrote off most of their bad loans. The U.S. government injected capital into the troubled banks, established programs to help get toxic assets off the banks' books, and worked to restart markets for asset-backed securities. Despite protest from those who thought the banks had been given too much, or too little, the crisis was deep enough to allow agreement on the need for decisive action.

However, many of these steps were less aggressive than the ones taken in the very successful Swedish approach. Insolvent banks were sometimes propped up rather than nationalized, and the capital injections may have been too small. There was a fair amount of regulatory forbearance, including some convenient accounting sleight of hand. Accounting rules that required banks to mark their asset-backed securities to market were suspended. While this measure slowed the workings of the adverse feedback loop, it also obscured the extent of the problems the bad assets were likely to cause.[34]

As in Japan, the modified American financial response was attractive to politicians because it reduced the direct costs of the intervention to the government. It also helped them address the concerns of the bankers themselves that the government would limit their room to maneuver. By the end of 2010 the most serious problems in the American financial system appeared resolved. The major banks were making profits and had paid the government back its TARP money. The administration did not have to go back to Congress for more bailout money, which it probably would not have obtained. Fears of an outright collapse of the financial system receded.

But the American solution risked replicating Japanese-style problems with zombie banks. For it was not at all clear that the banks were on a solid footing. They had rushed to repay TARP money, in large part because they found TARP commitments onerous, including restrictions on executive pay. Yet their repayment of TARP capital injections meant that they now had less capital, thus less ability to lend. In addition, the major banks had not written off all of their bad loans, in large part because of the mark-to-market regulatory forbearance. Their balance sheets were still quite weak. And when banks are saddled with lots of bad loans, so that they are in constant danger of tipping into insolvency, they will pull in their activities, avoid lending to any but the safest firms, or purchase risk-free assets like government bonds. This is not conducive to a resumption of normal business conditions.

For all its weaknesses, the American financial response had avoided an outright collapse of the financial system. But between pressures from the banks to give them more freedom, and electoral pressures to avoid further government involvement in financial markets, the Obama administration found itself limited in what it could do given the existing regulatory framework. For this reason, and because it was clear that the crisis demanded a more lasting fix for the banking system, the administration turned to a broader reform of financial regulation.

Re-regulating finance

While the ultimate roots of the crisis and ensuing recession had much to do with the capital inflows, and with the government's fiscal and monetary policies, the financial meltdown had unmistakably made matters a lot worse. And while the financial meltdown had many sources, an abject failure of regulatory oversight was unquestionably critical. More vigilant regulators could have spared the country some of the worst excesses of the capital flow cycle. Thirty years of almost continual deregulation of finance would have to be reconsidered, and some of it would have to be reversed.

In July 2010 Congress passed, and President Obama signed, sweeping financial reform legislation. The Dodd-Frank Wall Street Reform and Consumer Protection Act was named after Christopher Dodd (D-Conn.) and Barney Frank (D-Mass.), the bill's principal Senate and House authors, respectively. The legislation ran to 2300 pages and included a wide array of provisions. At its core were attempts to address some of the flaws in the system that had brought global finance to its knees. In all, it amounted to the most significant transformation of American finance since the Great Depression of the 1930s.

At the center of the new regime were several major changes.[35] The first was a mandate to increase the amount of capital large banks were required to hold. The act also delegated to regulators the authority to increase capital requirements for other banks. Many of the new provisions aimed to limit leverage to levels well below those that prevailed in the years before the financial collapse. This applied particularly to banks large enough to have a broad impact on the financial structure—"systemically important financial institutions." Banks considered systemically important are now required to have leverage ratios no greater than 15 : 1. Additional restrictions were agreed on in the international agreement known as the Basel III accord, negotiated among major financial center regulatory agencies. This international agreement sets forth a framework that will eventually require all international banks to maintain capital ratios of 7 percent, adjusted by the riskiness of a bank's assets, more than double the effective 2 percent to 3 percent currently in place.[36]

The second major set of provisions extended government regulation to the "shadow banking system," the previously unregulated complex of hedge funds, special purpose entities, conduits, special investment vehicles, and the like. All but the smallest private equity companies and hedge funds will now have to register with the Securities and Exchange Commission. Banks will be prohibited from shifting substantial portions of their assets and liabilities off their regular balance sheets and onto associated conduits or funds. While they will still be permitted to use these affiliates for some purposes, the regulators will limit how much a bank can invest in these entities.

The legislation also requires that most credit default swaps, the derivatives that forced the government to bail out AIG, will now trade on formal exchanges or central clearinghouses. This will allow market participants to see the prices at which these instruments are being traded. The legislation also directs the regulators to determine the method by which these trades will be managed, the amount of collateral firms will have to offer, and the amount of capital that will have to be held.

Related changes aim to address some of the features of the "originate-to-distribute" model of mortgage lending, which has been blamed for some of the uncertainty that helped shut down financial markets in 2008. This model is one in which one entity originates a mortgage and then promptly sells it off to be sliced and diced for mortgage-backed securities. Apart from the lack of transparency, the process of packaging loans and selling them off removed much of the incentive for banks to scrutinize borrowers and to watch what they were doing over time. The reform requires that whenever a bank securitizes loans, it has to keep at least 5 percent of the debt on its own books, so that it has some of its own "skin in the game," as the market saying goes.

The Dodd-Frank Act also sets up a consumer financial protection bureau. This is a real novelty, the first time a financial regulator has been primarily charged with defending the consumer. The legislation leaves many of the details about the direction and organization of the bureau to the regulators. It remains to be seen whether the new agency will be able to limit the illegal practices that abounded in the years before the crisis, including the frauds perpetrated by industry insiders in the subprime mortgage business.

A final major feature of the legislation attempts to minimize a particularly noxious form of moral hazard, the "too big to fail" problem. This is the issue highlighted by the experience of such enormous, highly complex, financial institutions as Citigroup, Bank of America, and the other major banks that were included in the government bailout of October 2008. The size of these banks did not itself cause the crisis—plenty of smaller regional banks were equally reckless and eventually equally insolvent. But the size and interconnections of these systemically important institutions tightly constrain the options available to regulators in a time of crisis, because the banks can effectively hold government policy hostage: either bail us out, or we take everyone else with us. To mitigate the impact of this type of moral hazard, the legislation forces banks to create "funeral plans" that provide advance planning for closing them quickly. The government would pay to wind up the bank in the short term, but would recoup the costs by selling off the firm's assets. This sort of mechanism would help reduce the panic that gripped markets in the aftermath of the Lehman and AIG failures, and it would also limit the impact of moral hazard by imposing clear costs for failure.[37]

Not everyone agreed with the regulatory changes adopted in 2010. Some felt they went too far in imposing restrictions on the private sector. One group of conservative leaders argued against the Dodd-Frank legislation on the grounds that it "would increase the size and scope of the federal government, regulating every phase of economic activity." For them the proposal was another misguided attempt to overregulate businesses. "Due to the bill's excessive taxes and government red tape," they argued, "families and small business owners would no longer have access to low cost credit, and a bureaucrat would stand between them and living the American dream."[38]

Conservative activist Grover Norquist charged that the reform put in place "costly and colossal new regulations . . . burdens banks with billions of dollars in new fees and restrictions . . . creates a massive new government agency with the power to monitor virtually any American citizen's or business's bank accounts."[39]

Other critics felt the regulatory reform did not go far enough, leaving bankers with too much power and too much leeway. Simon Johnson complained that no matter how one looks at the Dodd-Frank Act, "it is hard to find anything that will substantially change how Wall Street operates." As to who came out ahead with the reform, Johnson was categorical: "The big banks have won. They won with a terrific smokescreen, so there's a lot of pretense. . . . But it's hats off to them. Too bad it hurts the rest of us."[40]

The Dodd-Frank Act was certainly a compromise, and given the powerful interests on all sides of the issue, it was never going to satisfy everyone. But it did aim to restructure the nation's finances so as to reduce some of the regulatory and legislative defects that had contributed to the recent financial crisis. Nevertheless, the financial reform addressed only some of the causes of the crisis. Massive borrowing, by the government and by households, was central to the boom, bubble, and bust that nearly brought down the world economy. And as the United States gradually recovered from the deepest recession since the 1930s, the country's burgeoning debt burden emerged as a major dilemma—one even more politically contentious than banking reform.

Zombie nation?

If the continued operation of fatally impaired banks threatened the health of the financial system, a growing debt burden endangered the operation of government and the welfare of the country as a whole. The federal government had been borrowing massively ever since the 2001 and 2003 tax cuts, and federal deficits soared even higher as the economy deteriorated after 2007. They persisted through the lackluster recovery and in 2010 remained at $1.35 trillion, more than 9 percent of GDP.[41]

After a decade of casual acceptance of budget deficits, hard times led Americans to focus on the issue. Some politicians were quick to insist on immediate measures to limit spending. Republican Senator Bob Corker of Tennessee voted against an extension of unemployment insurance in June 2010, explaining, "My heart goes out to Americans who are hurting because Washington can't agree on a way to pay for an extension of unemployment benefits. . . . I cannot in good conscience continue voting for bills that aren't paid for."[42]

Representative Paul Ryan, a Republican from Wisconsin, was more dramatic. He called for a major round of spending cuts: "I would rescind the unspent stimulus funds, I would rescind all the TARP funds they aren't spending, I would do a federal hiring freeze and pay freeze for the rest of the year, and I would go back and cut discretionary spending back to '08 levels and freeze that spending going forward."[43]

To some extent, the antagonism was predictable posturing in a midterm election year. Ryan's measures would barely have made a dent in the budget deficit and would have had little or no impact on longer-term fiscal challenges. But the controversy highlighted two crucial issues: what to do about government spending in the short run, and what to do about it in the long run. Strangely, these were two quite separate questions, which suggested two very different answers.

In the short run, the federal government was running large deficits and would continue to do so for several years at least. These deficits were largely a result of an extremely deep and protracted economic slowdown. In part, they reflected the reduced revenues and increased expenditures that come automatically with any recessionary conditions. But they also represented a response to the continued sluggishness of the macroeconomy. With unemployment stuck near or above 9 percent, and long-term unemployment at record highs, it would almost certainly have been self-defeating to reduce the deficit immediately. A substantial reduction in spending, or a substantial increase in taxes, might well have plunged the already limping economy into yet another downward spiral, which would in turn have pulled tax revenues down with it. In the end, the government could well have ended up even more deeply in debt.[44] So in *the short term*, budget deficits were a necessary evil. Calls to rein them in prematurely may have been politically expedient, but actually responding to these calls would have been economically unwise.

The long run is another matter. The nation confronts a fundamental fiscal challenge, which has little or nothing to do with the crisis-era deficits of the years since 2007. Before the financial crisis and the Great Recession, before the 2001 and 2003 tax cuts, the United States was already facing a long-term debt problem. The tax cuts and recession did move up the date of judgment. Even in 2001, after a dramatic improvement in government finances in the late 1990s had provided the government with large surpluses, a look ahead indicated budget deficits of about 7 percent of GDP by 2035. The Bush-era tax cuts drove government debt rapidly upward, and the crisis drove it up even farther; by 2009, after the tax cuts and the crisis, that 7 percent level was expected to be reached fifteen years earlier, by 2020. And the fiscal dilemma is a political dilemma: it exists because of the political influence of powerful groups in American society, and its resolution will confront massive political opposition.

Ballooning entitlement spending is the main source of the increasingly ominous deficit. Neither TARP, nor the stimulus bill, nor other crisis-era measures matter much to the longer-term financial picture. The principal question is what to do about the entitlement programs—Medicare, Medicaid, and Social Security—which are going to consume ever greater shares of the budget. With no change in policy, by 2020 these programs will eat up nearly 12 percent of GDP and over half of all government spending. Medicare and Medicaid alone will cost as much as all noninterest discretionary spending by the federal government *combined*.[45]

The problem has been aggravated by policy changes that dramatically increased spending without providing for its financing. The Medicare Modernization Act of 2006, for instance, added a new program subsidizing prescription drugs for the elderly. The program has been extraordinarily popular and may well be desirable. But the Bush administration made little attempt to fund it, and over the course of seventy-five years its costs are expected to exceed revenues by $8.4 *trillion* if nothing changes.[46]

Unfortunately, the political system seems calibrated to change nothing—at least not to reduce spending or increase taxes—and to

ignore the danger signals. The broader effects of staying on this iner-
tial fiscal path are alarming. The nonpartisan Congressional Budget
Office has projected the impact of continuing to avoid substantial
change—not revising the Alternative Minimum Tax, not rescinding
the 2001 and 2003 tax cuts, not carrying out other politically difficult reforms. By 2020, according to these projections, the federal
budget deficit will be almost 7 percent of GDP, or $1.6 trillion; the
government's debt, over $19 trillion. By 2035, in this scenario, the
federal deficit will have reached 16 percent of GDP, and the government's debt would be about twice as large as the country's entire
economy. As deficits continue and debts accumulate, interest payments rise rapidly. By 2035, in this state of affairs, federal interest
payments alone would be almost 9 percent of GDP, six times their
current level; they would then be by far the single largest component
of government spending. While noninterest spending would be only
a bit larger as a proportion of the economy than it is today, the inter-
est-payment expenditures would push total federal spending up to
50 percent higher than today as a share of GDP.[47]

These numbers are staggering, almost unimaginable. But the
problems they cause are quite real. When a government *chroni-
cally* runs large deficits, it can divert the country's resources away
from the new factories, technologies, and education that are critical to improving living standards. Inasmuch as the borrowing
goes to increase current consumption rather than to finance productive investments, this borrowing simply postpones the day of
reckoning—and toughens the reckoning. Eventually, the country
will have to send trillions abroad to service the foreign loans. If
the loans have not been invested in increasing the country's productive capacity, these trillions will take an ever larger bite out of the
national economy.[48]

Another reason to worry about the government's long-term fiscal
condition is that it makes the United States increasingly reliant on
the favorable assessments of foreign investors. For now, foreigners
seem willing to lend the U.S. government as much as it needs, but
as the debt burden takes a larger share of the economy, foreigners
are likely to reassess their evaluation of the creditworthiness of the
American government—and, indeed, of the American economy

as a whole. How much longer will foreign investors be willing to add to the trillions of dollars they have already put into Treasury securities?[49]

All of these reasons to worry about chronic, large-scale deficits are subsumed by the most important reason: they impose massive costs on future generations, who did nothing to incur them. Excessive borrowing now means that our descendents inherit a smaller capital stock and a smaller economy. Massive foreign borrowing means that coming generations have to send ever greater portions of what they produce abroad, to service the foreign debt. The more our government delays getting control of spending on Social Security, Medicare, and Medicaid, the less likely it is that our descendents will be able to enjoy the full benefits of such desirable programs.

If current trends continue unabated, today's children are likely to grow up to a country with a reduced productive capacity, an oppressive foreign debt burden, and a degraded economic reputation. They will also have to tax themselves heavily, and deny themselves government benefits, in order to pay for their parents' and grandparents' profligacy. And the future generations who will suffer these indignities cannot have an immediate impact on the policies that affect them so powerfully. This is especially true in a political climate heavily weighted toward the next election and focused on blame rather than responsibility.

The country is full of politicians railing against the deficits and debts piling up. But virtually nobody appears willing to propose the only measures likely to make a real difference: substantial reductions in Medicare, Medicaid, and Social Security benefits, and substantial tax increases. The political realities appear to militate against meaningful change. The beneficiaries of these government programs are politically powerful enough to stand in the way of any attempts to reduce their benefits substantially. Meanwhile, the country's taxpayers appear unwilling to accept that higher taxes are the price a society pays for the programs it adopts.

Americans seem quick to anger over the trillions in liabilities that are piling up, but hostile to any meaningful proposal to address the problem. There are many reasons to worry about the future of America's fiscal position, but the most frightening reason is the *absence* of reason in the public debate over it. Diffuse popular anger, combined with powerful interests in conflict, have emptied the political system of meaningful analysis or deliberation. With nobody willing to help pay the price of getting the nation's fiscal house in order, the country as a whole risks having to pay an exorbitant price in the future.

It is not just Americans who were put at risk by the country's political deadlock. The future of the world economy depends on what happens in the United States, and informed foreigners are worried. Britain's Martin Wolf, probably the world's leading economic journalist, was glum: "US fiscal policy is paralysed," he observed in July 2010. The Republicans are "indifferent to deficits, provided they are brought about by tax cuts," while the Democrats are "relatively fiscally responsible (well, everything is relative, after all), but opposed to spending cuts on core programmes." This is a formula for disaster, and in some scenarios the result could be "to destroy the credit of the US federal government. . . . If so, that would be the end of the US era of global dominance." Faced with the prospect of "the destruction of fiscal credibility, " Wolf concluded that "a great deal of trouble lies ahead, for the United States and the world."[50] Part of the problem was Americans' increasingly antagonistic views about the rest of the world economy.

Globalization and inequality

Even before the crisis hit, Americans were becoming warier about the world economy. The 1990s had been the heyday of enthusiasm about the international economy. The cold war was over, capitalism had won, and the order of the day was ever greater economic integration among the nations of the world. But over the next decade, there was a noticeable change in American public opinion about globalization. By 2005 "globalization" had ceased to be a term of hope and promise and had instead become something of a swear word, used almost exclusively with negative connotations. Globalization threatened jobs; globalization destroyed traditional communities and lifestyles; globalization homogenized cultures.

Many Americans came to see globalization as largely responsible for the growing gap between the rich and the rest in the United

States. The collapse of unskilled and semi-skilled wages was generally associated with the onslaught of low-wage competition from poor countries that were joining the world economy. In a famous 1995 article, Harvard economist Richard Freeman asked, "Are your wages set in Beijing?"[51] and made the intuitive point that one could hardly draw 2 billion low-wage Asian workers into the world's labor force without driving down the wages of American workers who were competing with them.[52] One 2006 survey revealed that two-thirds of Americans believed that trade was bad for job security, and 60 percent believed it was bad for job creation. According to another survey, nearly two-thirds of the nation felt that the distribution of wealth and income in America had become more unequal, and more than four-fifths blamed globalization for this trend.[53]

Just as the collapse of working-class incomes seemed clearly connected to globalization, so too did the widening gap between the rich and the middle class. The extraordinary escalation in the earnings of the wealthiest 10, 5, or 1 percent of Americans was closely linked to the rise of what might be called a "headquarters society," an economy specializing in running global economic activities. Commercial and investment banks, hedge funds, accounting and law firms, multinational corporations all were paying their top American professionals and executives enormous sums. In 2007, it is estimated that the five best-paid hedge fund managers earned more than all of the chief executives of the country's 500 largest corporations combined. The top three, James Simon, John Paulson, and George Soros, made over $9 billion together.[54] At that point, America's 3 million millionaires had assets worth almost $12 trillion dollars—about one-fifth of the country's total wealth.[55]

Investors could too easily flee rich countries in search of more friendly regions. "In the global economy," the AFL-CIO averred, "multinational corporations move capital and jobs half-way around the world with the click of a mouse. These companies—many of them American—seek out the lowest possible labor costs and weakest worker protections."[56]

Many Americans shared this distrust of the world economy. Indeed, by 2007 Americans had become the least positive about world trade of all forty-seven nations surveyed; no industrialized nation even came close, not even France.[57] Poorer Americans were particularly hostile toward international trade and investment.[58] And Americans have grown only more unsympathetic toward globalization since the crisis. While in one 2002 survey, Americans rejected what the researchers called "isolationism" by a two-to-one ratio, in late 2009 a majority of respondents had come to endorse isolationist views.[59]

Many companies and industries have trouble competing with foreigners, and they clamor for protection. And many Americans are likely to resent paying taxes to serve the U.S. government's debt to foreigners. By 2013 interest payments on the government's debt will reach $500 billion, about half of which will go to foreigners.[60] Between foreign competition and foreign creditors, many Americans will find it hard to justify giving up valued markets or policies in favor of a nebulous commitment to the world economy.

Nevertheless, there are many interests adamant in their support of globalization. America's international bankers have long been a strong, insistent, powerful voice in favor of American international economic engagement. Going back to the 1920s, bankers were the country's principal opponents of isolationism and protectionism, for bankers' interests were tightly tied up with the world economy.[61] American multinational corporations also have decades of overseas experience and billions in overseas operations. In mid-2010, with much of the world still mired in recession, Apple reported that the firm's "international numbers are absolutely killer."[62] With a weaker dollar, and a weaker consumer in the United States, much of the earnings growth will be abroad. Rapidly growing economies in the developing world—such as Brazil, South Africa, China, and India—will be particularly important to American multinational corporations.

The United States is already a successful exporter of everything from heavy machinery and airplanes to environmental technology and computer software; it will need to build on this success. Knowledge- and capital-intensive manufacturing has long been a specialty of the United States, and such high-technology manufacturers as Intel, Hewlett Packard, and Cisco Systems have come to rely more and more on foreign sales as a source of growth. New types of exports will grow, especially in services. The United States already exports $500 billion in services, and it will be able to take advantage of its leading position in international trade in such sophisticated services as engineering, environmental services, and architecture.[63]

The need for more exports—whether by way of a weaker currency, lower wages, greater innovation, tighter management, or all of the above—will boost the importance of export industries. American multinational corporations and exporters, then, will join American international bankers as important domestic supporters of globalization.

As the American economy adjusts to the postcrisis reality, American society will adjust as well. One of the biggest questions for the future is whether the conflict between winners and losers bodes well or ill for the country's commitment to the world economy. For instance, the increase in America's exports of sophisticated manufactured goods and specialized business services will benefit highly skilled workers, but will do little for low-skilled laborers.

The United States, for all its economic weaknesses and recent financial follies, remains the linchpin of the world economy. As the American political economy goes, so is likely to go much of the rest of the world. But the future of globalization depends not just on what happens inside the United States; conditions abroad will have a profound impact. So what can we expect from the rest of the world?

The World's Turn

CHAPTER SEVEN

On the night of Monday, September 29, 2008, the Irish cabinet was called into emergency telephone session. The task was not simple. One minister, whose cell phone was either turned off or powered down, was woken at home by the police and told to call the prime minister. Another cabinet minister was transiting through Newark Liberty International Airport on the way home from the United Nations and had to take the call in a private room there.

The Irish prime minister and finance minister told the electronically assembled cabinet of the immediate problem. Ireland's housing bubble was quickly deflating, bringing its financial system down with it. Share prices of the country's banks were plummeting—that of the Anglo Irish Bank was in the process of falling 99 percent, from €17.00 euro a share to €0.17 a share. Many depositors understood that the housing bust would ruin at least some of the country's financial institutions, and they were feverishly pulling deposits out of the banks (Irish deposits were only guaranteed up to the European Union minimum of €20,000). A bank run seemed to have begun.

Irish government leaders had met with financial regulators, central bankers, and bank executives all afternoon and evening. Depositors were right to panic: one of the country's three largest banks was indeed on the verge of collapse, and the other two were not far behind. All private-sector avenues seemed closed, and a wave of bank failures would have savaged an economy that was already in recession. The prime minister and finance minister brought to the telephonic cabinet meeting their proposal: a blanket guarantee of all deposits in Ireland's banks, to the tune of €400 billion, an amount equal to twice the size of the country's entire economy.[1] Despite the size and haste, this was a reasonable choice: guaranteeing deposits is one classic way to stop a bank run. A guarantee is a gamble, for if the banks in fact fail, the government is liable for any uncovered deposits. But if depositors have faith in the guarantee, they leave their money in the banks, the banks have time to rebuild, and the guarantee costs little or nothing.

That night, the cabinet approved the plan, followed by Ireland's Parliament. With the guarantee in place, the markets calmed, bank shares rose, and a bank run was averted. But there was an immediate fallout across the Irish Sea. Savvy depositors in London realized that many British banks were also in shaky conditions and had very limited deposit insurance. So they pulled money out of British banks and deposited it in the British branches of the now-guaranteed Irish banks. Now Britain faced the prospect of a run on *its* banks.

British bankers were furious at the Irish deposit guarantee, arguing that this was unfair government aid to rival banks. "If this is legal, then I'm a banana," said one British financier. The British Bankers Association lodged a more stately complaint: "we need fair play for financial institutions across Europe," it insisted.[2] But after a few days, the British government was compelled to increase its deposit guarantees, eventually extending them implicitly to the entire banking system.

Within a matter of weeks all of Europe had been forced to follow Ireland's lead, as governments reluctantly provided worried depositors with similar guarantees. A country of 4 million people on the periphery of Europe had effectively driven the governments of the entire continent, with hundreds of millions of people, to extend trillions of dollars in bank guarantees. And it had done so without malice or artifice, simply in the attempt to prevent a national economic catastrophe.

This is how international cooperation breaks down, how well-meaning governments find themselves drawn into conflict. And these sorts of conflicts can turn a short global recession into a lengthy global crisis. Usually problems proliferate gradually, dragging governments and economies into a downward spiral. If national governments are unable to work together, or cannot agree on the way forward, the result can be disastrous. The quintessential example was the recession that began in 1929.

Lessons from the 1930s

For generations before 1929, the world economy was tied together very tightly—on some measures, such as immigration and a monetary standard, more tightly than the contemporary international economy. And this integrated economic order worked quite well. The world experienced more growth in the hundred years before 1929 than it had in the previous thousand. Many poor countries caught up with middle-income countries; many middle-income countries caught up with rich countries. Prices, currency values, and overall macroeconomic conditions were generally stable.

There were nonetheless regular crises over the course of the nineteenth and early part of the twentieth century, frequently beginning in the United States. When the vagaries of weather hit the enormous American farm sector, which dominated the country's economy in the 1800s, it often caused bank panics in the country's unstable financial system. Within weeks the panic would spread to Europe, where it threatened global trade and finance. But the governments of the major financial powers, and private financiers alongside them, would work together to calm markets, lending enormous amounts to each other as necessary. For a hundred years after the 1820s, the panics led to recessions, high unemployment, and much suffering, but they never came to threaten the very structure of the world economy.[3]

Then, in the middle of 1929, the American economy slowed into

what appeared to be a simple recession. Several European economies were also turning down, but even the most pessimistic observers expected little more than a repeat of the slump of 1920–1921,
which had been sharp but relatively short. In October the American
stock market plunged dramatically, but this seemed simply the correction of an unsustainable boom about which American economic
policymakers—and even President Hoover—had been warning.

As American and European economic activity decelerated, governments mostly did what they were used to doing in such conditions: nothing. The recession would, it was felt, take care of itself.
Economic downturns were regular occurrences, then as now, and
there was every reason to expect economies to recover within the
usual year or so.

The recession did lead American farmers and industrialists to
redouble efforts to get Congress to raise tariffs in the trade bill it
was considering, but this was nothing new from the traditionally
protectionist United States. And a series of debtor nations, especially in Latin America, fell behind in their payments, but this too
was hardly unusual. In May 1930, President Hoover asserted, "I
am convinced we have now passed the worst," and a few months
later his secretary of labor insisted, "We have hit bottom and are on
the upswing."[4] Even though American industrial production was
down one-fourth by the end of 1930, a return to normalcy seemed
imminent.

But around the world, things were more complicated. Germany's
heavy foreign debt burden was the thorniest international problem.
Europe's major debtor pleaded for relief, but the country's mostly
American creditors were reluctant to accept reduced payments. In
an attempt to resolve the dispute, over the course of 1929 European
policymakers and American bankers developed a new proposal,
called the "Young Plan" after the president of General Electric who
chaired the committee that developed it. Under the plan as adopted,
the major financial powers restructured Germany's obligations and
set up a Bank for International Settlements, a sort of central bank
for all the central bankers, to work out the continuing financial difficulties. Meanwhile, the League of Nations hosted an international
conference to reduce trade barriers, but it made little headway.

As 1930 ground on, the German problem got only worse: business conditions deteriorated and unemployment in Germany rose above 20 percent. The Nazis gained major ground in the September elections, running in large part against the world economy. Virtually all of the developing-country debtors were now in default, and as 1930 ended, the United States was hit by a wave of bank failures. Meanwhile, country after country was following the American lead and imposing higher tariffs. The League of Nations hosted another meeting in November to combat protectionism, but by now nobody was listening. By March 1931 the League gave up, calling a halt to the "Tariff Truce Convention."

The recession continued and worsened. Depressed conditions caused deflation; deflation triggered bankruptcies and foreclosures; these caused financial distress, currency disorder, and further depression. As the downward spiral gained speed, in late spring of 1931 Germany stopped paying its debts, which in turn provoked even greater disarray in the world's financial markets.

In the spring of 1931, Austria's Creditanstalt bank tottered toward insolvency. This was one of Central Europe's most important financial institutions, with many connections to other banks on the continent, and it was widely recognized that its failure could trigger a broader panic. The major European powers worked together to attempt to save the bank, with some success. But national political considerations made continued cooperation next to impossible. Eventually the French government refused to participate, complaining that Germany and Austria were taking advantage of the crisis to form a customs union that France opposed. The result was that the bank collapsed on May 11, 1931. Within weeks a currency and financial crisis erupted in Austria. Panic soon spread to Hungary and eventually Germany, driving Central Europe to the deepest point of the Great Depression and giving even more ammunition to the Nazis in Germany. President Hoover finally made a virtue of necessity and spearheaded an international effort, over French objections, to give the Germans some breathing space with debt relief. But it was too late.[5]

The financial distress continued through the summer of 1931. Country after country closed its banks in the midst of panic. Soon governments were driven to take their currencies off the gold standard. The gold standard had been the centerpiece of the international economic order since the 1870s, and participation was generally regarded as the essential indicator of national economic responsibility. To go off the gold standard was to admit incompetence, to retreat into the lower ranks of international financial reliability. But staying on it meant subjecting the economy to ever greater austerity. And so in September 1931 the United Kingdom, which had been on the gold standard (except in wartime) for over 200 years, abandoned it. Dozens of other countries followed suit. The central pillar of the classical international economy was crumbling. In the meantime even the Dutch, traditional free traders, were raising tariffs.

As the gold standard withered, governments began using currency values as weapons to defend their constituents. In normal times, this might have been a reasonable strategy. In fact, when a country faces an external shock that affects its export markets, it is common for economists to recommend that policymakers allow the currency to depreciate. This can help to maintain demand for export goods and avoid too severe a recession. But when countries followed this advice in conditions of a continuing breakdown of international cooperation, the result was usually counterproductive.

New Zealand and Denmark found themselves in a "butter war" over their currencies. The two countries were the United Kingdom's principal suppliers of butter, and butter was in turn the principal export of each nation. Early in 1930 the government of New Zealand devalued its currency by about 5 percent against the pound sterling, which gave its exporters a cost advantage over Danish producers. The Danes hoped that once they followed the British off gold and to a devaluation in September 1931, they would redress the balance, but the New Zealanders also followed the British pound downward. In September 1932 the Danes devalued their currency 5 percent more against the pound. Four months later the government of New Zealand retaliated with a further 15 percent devaluation, and a month after that the Danish government responded with yet another devaluation, of 17 percent. By the end of 1933 the two currencies were back to roughly where they had started against one another, but four years of competitive devaluations had heightened political tensions, financial distress, and protectionist pressures in both nations.[6] The policy itself was not the problem—there may have been good reason to devalue the two currencies—but when it was adopted in this uncoordinated, even conflictual, way, it probably left both economies worse off.

As the first globalized world economy twisted and turned in the wind, every attempt to bring governments together to stop the collapse failed. The Lausanne Conference in the summer of 1932 could not resolve the German problem, primarily because the U.S. Congress refused to allow any reduction in debts owed to the United States. The French government responded by unilaterally refusing to make payments on its war debts to the U.S. government, and within a few months so too had almost all the other war debtors. Meanwhile, Britain and its colonies and dominions were building tariff walls around the British Empire. Japan was invading China, fascists were taking power all over Central and Eastern Europe, and still the international economy kept declining.

By the end of 1932 it was clear that this was no normal crisis. The world economy was dead in the water. International trade was at barely one-third its 1929 levels. International financial markets were almost completely inactive. The world's leading trading nations had turned toward protectionism. Economic activity in every country was down by unprecedented amounts. In the United States, industrial production stood at half its 1929 levels, and unemployment was 24 percent; it was 44 percent in Germany. Economic warfare waged across Europe and the Atlantic: war debts were repudiated, trade wars declared, competitive devaluations and exchange controls celebrated, reparations denied. All this fed into an atmosphere of desperation, political polarization, and mutual recrimination.

When Franklin Roosevelt took office as president in March 1933, the United States was wracked by yet another bank panic. Roosevelt declared a bank holiday and took the dollar off the gold standard. A few months later he effectively shut down the World Economic Conference in London that had been trying to work out some form of international monetary cooperation. Domestic matters took priority, he insisted in his message to the conference: "The sound internal economic situation of a nation is a greater factor in its well-being than the price of its currency."[7]

And still the world economy stagnated, from 1929 until 1934, an unprecedented five calamitous years. Even after recovery began, almost everywhere unemployment remained two or three times 1920s levels, and a steep recession hit much of the world in 1937. What made this depression great was not only its depth but its breadth—it covered virtually the entire world—and especially its length.

The crisis was not an immediate descent into conflict and chaos. As the world economy slowed, there were continual attempts by the major powers to counteract the downturn. Governments held conferences, signed treaties, created international organizations, attempted to find ways to stop the bleeding—but nothing worked. The governments that failed so miserably were largely well meaning—including the Labour-Liberal coalition in the United Kingdom, the new Roosevelt administration in the United States, the last gasp of the Weimar Republic—and yet they were helpless to stop the world economy from spiraling downward through 1929, 1930, 1931, 1932, and 1933. The central problem was that governments were incapable of mustering domestic political support for the measures needed to sustain an integrated world economy.

Domestic constituents demanded that governments take action to reduce unemployment and restore economic growth, and policymakers had to respond, even at the expense of international cooperation. This often started governments, even governments with the best of intentions, down a path toward conflict. The Danes did not mean to impoverish farmers in New Zealand; the Germans did not intend to break American banks and ruin British pensioners. But currency devaluation and debt defaults had these effects. National policies to address desperate national conditions ended up imposing costs on other countries—not on purpose, but as an unintended consequence of measures undertaken in grave circumstances under serious political stress.

The experience of the 1930s makes clear that an integrated world economy requires purposeful cooperation among major economic powers. During much of the nineteenth and early part of the twentieth century, supporters of the reigning order believed that international markets were self-correcting. While in the narrow sense this view may have been accurate—markets do tend toward equilibrium—it was misguided. The integrated international economy of the era rested on the support of the world's major governments. This was especially true in times of stress, for no global government exists to confront a global crisis. Without determined cooperation among the principal powers, globalization could not survive the inevitable shocks to which it was subjected.

The collapse of the first era of globalization also demonstrated that international cooperation required, in turn, domestic political support for global economic engagement. If domestic publics, mass and special interest, were unwilling to compromise their national goals for international achievements, there was little reason to pursue cooperative policies. Governments were not willing, or able, to collaborate with one another if their constituents did not consider access to the world economy to be something worth working for. This is the true threat a crisis poses for globalization—now as in the interwar period. The danger is not a sudden plunge into trade wars, but a gradual erosion of support for compromise with commercial and financial partners, a gradual decline in patterns of cooperation and collaboration.

The Great Depression's global imbalances

Foreign indebtedness was a crucial problem of the interwar period, and a major obstacle to attempts to sustain international economic openness. Central to international economic affairs during the 1920s was what economists would now call a "global macroeconomic imbalance." One great power was running continual and very substantial deficits, borrowing from abroad; another, rising, power was financing that deficit by lending to the deficit country. The first country, Germany, was borrowing for largely political reasons. Its governments were weak and needed more money than Germans were willing to provide in taxes. The government had to pay unpopular reparations to the victors of World War I, to finance reconstruction, and to satisfy massive social demands. Fortunately for the German government, American bankers, led by J.P. Morgan and Company, had become the world's leading financiers during and after World War I and were happy to lend heavily to cash-starved Germans.

There was no inherent technical or economic problem with German borrowing and American lending. But there were political problems, for support for the relationship on both sides of the Atlantic was shallow. The German people resented the subordinate position defeat had put them in, the reparations they were forced to pay, and the social disruptions caused by the settlement imposed on them. On the other side of the ledger, although there were plenty of Americans willing to lend to and invest in Europe, the American public, in this heyday of American isolationism, rejected any official involvement of the United States in European political or economic affairs.

American lending helped sustain the German economy during the 1920s, a matter of no small importance when German social and political instability might have unsettled the rest of Europe. But the underlying conditions for this surplus-deficit relationship were extraordinarily weak, as neither country was really prepared for the implications of the capital flows. The United States was not willing to provide an open market for German goods that would allow the Germans to earn the dollars they needed to service their debts, nor were Americans open to the suggestion that they negotiate easier terms for their troubled debtors. For their part, the Germans seemed unwilling or unable to make the sacrifices necessary to meet their debt obligations.

In a 1932 presidential campaign speech, Roosevelt emphasized the contradictions of the incumbent Republican government's international economic policy, comparing it to the fantasy world of Alice in Wonderland:

A puzzled, somewhat skeptical Alice asked the Republican leadership some simple questions:

"Will not the printing and selling of more stocks and bonds, the building of new plants and the increase of efficiency produce more goods than we can buy?"

"No," shouted Humpty Dumpty, "The more we produce the more we can buy."

"What if we produce a surplus?"

"Oh, we can sell it to foreign consumers."

"How can the foreigners pay for it?"

"Why, we will lend them the money."

"I see," said little Alice, "they will buy our surplus with our money. Of course these foreigners will pay us back by selling us their goods?"

"Oh, not at all," said Humpty Dumpty, "We set up a high wall called the tariff."

"And," said Alice at last, "how will the foreigners pay off these loans?"

"That is easy," said Humpty Dumpty, "did you ever hear of a moratorium?"

And so, at last, my friends, we have reached the heart of the magic formula of 1928.[8]

When the crisis hit in 1929, the magic formula failed, and both Germans and Americans turned inward with a vengeance. Germany almost immediately collapsed into social disorder and political unrest; the foreign debt burden was a particularly sore point and strengthened the appeal of the Nazis' extreme economic nationalism and aggression. The United States, for its part, had no patience for debt relief or renegotiation and turned toward trade protection and a more general absorption with dire domestic conditions.

There were many such financial ties between borrowers and lenders in the interwar period, although the U.S.-Germany connection was the largest, most prominent, and eventually most disastrous. Virtually all of them ended badly, as debtor nations found the debt burden intolerable in a time of severe crisis and defaulted on their obligations, aggravating the financial crisis in creditor nations. The symbiotic surplus-deficit relationships of foreign borrowing and lending were popular in the Roaring Twenties, but not when it came time to turn the imbalances around and pay interest to foreign creditors. Most governments found it impossible to impose the sacrifices necessary to service outstanding debts, and the world's financial system collapsed into a jumble of defaults, bankruptcies, bank runs, and currency crises.

Mountains of debt

Massive international debts were central to the origins of the crisis that began in 2008, and debt levels increased further as governments scrambled to confront the crisis. The United States borrowed at least $5 trillion to get itself into a financial crisis, and it borrowed another $5 trillion to get itself out of the financial crisis.[9] The result is that the United States, along with many other nations, will emerge from the crisis with a huge debt burden. It will be difficult for debtor countries, and for debtors within these countries, to make good on their obligations.

The U.S. government will come out of the Bush boom and bust with a foreign debt well above $10 trillion.[10] Even if the private sector might be able to continue to borrow from abroad, the federal government will spend most of the coming decade attempting to control and reduce its deficit. Governments in the United States, as in other debtor nations—the United Kingdom, Ireland, Spain, and other countries in Southern, Central, and Eastern Europe—will have to implement serious austerity measures. Difficult as this will be domestically, it also can cause problems internationally.

Two countries on the edge of Europe—one small, one tiny—show how hard it can be to unwind a debt crisis, and how much one country's debt crisis can harm others. In the fifteen years before 2008, Greece borrowed massively from the rest of the world, mostly to finance a continual budget deficit and an American-style consumption boom. Borrowing by Greece—as by Ireland, Spain, Portugal, and Italy—was facilitated by membership in the euro zone, whose members shared very low interest rates and a generally creditworthy standing with international financiers. But Greek borrowing went beyond the sensible: at its peak, in one year Greece borrowed an amount equal to nearly 15 percent of GDP, so that more than one euro in seven spent locally was borrowed from abroad. By 2009, the country's 11 million people owed more than $500 billion to foreigners,[11] more than the foreign debts of Argentina, Brazil, and Mexico combined (with thirty times the number of people and ten times the economic output of Greece).

Of course Greece faced hard times dealing with the aftermath of its borrowing boom; but this one small country's travails caused huge problems for the rest of Europe. Late in 2009, investors began to worry that Greece might not make good on its debt. A new Socialist government revealed that the previous conservative government had cooked the country's books to mask its dismal fiscal condition, massively understating the true deficit. Investors began selling off Greek bonds, rating agencies downgraded the country's debt, and interest rates charged on new borrowing skyrocketed. The government announced austerity measures, provoking waves of strikes and protests and raising doubts about the country's ability to honor its debts.

The impact on the rest of Europe was immediate. Greece's partners in the euro zone found that uncertainty about the country was dragging down the entire region, despite the fact that Greece accounts for barely 2 percent of the euro area's economy. The value of the euro began to drop, amid fears that Greece's debt difficulties would affect conditions elsewhere in Europe. Many investors saw the Greek dilemma as a forerunner of broader problems among the continent's debtors. The unpleasant acronym eventually used to describe the potential problem countries was "PIIGS"—for Portugal, Ireland, Italy, Greece, and Spain, all facing massive debt burdens and serious austerity.

Greece was, in the words of New York University economist Nouriel Roubini, "the canary in the coal mine for the euro zone."[12] And if more of the heavily indebted nations ran into trouble, it could be extraordinarily costly for the rest of Euroland. For one thing, most of the debt was owed to Northern Europeans. British banks, German investors, and Dutch pension funds all stood to lose big if the debts were not serviced. More generally, worries about the debtors were likely to force higher interest rates on all members of the euro zone, to make up for the increased risk of debt problems—and for the increased risk of inflation and depreciation.

The Greek debt crisis provoked investors' fears, in part because it reminded them that one tried-and-true way countries make it easier to pay their debts is to inflate or depreciate some of them away. With just 5 percent inflation, €100 billion in debts loses more than a fourth of its real value in just five years. Government revenues keep up with inflation, but the debt doesn't—and so its real weight declines. This is why countries with heavy foreign debts typically run inflation rates double those without.[13] Many countries with foreign debts in their own currency reduce their real debt burden by allowing their currency to drop in value, so that foreigners get repaid in less-valuable currency. But Greece and the other PIIGS cannot pursue this option on their own, for they share the euro with other countries, including some of the countries to which they owe money. Given this dynamic, investors and others worried that the European Central Bank would be forced to allow euro-zone inflation to rise—and perhaps even to allow the euro to depreciate—in order to alleviate some of the pain and suffering caused by its members' debts.

An alternative was for the rest of the euro zone to bail out the debtors. The rationale here was like that of bailing out a bank: a collapse of Greek or Portuguese finances could harm the rest of the euro-zone financial systems. If Bank of America was too big to fail, then so was Greece. And since a deepening of the financial crisis that drew in the entire euro zone would affect the entire global financial system, the International Monetary Fund was also drawn into the rescue. So, just as American taxpayers got stuck with the bill for bailing out banks whose failure would have had dire effects on the economy as a whole, European and international taxpayers got stuck with a €110 billion bill for bailing out Greece. And because the Greek emergency triggered a crisis of confidence in other euro-zone countries whose failure could harm the region as a whole, the European Union was driven into a massive trillion-dollar package for other troubled European debtors.

Greece was not the only small country whose debts created large problems for itself as well as its neighbors. At the other end of Europe, the collapse of Iceland reverberated through the region almost as dangerously. Iceland dramatically opened up its economy and its banking system in the late 1990s. Its financial overexpansion during the next decade was remarkable even by the standards of the time. The tiny country's net foreign debt exploded from $8 billion in 2001 to $48 billion in 2007, equal to more than $150,000 for every man, woman, and child in the country of 300,000. In line with the standard pattern, the flood of foreign funds drove a boom and bubble: between 2001 and 2007, housing prices more than doubled, while the country's stock market soared, with share prices increasing more than sixfold.

The case of Iceland was almost a caricature of the other debt-financed expansions of 2001–2007, for it was largely engineered by the country's three principal banks. They borrowed tens of billions from foreign investors and financial institutions. They used branches abroad, especially in the United Kingdom and the Netherlands, to attract deposits from foreign residents—in effect borrowing tens of billions more from foreign depositors, including by way of Internet savings accounts available to foreigners. By 2007, the three banks' combined debts were more than ten times Iceland's GDP. The country had effectively turned itself into one enormous bank, with financial operations many times the size of the economy.

When the global crisis hit, Iceland's banks were among the first to go, failing within weeks in October 2008. The national economy collapsed, and by the spring of 2009 the previous conservative government had been thrown out and replaced by a Socialist-Green coalition. The bank failures left the banks' depositors hanging, including those in the United Kingdom and the Netherlands. As with Ireland's bank run and Greece's debts, a national problem became a European one, as British and Dutch citizens stood to lose billions of euros in unprotected deposits in Icelandic banks. The British were frantic enough that they used the Anti-Terrorism, Crime and Security Act to freeze all the assets of Iceland's banks in Britain. The next couple of years saw continued conflicts over who would be responsible for the damage to depositors. By early 2010, Iceland had negotiated a deal with the British and Dutch to pay about $6 billion to depositors of one of the banks—not much by global standards, but nearly $20,000 per person for the tiny country. But Icelanders hated the agreement and voted it down (by a 93 percent majority) in a national referendum. And so one more time, the crisis highlighted how politically controversial it can be to figure out who will pay the price of adjustment to the aftermath of a financial crisis.[14]

Greece and Iceland may seem like curiosities or anachronisms, but in fact they are prime examples of how heavily indebted nations can draw others—and even the whole world—into their problems. John Maynard Keynes is said to have remarked, "If you owe your bank manager a thousand pounds, you are at his mercy. If you owe him a million pounds, he is at your mercy."[15] The same is true of countries: debtors can hold their creditors hostage just as surely as the other way round.

By this standard, the United States, by far the largest international debtor the world has ever seen, holds the rest of the world at its mercy. Investors, financial institutions, pension funds, central banks, and sovereign wealth funds all over the world are owed huge amounts by the American government. Chances are that to some extent Americans will inflate and depreciate away at least part of its debt. It will shift some of the burden onto creditors, who won't get the full value of what they lent, not out of malevolence but because Americans will regard unemployment benefits, education, Medicare, and Social Security as higher priorities than debt service. This is true of all the principal deficit nations coming out of the crisis: their attempts to address the accumulated debts of a decade and more are almost certain to be costly to their creditors. Creditors can make things difficult for debtors, charging them higher interest rates or selling off their securities, but that path can, as in the 1930s, lead to an ever more severe financial breakdown.

The global macroeconomic imbalances of the past decade have left many nations with mountains of debt. Debtor governments will be hard-pressed to meet their obligations to their constituents and their commitments to their creditors. There will be powerful incentives to pawn at least some of the costs of the debt crises and their aftermaths off onto foreigners, but this could, as in the 1930s, set creditors and debtors on the path to conflict.

The enemy is not evil

Governments in times of crisis need to deal with pressing domestic concerns; it is this fact that constitutes the principal threat to international cooperation, rather than malicious nationalism or predatory protectionism. National measures that impose serious costs on others were called "beggar-thy-neighbor policies" in the 1930s, after a British card game in which two players take turns penalizing each other. The name is misleading: such outcomes are not normally the result of bloody-mindedness on the part of malevolent governments or of purposeful antagonism toward rivals. They are, instead, the outcome of desperate attempts to defend national economies.

When the American financial system was on the verge of collapse in September 2008, the U.S. government threw trillions of dollars into a rescue, or bailout, of the troubled banks. The policy was driven largely by the desire to avoid a further financial meltdown and damage to the American economy. From the standpoint of the rest of the world, however, the American bailout was an enormous subsidy to American banks. Just as the Irish deposit guarantee, made for domestic political and economic reasons, shifted real burdens onto other countries, so too did the American bank bailout make life more difficult for bankers and governments elsewhere.

Much the same was true of the American bailout of Chrysler and General Motors. In December 2008, the U.S. government spent $17.4 billion to prop up the American carmakers for straightforward, if controversial, domestic political and economic reasons. But from overseas, the measures appeared a massive interference with international markets. The American auto bailout was almost certainly a violation of the country's commitments to the World Trade Organization. It was also strenuously opposed by the other part of America's automotive industry, made up of Japanese, Korean, and European carmakers with factories in the American South. These producers—who employ over half a million Americans directly and indirectly, and produce two-thirds of the "imported" cars sold in the United States—did not benefit from the bailout, which went to improve the competitive position of their competitors.[16]

Actions of this sort fall into a category that economists call "externalities," or external economic effects, in which one country's efforts on its own behalf have an impact on another country. The impact could be positive, such as when two countries share a lake and one cleans it up; but in most instances the term is used to refer to negative externalities, such as when two countries share a lake and one pollutes it. A government (or firm, or household) does not impose externalities on others on purpose; they are an inadvertent result of self-interested behavior that does not take the well-being of neighbors into account. Countries have been inflicting negative externalities on one another since the financial crisis first broke in 2008.

The range of policies of this type—sincere national initiatives with counterproductive international implications—is virtually endless. It may seem natural for taxpayers to insist that the money from fiscal stimulus packages be spent on local products. Indeed, the American Recovery and Reinvestment Act of 2009 required the projects it funded to use American manufactures. But this sort of "buy American" provision looks to other countries like uncooperative protectionism. In response to foreign protests the Obama administration attempted to soften the requirements, but they remained almost certainly in violation of international trade law.[17] And the case of the Denmark–New Zealand butter war of the 1930s illustrates that reasonable policies of currency depreciation, a common recommendation for difficult times, can turn into a bitter race among commercial competitors or partners, leading to round after round of "competitive devaluations."

Even with the best of intentions, governments can act in ways that drive wedges among countries, block cooperative responses to a crisis, and ultimately make everyone worse off. And despite often flowery rhetoric, national policymakers find it very difficult to take into account the international implications of their actions. Yet such behavior can be a major obstacle to recovery and to the reconstruction of a healthy international economy.

Rebalancing on the backs of others?

For the past fifteen years, a core feature of the world economy was a massive symbiotic relationship between two sets of nations. One group of countries borrowed heavily from the rest of the world to finance big increases in consumption. The United States, the United Kingdom, Spain, Ireland, and a phalanx of other borrowing countries ran large deficits, sucking in foreign goods and relying on foreign capital to pay for these goods. The deficit countries relied on debt-financed consumption as the engine of their economic growth.

Another group of countries provided the goods and the financing. Japan, Germany, China, and the Persian Gulf states based their economies on exports to the big consumers. They used the money they earned from these exports to lend trillions to the deficit countries. This group of countries relied on exports as the engine of *their* economic growth. The result was a decade and more of "global macroeconomic imbalances," in which borrowing countries ran huge deficits, while lending countries ran huge surpluses.

This model of international economic interaction will almost certainly prove unsustainable in the future. The major debtor nations have exhausted their willingness, and perhaps their ability, to incur further debts, while the major lenders show increasing signs of uneasiness about further lending.[18] Once emergency short-term measures to address the current crisis are behind us, deficit and surplus countries alike will have to rework their relationship with the rest of the world economy. This "rebalancing," to reduce the previous imbalances, is not primarily a technical or purely an economic problem, but rather a political one. On whose backs will these national economies, and the world economy, be rebalanced?

The major deficit countries will no longer be able to rely on running massive current account deficits. This will especially be the case given the very large additional debt burdens their governments have taken on during the crisis. Every major debtor country will, like the United States, come out of the crisis with government debts larger than the size of the national economy—a level which, if the historical record can be trusted, means they face a long period of reduced consumption, flat or declining real wages, and a stagnant standard of living.[19] They will almost certainly push some of the adjustment burden onto creditors by inflating or depreciating away some of their debts. If, as in the case of members of the euro zone, they do not have this weapon in their macroeconomic policy arsenal, they can force their creditors to restructure their debts or bail out their governments. Either way, rebalancing will be controversial both within and among countries.

The United States, like other countries in similar positions, faces a very difficult next ten years. Most of the government's, and the society's, efforts will be needed to restore macroeconomic balance, create the conditions for future growth, and maintain a reasonable social consensus. If international economic commitments conflict with domestic objectives, the domestic aims are almost certain to prevail. Attempts to trim the trade deficit, for example, may stimulate aggressive measures against imports. In fact, in just the first two years after the crisis broke in full force in the fall of 2008, the United States imposed nearly four hundred protectionist measures affecting over three hundred types of products.[20] All in all, American policy and American politics are likely to be very self-absorbed, and when aimed at the foreign sector, heavily oriented toward improving the country's competitive position.

American attempts to reduce the current account deficit may take several forms. The government could use currency policy to make American goods more attractive on foreign markets, and foreign goods more expensive in the United States. The United States could purposely try to get the dollar to depreciate, perhaps by keeping interest rates much lower than elsewhere, or it could attempt to force other countries to appreciate their currencies. Another American strategy might be to try to pry open foreign markets, such as by using unilateral threats of retaliation that other nations resent and resist. American industries may increase their demands for import protection.

In the case of Chinese trade alone, since the crisis began the U.S. Congress has taken up scores of measures that would penalize China for alleged impediments to American exports or that would impose American impediments to imports from China.[21] In September 2010, the U.S. government filed two complaints with the World Trade Organization about Chinese attempts to keep out American goods and services; a few weeks later, the House of Representatives passed a bill that would punish China for manipulating its currency to keep its sales in the United States artificially cheap. These measures are almost certain to heighten conflicts over commercial, financial, and currency policy with the country's major partners.

The major lending countries will also face significant adjustments. Even if Germany, Japan, China, and others wanted to continue to run the kinds of surpluses they have gotten used to, their previous markets will be reducing their demand for imports. They have to reduce their dependence on exports, which implies that they have to increase domestic production for domestic consumption. Exporters will be less favored than they were in the upswing, as their economies turn away from relying on the export sector and toward the promotion of domestic consumption and the domestic service sectors. The surplus countries will of necessity turn inward.

Turning these export-oriented economies toward domestic markets may be politically difficult. In China, for example, the manufactured export sector has been at the center of the country's economic, social, and political order for decades, and it will not be easy to reduce its economic importance. In China and the other surplus countries, as in the deficit countries, rebalancing implies a fundamental change in the center of gravity of the economic, and therefore political, life of the societies in question. One reason why such countries as Germany have been less enthusiastic than the United States about running larger deficits to stimulate their economies is that they hope to get a boost from a revival in their export markets instead.

Rebalancing, then, raises again the problem of winners and losers. This was true in the 1930s. It was true after the debt crisis of the 1980s in Latin America, and that of 1997–1998 in East Asia. It will be true again in the decade to come. Now, as in the past, economic changes brought on by the crises may also lead to fundamental political change, as winners become losers, losers become winners, and political conflicts ensue. These domestic political conflicts are certain to spill over into conflicts among nations. Indeed, they already have.

Rebalancing and the renminbi

"We are opposed," Wen Jiabao said angrily in March 2010, "to countries pointing fingers at each other or taking strong measures to force other countries to appreciate their currencies."[22] The Chinese premier's irritation was provoked by American pressure on its trading partner to allow the Chinese currency, the renminbi, to rise in value. The United States needed, said President Obama, "to make sure our goods are not artificially inflated in price and their goods are not artificially deflated in price; that puts us at a huge competitive disadvantage."[23]

The specter of "competitive devaluations," so central to the trade and currency wars of the 1930s, again occupies center stage as the world economy rebalances, with China and the United States the principal actors. Since it opened to the world economy in 1979, China on occasion—and particularly in recent years—has kept the renminbi very weak or depreciated. This makes Chinese goods more attractive on foreign markets and makes it more attractive for people in China to produce for the foreign market. It also makes foreign goods more expensive in China.

The Chinese government has consistently regarded the weak renminbi as crucial to channeling the country's resources into producing manufactured goods for export. China's leaders have argued that they have hundreds of millions of people engaged in backward agriculture who are streaming toward the cities as the country modernizes, and that the only way to absorb 10 million and more new urban workers every year is by providing jobs in export manufacturing. And many analysts would agree that a poor country such as China can benefit by keeping its currency weak: it pushes domestic producers into foreign markets and forces them to bring their work up to global technological and quality standards.[24]

A weak, depreciated, renminbi is good news for consumers elsewhere, for it means that Chinese goods are that much cheaper. China is America's largest supplier of imports, sending hundreds of billions of dollars' worth of clothing, computers, toys, games, and video equipment every year. A weak renminbi helps keep these products cheaper. But it redoubles the already serious competitive pressures felt by manufacturers who compete with the Chinese. As one American steelmaker complained, "If their currency is 40 percent below its real market value, they can undercut US producers and that's what's eroding the manufacturing base here. That's their plan. Their government is basically subsidising that."[25] The growing chorus of protests by American manufacturers led 130 congressmen and senators to condemn China's currency practices in a March 2010 statement.[26]

This dispute is not simply between China and the United States, for it has different effects on different groups in the two countries. An artificially weak renminbi is good for American consumers who buy artificially cheap Chinese goods, as well as the American multinationals with Chinese operations, but bad for American producers and workers who have to compete with these goods. In China, the weak currency is good for anyone who competes with foreign goods, whether they are exporters or producing for the local market. A Chinese toy manufacturer gains a competitive advantage against other toy producers, both in the Chinese market and abroad. When a national currency goes down by 10 percent, for example, it makes foreign goods 10 percent more expensive at home and domestic goods 10 percent cheaper abroad. This makes a 10 percent devaluation the equivalent of a 10 percent tariff on imports and a 10 percent subsidy to exports. On the other hand, the weak currency depresses domestic purchasing power—Chinese money is worth less—and harms China's consumers. In this way, the weak renminbi helps American consumers but hurts American producers; it helps Chinese producers but hurts Chinese consumers.[27] In both countries, clearly, it's the producers who dominate currency politics; consumers are too disparate a group to play an organized role.

Currency values—and in particular the renminbi—were central to the global imbalances of the past decade. A weak renminbi helped China export more and import less; Chinese policies to keep the renminbi weak included lending trillions to the United States and others. By the same token, as the world economy moves toward rebalancing, currency values will again be central. A continued weak renminbi would encourage American imports from China and discourage American exports to China, at a time when the country needs to reduce its imports and increase its exports. Some might welcome the implicit subsidy to American consumers reflected by cheap Chinese imports. But at this point America's economic policy agenda is dominated by the need to reduce consumption, increase savings, reduce imports, and increase exports—all of which would be hampered by a weak renminbi. And as long as China keeps its currency weak, so too will the rest of East Asia, further exacerbating America's trade deficit.

Nonetheless, the Chinese insist, in the words of one foreign ministry spokesman, that "wrongful accusations and pressure will not help solve this issue."[28] And Premier Wen was blunt: "What I don't understand is the practice of depreciating one's own currency and attempting to press other countries to appreciate their own currencies solely for the purpose of increasing one's own exports. This kind of practice I think is a kind of trade protectionism."[29] The Chinese argued that they were not purposely manipulating their currency, and that even if they were, that was a matter for national policy, not foreigners, to decide. In language reminiscent of the currency wars of the 1930s, Wen insisted, "A country's exchange rate policy and its exchange rates should depend on its national economy and economic situation."[30]

But from the American standpoint, this was simply rubbing salt in wounds, many of them originally inflicted by China's currency policy. New York Senator Charles Schumer (D) was furious at the Chinese premier's dismissal of American complaints: "That was the last straw. We are fed up, and we are not going to take it any more." He explained the congressional anger behind the two chambers' March 2010 joint statement: "China's currency manipulation would be unacceptable even in good economic times. At a time of 10 percent unemployment, we will simply not stand for it."[31] The members of the House and Senate wanted the administration to declare formally that the Chinese were manipulating their currency and to bring formal complaints to the World Trade Organization if the Chinese did not relent.

The pressure on China to allow the renminbi to rise in value was coupled with aggressive American words, and some action, on trade policy. In September 2009, the Obama administration imposed very high tariffs on Chinese tires, effectively pricing them out of the American market for inexpensive tires. The Chinese retaliated by threatening to investigate some American imports into China. As one Chinese editorialist wrote, "A trade war would be regrettable, but creating a long-term deterrent to U.S. protectionism may require retaliation."[32] Nonetheless, undoubtedly in part due to foreign pressure, the Chinese government has proclaimed its willingness to let its currency appreciate gradually, over time.

The U.S.-China currency conflict is emblematic of the domestic and international conflicts the Great Recession will spark and deepen. A weaker dollar would aid American adjustment to the aftermath of the crisis: it would spur exports, reduce imports, restrain consumption, and reduce the real debt burden. A weaker renminbi would aid Chinese adjustment, by continuing to help Chinese producers penetrate foreign markets. But the two currencies cannot simultaneously weaken against each other. Each country has good domestic, economic, political, and social reasons to depreciate its currency; neither has much incentive to work with the other to impede this process.

All this runs in the direction of reducing the interests of major governments in international economic cooperation. The global economy will not become irrelevant, for the depth and breadth of international commercial and financial ties is extraordinary. But the goals of major governments are likely to become more inward-looking than they have been. Their constituents will be more concerned about domestic matters, and less concerned about international ones, than they have in the recent past.

Can a global economy survive a global crisis?

The global economic, social, and political changes ahead will threaten powerful groups with vested interests in minimizing the extent of their sacrifice. Interests under threat will resist the economic transformations needed to rebalance national economies and maintain collaborative international relations. It will be difficult to sustain domestic support for global economic engagement.

There are constructive ways forward. In the United States and elsewhere, there remain many groups with a strong interest, real or potential, in an open international economy: exporters, multinational corporations, investors. The American economy will become more reliant on export markets over the next decade, especially as economic growth accelerates in regions, such as East Asia and Latin America, that are large consumers of America's sophisticated manufactures and high-end services. Americans whose fortunes are tied to those markets will discover how vibrant they can be. American multinational corporations—from Apple to Xerox—already have trillions of dollars invested abroad. American farmers are among the most important providers of food to the world. And even many of those who believe that the world economy holds more threats than promises may find that a revitalized, reformed version of globalization presents many opportunities. Whether the world, and the United States, can make these opportunities available remains to be seen.

What Is to Be Done?

America faces a long and painful recovery from the follies of the past decade. The right choices will shorten and lessen the pain and guide the economy onto a sustainable and equitable growth path. To make the right choices, however, Americans need to draw appropriate lessons from the financial crisis and the Great Recession. If the macroeconomic imbalances and financial distortions that caused the crisis are allowed to persist and re-create themselves, the United States will experience a repeat performance. Future policies must cure the disease rather than merely treat the symptoms.

Government policies enabled, catalyzed, and fueled America's crisis. The Bush administration's tax cuts and spending splurge drove the federal budget from surplus to deficit, beginning the most recent cycle of foreign borrowing boom and bust. The Federal Reserve's excessively loose monetary policy encouraged households to take advantage of very low real interest rates to embark on a debt-financed consumption spree, with much of the debt borrowed from abroad. Neither the government nor the households that did the borrowing used enough of the borrowed funds to increase the nation's productive capacity and its ability to eventually service the debt without sacrifice. Lawmakers disarmed financial regulators, who in turn used few of the weapons left in their arsenals, allowing financial institutions to develop new instruments that were largely untested and wholly unsupervised. Financial institutions worked madly to increase their profits in a low-interest-rate environment by taking on ever riskier assets, insisting that they had mastered risks they barely understood.

Any one of these policies might have gotten the United States into serious trouble. Together they created a financial perfect storm, driving the American economy to the brink of financial collapse and dragging much of the rest of the world with it.

American decision makers have a difficult task. They develop policies in an environment fraught with political pressures, from special interests and the general electorate at home and abroad. We do not fault policymakers for an excess of democratic accountability, but rather for a shortage of political responsibility. The public was largely unaware of many of the policies that made the first lost decade possible. When people were aware, they were not informed about the implications. But conscientious politicians have a duty to use their access to greater information and greater authority to avoid policy traps, not to exploit them. For a decade politicians were all too willing to evade responsibility: to delay action on deficits, to make the most of readily available foreign lending, to revel in asset bubbles. Now they have to address the results of a decade of failed policies. And they have to do so in an atmosphere charged with partisan, special interest, electoral, and international political pressures that threaten to paralyze the American government.

A sustainable and responsible fiscal policy

America's prosperity requires fiscal responsibility. The phrase "fiscal responsibility" has been used so much that it is something between an obligatory buzzword and a code word for cutting government spending. In our view, true fiscal responsibility involves a willingness to raise sufficient tax revenue, over the longer term, to pay for the programs the government implements. Fiscal responsibility should not be equated with a small government, but rather with a commitment to pay for the government services provided. If the nation affirms that enhancing national defense and improving health care for the poor are legitimate goals, fiscal responsibility entails raising the revenue to fund these programs, rather than borrowing for them.

We certainly know what fiscal responsibility doesn't look like. It is what the country has experienced over most of the past several decades.[1] For years, even before the financial crisis and the last recession crushed tax revenues, government debt grew more rapidly than the overall size of the economy. Most recently, the ratio of debt to GDP rose from 34 percent at the beginning of the Bush administration to 48 percent by the beginning of the Obama administration, and 54 percent by the end of 2009.[2]

Not all borrowing is undesirable, and not all budget deficits are bad. Sometimes the government needs to step in to counter economic downturns, and in those instances expenditures should exceed revenues. The deepest recession since the Great Depression required an aggressive response from the government. Otherwise, economic activity would have continued to spiral downward, along with tax revenues, and the government would have ended up in a deeper hole of debt.[3]

In *the short term*, there was no choice but to act decisively, with temporary tax cuts, spending increases, and transfers to the states. And with the economy growing only modestly as recovery began, too rapid a retrenchment in spending and an increase in taxes could very well be counterproductive, throwing the economy back into recession and further accumulation of debt. However, the politics of countercyclical fiscal policy can be perverse, as the Obama administration found. Recessions hit hardest at poor and working-class families, who would benefit most from stimulative fiscal policy. But attempts to undertake these policies face opposition from upper-income taxpayers who are less affected by the recession and more concerned about the impact on their future taxes. This opposition can impede an effective fiscal response to cyclical downturns.

Whatever the difficulty with devising appropriate short-term fiscal policy, government finances over the next two decades need everyone's focused attention. The big problems are Americans' unwillingness to tax themselves, ever since the Bush tax cuts of 2001 and 2003, and the entitlement programs—Medicare, Medicaid, and Social Security—which are going to consume ever greater shares of the budget. There are many ways to set the federal government on a more responsible and sustainable fiscal path. All of them involve some mix of increased taxes and reduced spending.

Increase taxes. A simple and important step would be to allow the tax cuts enacted by the Bush administration in 2001 and 2003 to lapse as soon as the economy has fully recovered. According to the Congressional Budget Office, the resulting revenue increases would amount to over $300 billion in 2015 alone. Combined with other feasible (but unpopular) measures, such as allowing the Alternative Minimum Tax (AMT) to take effect, the revenue increases would total close to $500 billion.[4]

Given the fractious nature of American politics, is there hope for action on the tax front? There is powerful political opposition to tax increases. As with countercyclical fiscal policy, many upper-income taxpayers feel that government spending is targeted at lower-income Americans or at public programs that are of little importance to them, and resist attempts to increase taxes to fund these programs.

Nonetheless, the debate over the extension of the 2001 and 2003 tax cuts gives us some reason to hope that opposition to a more responsible fiscal stance can be overcome. Even a number of Republicans have come out against unlimited tax cuts. Ronald Reagan's first budget director, David Stockman, issued a call to arms:

> If there were such a thing as Chapter 11 for politicians, the Republican push to extend the unaffordable Bush tax cuts would amount to a bankruptcy filing. The nation's public debt—if honestly reckoned to include municipal bonds and the $7 trillion of new deficits baked into the cake through 2015—will soon reach $18 trillion. That's a Greece-scale 120 percent of gross domestic product, and fairly screams out for austerity and sacrifice. It is therefore unseemly for the Senate minority leader, Mitch McConnell, to insist that the nation's wealthiest taxpayers be spared even a three-percentage-point rate increase.[5]

Another way to increase revenues is to augment the current tax system with a value added tax, or VAT. Unlike a sales tax, which is collected at the final point of sale, a VAT is levied at each stage of production. The VAT is a major part of tax systems in over 130 countries. In many developed countries, the VAT accounts for a large share of tax revenues. The United Kingdom and Germany raise about one-fifth of their taxes with a VAT and similar taxes on consumption, while the United States raises only about 8 percent by way of sales taxes.[6] Economists are widely agreed that the VAT is a particularly efficient way to collect revenue.[7]

There is substantial resistance to a VAT, and not just for the general reason that it is a tax. To consumers, the VAT looks like a sales tax and therefore is a visible target for opposition. Some conservatives fear the tax exactly because it is so effective at raising revenue, inasmuch as they worry that this will encourage greater public spending.[8] On the other hand, corporations with overseas interests typically prefer a VAT over income taxes. This is because firms have to build the cost of paying income taxes into the price of exports, making them less competitive, while they can get the VAT rebated on exports.[9] In a period in which the United States needs both to increase exports and to increase government revenue, perhaps policymakers will find it easier to overcome resistance to the VAT.

Restrain spending. For too long, words have not been matched with deeds when it comes to restraining spending. Americans need to decide which services they want their government to deliver and then pay for those services. Over the past decade, the U.S. government increased spending to safeguard the country from terrorist attacks, and cut taxes. It went to war with Iraq, and did not raise taxes to pay for it. It enacted a huge new entitlement in the form of a Medicare prescription drug program without properly funding it. At the beginning of the program, the government estimated that over the next seventy-five years, the costs would exceed revenues by $8.4 *trillion.*[10] There is no wonder that the deficit rose during the 2000s.

We have plenty of examples, including some recent ones, to show that this is not the only way for government to act. Over the course of the 1990s the federal government reduced its budget deficit and eventually began running large surpluses. This success was made possible in part by congressional pay-as-you-go (PAYGO) rules for nonemergency expenditures. PAYGO rules require that new discretionary spending or tax cuts have to be offset with some sort of revenue enhancement. In some cases the offset can extend over several years: for example, a spending increase in one year would be permitted so long as it did not affect the deficit over a five-year horizon.[11] PAYGO seems to have deterred some deficit-increasing measures.[12]

A more fundamental spending problem involves entitlement programs. All of them face serious challenges. Social Security is the easiest to deal with. There are several straightforward policy changes that would have a big impact: lifting the cap on the earnings on which workers and employers pay Social Security taxes, scheduling rate increases, gradually lowering some future benefits, and raising the retirement age. All of these could easily make Social Security solvent for the next seventy-five years. For instance, simply raising the retirement age to seventy would eliminate half the shortfall, while making all earnings taxable would eliminate all of it.[13]

Medicaid, and especially the Medicare program, pose much more serious challenges. Medicare spending is set to explode starting in the next decade, due to both the aging of the population and the rapidly rising price of health care services. Under current policy, these programs will account for 11.8 percent of GDP, and over half of all government spending, by 2020. Medicare and Medicaid alone will equal all noninterest discretionary spending *combined*.[14] The only way to deal with this problem is to "bend the curve," that is, reduce the growth rate of national health expenditures and its resultant drain on the federal budget.[15] These are serious challenges for the future. There are plenty of reasonable and realistic proposals, ranging from taxing health care benefits to finding ways to cut waste and duplication; all of them have to be considered. But the harsh fact is that almost any realistic attempt to restrain Medicare spending involves reducing the real benefits received by its beneficiaries. And the political opposition to such reductions will only gain in power as the American population ages and the ranks of the elderly swell.

Nevertheless, the longer the country delays in dealing with entitlement expenditures, the more complicated, costly, and difficult the task will be. Delay could be costly in other ways as well. If foreign investors perceive that the American political system cannot handle the relatively easy challenges of raising taxes and cutting discretionary spending, they are likely to start losing confidence in Treasury bills and bonds as a store of value; this in turn would raise the government's cost of borrowing and thus worsen the problem.

Ending overborrowing

It is not just the U.S. government that has relied too heavily on borrowing to finance its activities. Between the end of 2000 and early 2008, consumer debt nearly doubled to $13.9 trillion, rising from 80 percent to 114 percent of personal income.[16] To be sure, there is nothing wrong with households and firms borrowing against their future earnings in a well-functioning credit market. But just as the federal government overextended itself over the past decade, many American households came to depend too heavily on borrowing to finance current consumption.

If borrowing responds to important opportunities for investments that enhance the nation's economic efficiency and productivity, it is both justifiable and profitable. Unfortunately, much recent borrowing responds less to inherent economic opportunities and more to government tax policies that actively *promote* borrowing by households and businesses.

The housing boom is an example of how government policy can heighten the ill effects of misguided overborrowing. Those who had previously rented now found loans readily available, and on top of that they could take advantage of a tax code that makes interest payments for home mortgages tax deductible. More generally, since interest payments are tax deductible, it pays to borrow more than one would otherwise. In fact, if one borrows enough, the deductibility of mortgage interest means that the effective tax rate on owning one's own home is negative.[17] The result is that many Americans buy bigger houses than they otherwise would, at enormous fiscal cost—around $80 billion in 2009.[18] The subsidy is not limited to one home per household; it even extends to second homes.

The tax code's encouragement of borrowing is not restricted to the housing market. Since firms treat interest payments as a cost, they

too have strong incentives to load up on debt. Consider a corporation that can finance a new factory either by issuing new shares of
equity or by issuing debt. The corporation cannot deduct payments
of dividends to the shareholders from its taxes, while it can deduct
payments to creditors. This makes the firm's cost of financing itself
by borrowing lower than by selling shares. The higher the corporate
tax rate, the greater the bias toward debt, holding all else constant.
Even in the wake of the most serious financial crisis in memory, the
American tax code continues to encourage households and firms to
leverage heavily and take many financial risks. It is up to the political system to evaluate the desirability of any particular tax break, but
it should be understood that the path to fiscal moderation will probably include eliminating at least some of these special exemptions.

The overall structure of the tax system also pushes consumers
to borrow. Because the government taxes income rather than consumption, it makes consuming today more attractive than saving
for the future. In the absence of an income tax, a person who saves a
dollar today would get the dollar plus interest next year. But with an
income tax system in place, an American who saves gets the dollar
with interest back but has to pay tax on the interest earned. Since
the federal tax code relies more heavily on income taxes than do tax
codes in many other developed economies, it is not surprising that
U.S. household savings rates are so low.[19]

Putting into place a VAT, which feels like a sales tax to consumers, would help remove this pro-debt bias in the tax system. The
VAT would be a very useful adjunct to the income tax, not a replace-
ment for it. If the government implemented a VAT at the same time
as it ended the Bush tax cuts, the progressive nature of the overall
tax code could be reestablished.[20] An additional benefit is that tax
revenues would become less volatile, because income tax receipts
have become increasingly sensitive to capital gains and therefore
increasingly unpredictable.[21]

The government's "hidden debts"

In the Latin American crisis of the 1980s and the East Asian crisis of
the 1990s, the full magnitude of indebtedness was not clear until the

crisis hit. There were tens of billions of dollars in "hidden debt"— in particular, debts that governments did not realize they had, but that they had to assume once the crisis struck. In Korea, corporations that had overborrowed in foreign currency had to be bailed out by the government. In Thailand, the government had to bail out the banks. Once the crisis made these hidden debts evident, forcing the government to take on even more debt, the crises became even more challenging.[22] The current American debt crisis is no exception: once again government has stepped in to bail out financial institutions, revealing debts previously out of sight.

Hidden debt often takes the form of "contingent liabilities," so called because they are contingent on economic events, often the general state of the economy. For instance, as long as Fannie Mae and Freddie Mac were solvent, they cost the federal government nothing. After all, these government-sponsored enterprises enjoyed no *formal* federal guarantees. However, they were so inextricably interlinked with the operation of the rest of the economy that the government found it could not allow them to fail. This put the government on the hook for their bailout—for what ultimate amount depends on how quickly the housing market recovers.[23]

This hidden debt explains the large jump in government debt at the end of the Bush administration, when AIG was bailed out and the major banks were recapitalized under the Troubled Asset Relief Program (TARP). As the federal government and the Federal Reserve intervened massively in financial markets, contingent liabilities were realized as actual liabilities. The Congressional Budget Office estimated the eventual cost of TARP alone to be $99 billion.[24]

Some of the contingent liabilities are less well hidden. Still, with the cost of these programs contingent on events, it is difficult to determine their ultimate cost. In 2009 the *Financial Report of the U.S. Government* set probable costs of the financial insurance programs at $166.2 billion. But a more inclusive House of Representatives report placed the range of contingent liabilities—from TARP to the National Flood Insurance Program—at anywhere from $170 billion to $986 billion.[25]

Contingent liabilities will be even more important in the future, for the government faces the possibility of hundreds of billions more dollars in federal explicit or implicit guarantees of everything from farm crop insurance to student loans. Of greatest concern are contingent liabilities in the financial sector, because the underlying problems of financial excess have not been solved. And there are powerful interests with much at stake in ensuring that the government continue to backstop their activities. As former IMF chief economist Simon Johnson observed, "As long as massive financial institutions continue to take on huge amounts of risk, there remains a strong possibility that governments in the US and other countries will once again face unexpected liabilities and collapsing tax revenues in a financial crisis—pushing up debt by another 40% or so of GDP."[26]

The contingent liabilities that arise from the financial sector are a particularly important challenge. The U.S. government needs to limit their growth, and limiting their growth means getting financial regulation right.

Financial system, financial regulation

Before the financial crisis, hedge fund managers and investment bankers proudly claimed to be the fittest in a Darwinian world of free-wheeling financial markets. Their enormous profits were justified, at least in their view, by their imaginative searches for the next best deal and their innovative uses of modern financial engineering. There was, they and their supporters argued, little or no role for government. Each institution would rise or fall on its own merits, and the new tools of risk management would ensure that no large firm would fail and threaten the financial system as a whole.

This worldview, which justified little or no regulation for large portions of American finance, came to a spectacular end in September 2008. It turned out that neither quantitative analysis, nor financial engineering, nor modern risk management had made obsolete the traditional understanding of the role of private and public interest in financial markets. Individual firms pursued their own interests with vigor. However, this pursuit had the potential to impose costs on financial markets more generally and on society as a whole. Competition among modern profit-seeking financial institutions could—just as a century ago—cause bubbles, bank runs, panics, and other dangers to the entire economy. There was still a gap—an enormous gap, it turned out—between the private interests of financiers and the public interest. The American taxpayer will be paying the price of this rediscovery for years to come.

In the aftermath of the government rescue of modern finance, it was inevitable that policymakers would discard the dogma of the self-regulating financial system and would rethink financial regulation.[27] The sweeping financial reform of the Dodd-Frank bill passed in July 2010 was the result. Financial markets will be re-regulated. Although the Dodd-Frank Act sets out many regulatory specifics, in practice the future of American financial regulation will not be governed by attention to the particular proximate causes of the financial crisis. After all, the next crisis will *not* involve credit default swaps and collateralized debt obligations, but will involve new financial issues. Regulators will have to move forward into new financial territory, focusing on some core principles on which the new regulatory framework is based.

The first core principle is that investors must put up some of their own money when making bets. Those making the bets have to have something of their own at stake, rather than gambling with the taxpayer money that stands behind implicit or explicit guarantees. In the most recent boom-bust cycle, financial firms leveraged up well beyond reasonable levels—investment banks put in only $1 for each $30 they borrowed.[28] The result of this strategy motivated the call for higher capital requirements and a widening of regulation to encompass previously unregulated (hedge funds) and lightly regulated (investment banks) portions of the shadow financial system. The new framework also makes off-balance-sheet activities—such as the warehousing of collateralized debt obligations in special investment entities—subject to capital requirements.[29] This requires extending lender-of-last-resort facilities to hedge funds and investment banks, which in turn expands the range of emergency powers available to the Federal Reserve.

The second principle is to discourage certain types of financial intermediation, especially those prone to cause financial disruption and costs to the taxpayer. Many of the financial activities of the last decade did not directly increase the productive capacity of the nation. All of the energy, and all of the resources, devoted to creating securities out of other securities that were backed by other securities—such as CDO^2s—did not in the end increase the capital available for productive investments, like new factories.

The third principle is to avoid the emergence of financial institutions that are too big to fail, such as AIG, Citibank, and other institutions whose potential collapse threatened the entire financial system in 2008. Institutions of this "systemically important" size can take on excessive risks and reap higher profits for shareholders, taking advantage of the knowledge that the government will have to bail them out if they get into trouble. Institutions too big to fail create the possibility of "private profits and socialized losses."

The fourth principle requires transparency in financial transactions. One prominent example of an area in which transparency was all too absent was in the market for credit default swaps. These products were billed as a way in which firms could buy a form of insurance on their investments. But the way these insurance contracts were sold—on a bilateral basis, rather than on an exchange like the stock market—meant that nobody knew if the insurance company (AIG) could pay up. Financial institutions that held large amounts of asset-backed securities were lulled into a false sense of security because they thought they had insurance. Eventually, the collapse of AIG saddled the government with tens of billions of dollars in obligations. Although such over-the-counter derivatives as credit default swaps did not cause the boom and resulting bust, they certainly encouraged excess risk taking by financial market participants. This is why the Dodd-Frank Act requires most credit default swaps to be traded on organized exchanges, which is an indication of the need to ensure that such contracts are standardized and are traded openly in a transparent fashion.[30]

A final principle is to temper the financial system's tendency to lend freely when times are good and to pull back when times are tight. Financial regulation as it stood in September 2008 focused on the conditions of *individual* financial institutions. This traditional approach emphasizes "micro-prudential" concerns, those associated with specific firms. But the events of 2007–2009 demonstrated that regulation needs to address *systemic* issues as well. After all, a good thing for a single bank to do might not be a good thing for *all* banks to do simultaneously.

Systemic or "macro-prudential" regulation looks at the aggregate effects of financial behavior. Micro-prudential regulation, for example, might limit the extent to which a financial institution could use borrowed money to fund the lending operations of the bank, requiring that it be a relatively small multiple of the bank's capital. The capital required typically depends on the riskiness of the investment made with the borrowed money: a riskier portfolio of assets requires holding more capital. This approach makes perfect sense if the problem has to do only with individual banks in isolation, whose activities are unrelated to one another, and whose business is not complicated by the possibility of a countrywide, or worldwide, business cycle.

But there *are* business cycles, and financial activities are very sensitive to cycles. Banks lend more when potential borrowers look like good prospects, as in booms; they pull back when borrowers' prospects sour, as in recessions. This means that bank lending can intensify and aggravate the ups and downs of the business cycle. The effect can be magnified by bank attempts to manage risk in a slump. As the economy turns down, some of the loans go bad. As loans, and the securities they back, lose value, they have to be considered riskier. Banks thus need to back them up with more capital, which forces banks to raise more capital and reduce their lending. This in turn depresses economic activity further, which again degrades the quality of bank assets, and feeds a downward spiral.[31]

To mitigate the boom-bust cycle in lending, regulators need to go beyond the traditional approach that focuses on individual banks, to look at the evolution of loan portfolios over the business cycle. One way of doing this would be to raise required capital ratios during booms and reduce them in downturns. This would mute the tendency to lend more during the boom, and the tendency to pull back during downturns.[32]

The financial reform passed in 2010 put into place a framework for addressing the first four core issues. While the framework has many positive aspects, it will take many years for regulators to figure out how to apply it in practice.[33] Much of what actually happens in American finance depends on how the country's regulators interpret and implement the legislation, so that the new regulatory environment remains a work very much in progress.[34] In addition, the new legislation covers only banks with major operations in the United States. Finance is now global, as was the financial crisis; meaningful reform must also be global.

Global rules for global finance are only now being shaped under the auspices of the Basel Committee, an international group of bank supervisors that coordinates international banking regulations.[35] In September 2010, members of the Basel Committee agreed on the outlines of a new regulatory accord, called Basel III. Some features of Basel III are clear. It requires a gradual transition to higher levels of capital for large banks, two to three times higher than at present. It will probably insist on a stricter definition of what counts as capital, and require capital to be held against assets that are off banks' balance sheets. All of these provisions will effectively reduce the leverage that financial institutions can take on. The parties to the Basel III negotiations have also agreed to work toward a countercyclical system of prudential regulation. The mechanism proposed would be to require "buffers," additional capital that could be called on as needed depending on business conditions.[36] This would address the fifth core principle we described, and help mitigate the boom-bust cycle that has been so much a part of international banking.[37]

At the international level, agreement on common standards is crucial. If banks are treated differently in different countries, they will migrate to regions where regulations are least onerous.[38] And banking interests are certain to try to weaken the capital standards as much as possible.[39] It is useful to recall that the United States, an enthusiastic proponent of the earlier Basel II agreement, was itself a laggard in finally implementing the provisions.[40] This leaves it still uncertain whether the most prominent aspects of global financial reform—a more capitalized, less leveraged, international financial system—will actually be achieved.

Despite the ambitious new legislation, financial reform remains in its early stages. Financial regulation affects powerful interests with great political power. Historically, the major financial institutions have had a great deal of influence over regulators. As the details of the new structure are worked out, there will certainly be tremendous pressures brought to bear on the regulatory agencies to bend the rules to favor entrenched interests. Many observers believe that the major financial institutions will be able to weaken or reverse some of the regulatory reforms as they are put into practice. As Bill Gross, the founder of PIMCO, the world's largest mutual fund, said, "Wall Street still owns Washington."[41]

The conduct of monetary policy

The low-interest-rate policy of 2001–2004, and the belated increase in interest rates in 2004–2006, are part of the reason why the world suffered a financial crisis. For the last quarter century, monetary policy in developed countries has largely followed some form of the Taylor rule, where short-term interest rates are raised and lowered in response to the level of economic activity and inflation rates. Financial conditions were of secondary importance, except insofar as they informed policymakers about the state of the economy. Many critics blame the Federal Reserve for either building the housing bubble or being insufficiently aggressive in raising interest rates in order to deflate the bubble, or both. Former Undersecretary of the Treasury John Taylor has been one of the more forceful proponents of the view that an excessively easy monetary policy was the principal cause of the crisis.[42]

We do not subscribe to this monocausal view, but we do believe the Fed could and should have stepped in more quickly and more forcefully to raise interest rates and counteract the bubbling housing market.[43] This suggests that in the future, the Fed should focus more on affecting asset prices—in particular on pricking bubbles—than it has in the past. (Of course, there were regulatory measures the Fed could have imposed as well.)

Implementing such a change is not straightforward, but we think it is feasible. Congress has given the Federal Reserve a dual mandate: to aim for both full employment *and* price stability. The modern interpretation of this dual mandate has been to try to stabilize inflation over the medium term, while minimizing fluctuations in economic growth around the long-term trend. The only way asset prices have figured into this calculation in the past is when the Fed used them as indicators to help inform itself about what to expect about future inflation and output growth. This led to circumstances, such as during the boom in housing prices in the years before 2008, when the Fed observed the asset bubbles but did nothing to attempt to limit them.

Inasmuch as "bubbles" or "manias" destabilize the overall economy, the Fed would improve its chances of achieving the twin goals of price stability and full employment if it targeted, and minimized, asset booms and busts.[44] The task is, like so much else, politically difficult: during an asset boom, the overwhelming weight of political pressure is normally to keep it going, not to rein it in. Nonetheless, in the postcrisis environment it seems likely that the Federal Reserve and other central banks will pay much more attention to financial factors in the future.

Global rebalancing, global growth

Massive lending by East Asia and the oil exporters played a large part in creating the conditions for the financial crisis and the Great Recession. This was part of a global growth pattern in which savings from one large group of countries flooded into another group of countries. While international financial flows are normally a positive feature of an integrated international economy, the experience of the past decade demonstrates the danger of excessive reliance on debt-financed consumption as an engine of economic growth. The world needs a new growth model to avoid a replay of the crisis, while establishing the foundations for sustained recovery.

The work begins at home. The United States must reorient its economy toward exporting more and importing less. Some portion of this objective will be achieved by getting fiscal policy on a sounder footing, which will encourage saving on the part of households and the government. Reduced consumption will reduce imports, while reduced foreign borrowing will lessen upward pressure on the value of the dollar so as to discourage imports and encourage exports.

A smaller trade deficit will diminish America's foreign borrowing needs. And as the country's demand for foreign credit declines, both American interest rates and the value of the dollar are also likely to decline. Both of these will help stimulate growth, and a weaker dollar will facilitate adjustment to less reliance on imports and greater orientation toward exports.

The Fed's monetary policy can assist the decline in the dollar's value, but only as long as other countries do not push their own currencies downward as well. This highlights the close connections between recovery in the United States and the rest of the world. This makes it particularly important to persuade policymakers abroad to move away from the old policy framework in which one set of countries relied excessively on exports and foreign lending, while another set of countries relied excessively on imports and foreign borrowing.[45] More balanced growth will be good for national economies and the world economy. The United States needs higher levels of domestic saving and domestically financed investment; East Asia needs to rely more on internal sources of demand. Attempts to maintain the old framework—through new tax cuts in America, continued weak-currency export-led growth in East Asia—will fail. For one thing, East Asian exports would have far fewer places to go in a world of slower growth. For another, other governments will be much more determined to penalize China and the other East Asian countries for keeping their currencies perpetually weak so as to shift employment their way.

China is critical to rebalancing the world economy. Although the country has grown very rapidly over the past decades, consumption has actually declined substantially as a share of total output. This is aberrant behavior for a rapidly developing economy. And while the export-led growth strategy has served China well in the past, the resulting imbalances have become a clear threat to China's economy, and to social stability more generally. China's export sector is relatively capital intensive, in a country awash with labor; industries servicing domestic demand are much more labor intensive. A refocus on domestic goods and services not only would be more sustainable, but also would make it easier to maintain employment growth.[46]

It is in the interest of most of China's people to reorient the country's economy away from exporting and toward private and public consumption. In addition to ending the policy of currency under-valuation, the Chinese government can accelerate government spending to spur aggregate demand. It has taken some steps in this direction, increasing spending on infrastructure, health, and welfare. These changes will also allow Chinese households to consume more: they have been reluctant to increase spending in part because they have to save to provide for medical or economic emergencies. If the country had a better-developed system of social programs, households would need to save less for these sorts of precautions.[47]

China's longer-term challenges are much more daunting. The Chinese financial system now acts largely as an adjunct to the government at both the national and the local level. Even banks that have been privatized are subject to considerable influence by the authorities. The financial system needs to develop into a mechanism that funnels savings from households and firms to economic activities where those savings can be most efficiently deployed.

There is hope that China is moving onto a more sustainable path. Wages are beginning to rise as labor becomes scarcer. Higher wages may increase the share of national income going to households rather than firms, finally reversing the perverse trend of recent decades. If personal incomes rise, consumption may finally rise to help drive Chinese growth.[48]

China played some part in America's debt binge, but the borrowing was largely America's own doing. American oil imports accounted for a large share of the country's trade deficits during the Bush boom years. Like East Asian and Northern European exporters, the Persian Gulf oil producers put much of the proceeds of their oil sales into American Treasury securities, helping in turn to fuel the borrowing boom. In recent years American oil imports have approached $500 billion a year, about 3 percent of GDP, accounting for well over half of the trade deficit. Current projections anticipate no decrease in oil imports over the next two decades.[49]

Reducing oil imports would reduce sensitivity to oil price shocks in general. This could be accomplished by enhancing domestic supply and reducing demand. Demand-side measures, such as encouraging energy-saving investments and taxing consumption, are the most effective means to accomplish this goal. For instance, a $1 per gallon tax on gasoline would reduce annual petroleum imports by between $43 and $117 billion.[50]

The United States, like other countries, also has a major stake in the maintenance of an open trading system. Open markets are critical to expanding U.S. exports. For the country to fully exploit its comparative advantage in high technology, biotechnology, and advanced services, it needs to be able to import cheaply the inputs, such as semiconductor chips, that are produced more efficiently abroad. Restoring American economic growth, including growth in productivity and wages, requires an open trading regime. International trade is also essential to the rapid growth of other countries, especially the developing nations.

The United States can and should lead by example and by initiative to maintain the openness of the global trading system. It should refrain from further protectionist measures. U.S. law allows the government to erect trade barriers in response to unfair competition, or in situations where American industry is being injured mostly as a consequence of imports. But the president has discretion in many of these cases and can decline to impose trade restrictions. While imposing protection is tempting, it is ultimately self-defeating, as other countries will retaliate. Given the tremendous export potential of the U.S. economy, the country has much more to lose than to gain from protectionism.[51]

The United States should rededicate itself to negotiating a new round of trade liberalization under the auspices of the World Trade Organization. High unemployment and slow growth are fertile conditions for protectionist backsliding. The key to deflecting protectionist pressures is to motivate export-industry firms and labor interests. This can best be accomplished by providing opportunities to gain access to the new markets that come from trade liberalization.

The U.S. government should also expand and deepen its system for easing adjustment to trade dislocation. This is important to sustaining a coalition in favor of trade openness, where workers and firms believe they have a stake in the international trading system. For the past forty years, the government has relied on a relatively small program—Trade Adjustment Assistance—to compensate workers who lose their jobs due to import competition. That pro-

gram has provided meager benefits for retraining, and only for manufacturing industries, even as trade has been hitting more and more
nonmanufacturing sectors over time. Policymakers need to rethink
how the country deals with trade dislocation, and to consider more
serious measures to ease the uncertainty associated with working in
trade-sensitive industries.[52]

The end of American exceptionalism

Americans have discovered that they are subject to the vagaries of
the international economy and to the volatility of international capital markets. As in Argentina, and dozens of other developing-country
debtors, for years "the money kept rolling in."[53] And for years, this
seemed to be a happy arrangement. Foreigners were willing to lend
to America, buying what seemed extremely safe bonds issued by
Fannie Mae and Freddie Mac, or purchasing high-yielding but pur-
portedly safe derivatives. The U.S. government paid for two massive tax cuts and two wars with the low-cost financing that foreign
investors and foreign central banks provided. And Americans rode
a wave of rising asset prices, from houses and land to stocks and
derivatives.

American policymakers deluded themselves into thinking that
massive current account deficits and massive borrowing to finance
them would not matter in today's era of globalization. They believed
that the United States was immune to the troubles that have afflicted
major foreign borrowers for centuries. They ignored the advice they
have given other countries for decades, about the dangers of excessive deficits, debt-financed consumption, and lax regulation. The
new financial managers assured policymakers that their modern,
computer-assisted methods had relegated risk to the dustbin of history. Policymakers in turn reassured themselves that all that was
necessary was for the wizards of finance to take good care of themselves and their financial institutions, and that this would take good
care of the rest of the country. These fables have been put to the test,
and by now put to rest.

The events of the past several years demonstrate that international finance is too important to be left to international financiers.

Empty homes and unemployed workers testify to the past decade's foolhardy experiment in excessive deregulation, excessive deficits, and excessive borrowing. Private and public interests are not the same, and their divergence has been demonstrated at great cost to America, and to the world.

Americans face serious economic challenges. They lost the first decade of the century to a boom that enriched the wealthiest, and a subsequent bust that impoverished the rest. Now they risk losing another decade to an incomplete recovery and economic stagnation.

None of the changes necessary to avoid a repeat of this disaster will be easy. At every turn there are major political obstacles. Financial interests resist regulations that shift the burden of risky behavior back onto them and off of taxpayers. Beneficiaries of government programs fight against attempts to curb their benefits. Taxpayers refuse to pay the taxes needed to pay for the programs they want. Partisan politicians block reasoned discussion, suggesting absurd pseudo-solutions instead of realistic alternatives. Ideologues and political opportunists encourage Americans to cling to the childish things that have served them so poorly in the past: a mindless belief that markets are perfect, that tax cuts solve every ill, that borrowing is to be encouraged. Despite the great trouble these policies have caused, their attractions continue to be touted and spouted by unprincipled pundits.

It is extraordinarily difficult for even the most well-meaning of policymakers to resist these pressures. But while giving into them may be good for a politician's electoral prospects, they are bad for the country and for its future. A skeptic might conclude that nothing can change for the better, that neither the interest groups nor the taxpayers nor the policymakers have any reason to act differently. We prefer to think that there are times when citizens, voters, interest groups, and policymakers are able to rise above their own self-interested concerns. We hope that now is one of those times, and that Americans learn from this painful episode to avoid another lost decade.

CHAPTER NINE
Conclusion

Borrowing and lending are important features of an open world economy. Capital can, and should, move from where it is less needed to where it is more needed, from areas that are flush with savings to areas with valuable investments to finance. Careful lending for productive investment is central to a successful economy, both within one country and across borders.

Over the course of the past decade, the potential benefits of the international financial machinery were swamped by its malignant misuse. Lenders were irresponsible, borrowers were reckless, and regulators were negligent. The results were disastrous. Instead of putting scarce capital to good use, Americans squandered it on unnecessary tax cuts, indefensible budget deficits, and unwise purchases. The United States lost a decade by living on borrowed time and spending it badly.

Many of the decade's failures were the result of a perversion of otherwise reasonable ideas, distorted for suspect motives. There are legitimate reasons to reduce taxes: to fuel spending and promote entrepreneurship. There are valid grounds for a government to run deficits and finance them abroad: to stimulate the economy and further investment. There are sensible arguments in favor of promoting home ownership: to stabilize communities and reward thrift. And there are defensible motives for deregulating finance: to increase competition and foster efficiency.

But in America's lost decade, taxes were cut to curry favor with wealthy and middle-income voters, to make it easier to starve programs the ruling party did not like, and to tie the hands of future governments. Budget deficits and foreign borrowing were encouraged to allow Americans to engage in politically popular spending sprees. Home ownership was promoted to cater to electoral constituents and special interests in pivotal regions. And finance was deregulated to kowtow to powerful interest groups. The people responsible for all of this compounded their failings by cynically abusing philosophical principles, espousing pseudo-theories and misrepresenting real ones, in order to provide an ideological pedigree for policies that were patently political and openly opportunistic.

Whose fault was it all? Bankers and their allies among the regulators are perhaps the most common, and most satisfying, culprits. Financiers did, after all, get rich as they led the country to reckless levels of debt, and they did eventually bring the entire system down with them when they fell. Certainly there is much foundation to the fury directed at financial shenanigans. Nonetheless, it should not be exaggerated. For one thing, countries with much more tightly regulated banking systems, and many fewer reckless bankers, got into just as serious trouble (Spain). For another, American financial institutions were largely playing with the cards they had been dealt. The country's foreign borrowing brought $5 trillion into the American financial system over the course of a few years; the need to lend out these additional trillions inevitably reduced the average quality of loans. America's lenders and borrowers were responding to incentives created by others.

It is tempting to blame Americans in general, or the electorate in particular. The country at large enjoyed the debt-financed expansion, and it might well have been politically difficult to rein it in. But this blame is misplaced. It is unreasonable to expect average citizens to understand international macroeconomic relations, or the intricacies of fiscal and monetary policy, or financial regulation. It is the job of politicians and their appointees to guard against economic excess and financial distress, drawing on the advice of experts who do understand the complexities of a modern economy.

And the experts did warn. While the Bush boom was gathering, academic authorities sounded plenty of cautionary notes.[1] The country's leading specialists in international macroeconomics attempted to alert policymakers to the dangers of the global macroeconomic imbalances driven by American borrowing. Analysts of fiscal policy expressed rising concern over the federal government's deficits, while many monetary analysts warned that uncommonly low real interest rates were fueling unwarranted increases in asset prices. America's most prominent housing economists cautioned that the real estate market was in a classic bubble. Those with knowledge and experience of debt cycles past and present pointed out that the United States was following a well-known path from borrowing boom to bust.

Policymakers did not listen. As alarm bells about the future rang, they ignored them and justified inaction by pointing to the happy present. This is hardly rare, and is understandable: voters do not normally reward politicians for slowing growth or restraining the economy. Nonetheless, it is the job of policymakers to make difficult choices, informed by knowledge and understanding that the average citizen does not have. It would have been politically costly for the Bush administration and the Federal Reserve to brake the economic expansion. But it turned out to be far more costly to ignore the signs of impending problems—more costly for the country as a whole, and probably even for the policymakers in office at the time.

The Bush administration focused far too much on its short-term political ambitions and far too little on the impact of its decisions on the nation's long-term future. In this they were not alone: many other governments made similarly short-sighted choices. But there were also governments that were more cautious and judicious, that recognized the limits of a debt-financed growth model and avoided the worst excesses of the Bush boom and bust. Canada, a country that is as similar to the United States as can be imagined, had a responsible fiscal policy and vigorous regulators and escaped

American-style problems (although, like other countries, it was caught in the backwash of the American disaster).

There was nothing inevitable about the loss of the last decade. Its loss was due to decisions made by governments, decisions that were too little motivated by concern for the public interest and too much motivated by political expediency. Certainly citizens could have been more vigilant, bankers more conscientious, and regulators more watchful. But the root of all the evil that befell the country was irresponsible government policies, policies that encouraged a foreign borrowing binge and consumption boom, policies that allowed financial institutions to take inordinate risks with an implicit government guarantee, policies that gambled with taxpayer money.

The general contours of lost decades, such as the one just lost, are well known and well understood. Over the past hundred years and more, the world has experienced scores of financial crises that were strikingly similar to the current American debt crisis. Governments from Argentina to Zambia, from Thailand to Mexico, from Russia to Ireland have made the same easy choice to encourage indebted expansions, and have then allowed their economies to collapse into debt-ridden crises. In historical and comparative perspective, the American crisis is only unusual in its size; the country's government policies exhibited the same pathological proclivities that have produced a procession of lost decades.

The losses of the past decade will be felt for most of the current one. Trillions of taxpayer dollars will be spent repairing the damage to the nation's financial system. On top of this, the country is giving up the equivalent of years of economic activity, with factories and millions of workers idle. The cost in lost output of the downturn and slow recovery is calculated at $4 trillion, about $50,000 for the average family of four. Current estimates are that it will take at least until 2014 before the economy is back where it would have been without the collapse that began in 2007.[2] That is at least seven lean years, perhaps a suitably biblical result of the seven artificially fat years that preceded them. But the fat years were hardly worth it: it will take many more than seven years to repair the damage done to the American economy and to the American political system.

One decade has been lost, and the country risks losing another.

Whether it does is up to Americans. As the American people rebuild their lives, and their economy, from the crisis, they can and should learn from the past. The government has important and useful functions to perform, but citizens need to be willing to pay for them. The financial system is crucial to the national economy, but it requires supervision by regulators who see more broadly than those inside one bank. Monetary policy is a powerful tool to stabilize the macroeconomy, but it should not be misused for political gain. The nation has a great deal to gain from engaging with the rest of the world economy, but it must also cooperate with its partners to devise a more stable and equitable economic order. The economy can return to rapid growth, but the fruits of this growth should be shared widely. If Americans, and their leaders, do not pay careful attention to these considerations, the nation risks losing another decade to stagnation and social conflict.

The financial crisis is one of the defining events of the early part of the twenty-first century, both for America and for the world. It marks an intellectual and political watershed in the history of the modern world economy. The ways in which Americans and others address the crisis and its aftermath will mold the American, and the global, political economies for decades.

NOTES

Preface

1 The causes of the recession are still hotly debated, although most scholars regard fiscal and monetary policy as the primary factors. For an excellent summary and analysis, see François Velde, "The recession of 1937—a cautionary tale," *Federal Reserve Bank of Chicago Economic Perspectives* no. 4 (2009): 16–37.

Chapter 1: Welcome to Argentina

1 John Tempalski, "Revenue effects of major tax bills," Office of Tax Analysis Working Paper 81 (Washington, DC: U.S. Treasury Department, 2006).

2 Paul Volcker and Toyoo Gyohten, *Changing Fortunes* (New York: Times Books, 1992), 177–178.

3 Jeffry A. Frieden, *Global Capitalism: Its Fall and Rise in the Twentieth Century* (New York: W. W. Norton, 2006), 380.

4 Ibid., 397.

5 George A. Akerlof and Paul M. Romer, "Looting: the economic underworld of bankruptcy for profit," *Brookings Papers on Economic Activity* no. 2 (1993), provides a good example of how firms exploit explicit or implicit government guarantees for profit, at the public's expense. They term this behavior "looting."

6 For two good summaries of the crisis and its aftermath, see Timothy Curry and Lynn Shibut, "The cost of the savings and loan crisis: truth and consequences," *FDIC Banking Review* 13, no. 2 (2000); and Frederic Mishkin, *The Economics of Money, Banking, and Financial Markets*, 9th ed. (New York: Prentice Hall, 2010), appendix 1 to chapter 11.

7 "Showing this week: the tax cut," *Economist*, February 8, 2001.

8 "Surplus alarm," *Wall Street Journal*, June 28, 2000, A22.

9 Testimony of Chairman Alan Greenspan, Current Fiscal Issues, before the Committee on the Budget, U.S. House of Representatives, March 2, 2001, http://www.federalreserve.gov/boarddocs/testimony/2001/20010302/default.htm.

10 Erick Bergquist, "Fed seeks other bonds for monetary policy," *American Banker*, May 25, 2000, 14.

11 "Please sir, the dog ate my surplus," *Economist*, August 2, 2001, 41.

12 Total foreign holdings of U.S. federal government securities rose from $1137.8 billion at the end of 2000 to $4115.1 billion at the end of 2008, according to international investment position data from the Bureau of Economic Analysis (BEA). These figures compare to a cumulative deficit over those years of about $3.3 trillion, or to a $3.0 trillion increase in federal debt held by the public overall, or to $1.8 trillion cumulative deficit if the Social Security surplus is taken into account. The cumulative deficit figures are by fiscal year, from CBO, "Budget and economic outlook: Fiscal years 2010 to 2020" (Washington, DC: Congressional Budget Office, January 2010).

13 Total foreign holdings of U.S. government securities at the end of 2008 amounted to $4115.1 billion, while federal debt held by the public was $6372.7 billion, according to the BEA's international investment position data, and the Treasury's Financial Management Service.

14 Ben Bernanke, "The global saving glut and the U.S. current account deficit," Speech delivered at the Homer Jones Lecture, Federal Reserve Bank of St. Louis, St. Louis, April 14, 2005.

15 Lisa Stein, "Business: hot economy," *U.S. News & World Report*, November 10, 2003, 12.

16 Jeffrey Frankel, "Snake-oil tax cuts," Paper written for the Economic Policy Institute (Washington, DC: Economic Policy Institute, September 16, 2008), 36, 38.

17 See ibid. for ample examples.

18 Bruce Bartlett, " 'Starve the beast': origins and development of a budgetary metaphor," *Independent Review* 12, no. 1 (2007): 5–26 (quotes on 9, 16–17).

19 In fact, as shown in Christina Romer and David Romer, "Do tax cuts starve the beast? The effect of tax changes on government spending," *Brookings Papers on Economic Activity* no. 1 (2009), the principal effect of tax cuts is to force subsequent tax increases. This fits with the general discussion here, assuming the tax increases are forced on subsequent (presumably opposing-party) administrations.

20 Daniel O. Beltran, Laurie Pounder, and Charles Thomas, "Foreign exposure to asset-backed securities of U.S. origin," International Finance Discussion

Papers no. 939 (Washington, DC: Board of Governors of the Federal Reserve System, August 2008), http://www.federalreserve.gov/pubs/ifdp/2008/939/ifdp939.htm.

21 Thomas Piketty and Emmanuel Saez, "Income Inequality in the United States, 1913–1998," in A. B. Atkinson and T. Piketty (eds.), *Top Incomes over the Twentieth Century: A Contrast between European and English Speaking Countries* (New York: Oxford University Press, 2007), 141–225. Data set available at http://elsa.berkeley.edu/~saez/TabFig2007.xls.

22 Raghuram Rajan, *Fault Lines: How Hidden Fractures Still Threaten the World Economy* (Princeton: Princeton University Press, 2010), makes a forceful case for the importance of this in explaining the borrowing boom.

23 For an assessment of the role of manufactured exports in job creation in China, see Robert C. Feenstra and Chang Hong, "China's Exports and Employment," in R. Feenstra and S.-J. Wei (eds.), *China's Growing Role in World Trade* (Chicago: Chicago University Press, 2010).

24 When foreign exchange reserves increase, then in the absence of offsetting actions, the money base (bank reserves and currency) will also increase. The Chinese central bank has sterilized a large amount of the foreign exchange reserve accumulation by raising the bank required reserve ratio (the proportion of bank deposits that have to be held back and can't be loaned out), and by selling its own debt securities, taking in exchange currency. See Nicholas R. Lardy, "Financial repression in China," Policy Brief 08-8 (Washington, DC: Peterson Institute for International Economics, 2008), for a discussion of the mechanics of sterilization.

25 Peter L. Bernstein, *Wedding of the Waters: The Erie Canal and the Making of a Great Nation* (New York: W. W. Norton, 2005).

26 Letter from Alexander Hamilton to Robert Morris, April 30, 1781, according to Wikiquotes, http://en.wikiquote.org/wiki/Alexander_Hamilton, and Notable Quotes, http://www.notable-quotes.com/n/national_debt_quotes.html.

27 Council of the Corporation of Foreign Bondholders, *Annual Report* (London: Council of the Corporation of Foreign Bondholders, 1980), 17. More details are in Namsuk Kim and John Joseph Wallis, "The market for American state government bonds in Britain and the United States, 1830–43," *Economic History Review* 58, no. 4 (2005): 736–764.

28 Maurice Obstfeld and Kenneth S. Rogoff, "The Unsustainable US Current Account Position Revisited," in R. Clarida (ed.), *G7 Current Account Imbalances: Sustainability and Adjustment* (Chicago: University of Chicago Press, 2007), 339.

29 Lawrence H. Summers, *The U.S. Current Account Deficit and the Global Economy, The Per Jacobsson Lecture* (Washington, DC: International Monetary Fund, 2004), 10.

30 Menzie D. Chinn, "Getting serious about the twin deficits," Council Special Report no. 10 (New York: Council on Foreign Relations, September 2005), 21, 27.

31 Nouriel Roubini and Brad Setser, "The US as a net debtor: the sustainability of the US external imbalances" (November 2004), http://pages.stern.nyu.edu/~nroubini/papers/Roubini-Setser-US-External-Imbalances.pdf.

32 See, for example, Raghuram Rajan, "Global current account imbalances: hard landing or soft landing," Speech at the Crédit Suisse First Boston Conference, Hong Kong, March 15, 2005, http://www.imf.org/external/np/speeches/2005/031505.htm.

33 Some were lulled into complacency by the observation that while the United States kept on running current account deficits, the country's net international investment position—the difference between U.S. assets held abroad and liabilities to foreigners—actually *improved* from 2002 to 2007, despite the record-breaking current account deficits. This was due to changes in the value of American overseas assets, and led some to the view that the United States was exceptional. See Ricardo Hausmann and Federico Sturzenegger, "The valuation of hidden assets in foreign transactions: why 'dark matter' matters," *Business Economics* 42, no. 1 (2007). We now know that this was a temporary illusion, since reversed.

34 Michael P. Dooley and Peter M. Garber, "Is it 1958 or 1968? Three notes on the longevity of the revived Bretton Woods system," *Brookings Papers on Economic Activity* no. 1 (2005). Richard Cooper, "America's current account deficit is not only sustainable, it is perfectly logical given the world's hunger for investment returns and dollar reserves," *Financial Times*, November 1, 2004, 19.

35 Sometimes the foreign investment was induced by generous tax incentives. Intel's investment in Ireland is one case. See Frank Barry, "Tax policy, FDI and the Irish economic boom of the 1990s," *Economic Analysis & Policy* 33, no. 2 (2003): 221–235.

36 Central Bank of Ireland, *Quarterly Bulletin* (Dublin: Central Bank of Ireland, various years), table C3.

Chapter 2: Borrowing, Boom, and Bust

1 John Quigley, "Real estate and the Asian crisis," *Journal of Housing Economics* 10 (2001): 439–458; Hali Edison, Pongsak Luangaram, and Marcus Miller, "Asset bubbles, leverage, and 'lifeboats': elements of the East Asian crisis," *Economic Journal* 110, no. 460 (2000): 309–334; and "Thai banking: draw the blinds," *Economist*, February 1, 1997, 78 (quote from banker).

2 Ayn Rand, *The Virtue of Selfishness* (New York: Signet, 1964), 29.

3 John Taylor, "Housing and Monetary Policy," in *Housing, Housing Finance, and Monetary Policy: A Symposium Sponsored by the Federal Reserve Bank of Kansas City*, Jackson Hole, Wyoming, August 30–September 1, 2007 (Kansas City: Federal Reserve Bank of Kansas City, 2008), argues that using his formulation of the Taylor rule, the target rate should have been on average about 4 percent. Other rules that rely on estimated Taylor rules lead to slightly lower estimates, averaging in the range of 3 percent according to Glenn Rudebusch, and as far down as 1.5 percent, when using data and forecasts available to policymakers at the time of decision making according to Athanasios Orphanides and Volker Wieland. See Glenn D. Rudebusch, "The Fed's monetary policy response to the current crisis," *FRBSF Economic Letter*,

2009–17 (San Francisco: Federal Reserve Bank of San Francisco, May 22, 2009), http://www.frbsf.org/publications/economics/letter/2009/el2009-17.html; Athanasios Orphanides and Volker Wieland, "Economic projections and rules of thumb for monetary policy," *Federal Reserve Bank of St. Louis Review* 90, no. 4 (2008): 307–324.

4 Total debt figures are the sum of domestic nonfinancial debt and financial debt from the Federal Reserve Board's *Flow of Funds Accounts of the United States* (Washington, DC, June 11, 2009). The 2000 and 2007 amounts were $26.3 and $47.9 trillion, respectively.

5 Gross federal debt at end of fiscal year, from Council of Economic Advisers, *Economic Report of the President* (Washington, DC: Government Printing Office, 2010), divided by total population as of September 2010.

6 See graph 1 in Malcolm Knight, "Challenges for financial institutions," Speech at a European Financial Services Roundtable Meeting, Zurich, February 7, 2006.

7 Ibid.

8 Federal Reserve Statistical Release, Consumer Credit, http://www.federalreserve .gov/releases/g19/hist/cc_hist_sa.html (accessed December 28, 2010).

9 Charles Morris, *The Trillion Dollar Meltdown: Easy Money, High Rollers, and the Great Credit Crash* (New York: PublicAffairs, 2008), 65–66, 168.

10 Robert Friedman, "Going like hotcakes," *South Florida Sun-Sentinel,* June 16, 2002.

11 Median home prices available at Housing Bubble Graphs, http://mysite .verizon.net/vzeqrguz/housingbubble/ (accessed December 28, 2010).

12 William Field, "Policy and the British voter: council housing, social change, and party preference in the 1980s," *Electoral Studies* 16 (1997): 195–202.

13 The Community Reinvestment Act, originally passed in 1977 to encourage banks to lend to historically underserved communities, occupies a special place in this narrative. In 1995, under the auspices of the Clinton administration, the regulatory implementation of the act was considerably strengthened, with the aim to reduce the extent of "redlining," lender discrimination on the basis of geographic attributes, such as zip codes.

14 George W. Bush, "President's remarks to the National Association of Home Builders" Columbus, Ohio, October 2, 2004, http://georgewbush-whitehouse .archives.gov/news/releases/2004/10/20041002-7.html.

15 The estimated per-dollar impact is from Daniel Cooper, "Impending U.S. spending bust? The role of housing wealth as borrowing collateral," Federal Reserve Bank of Boston Public Policy Discussion Paper no. 09-9 (Boston: Federal Reserve Bank of Boston, 2009).

16 Thomas Philippon and Ariell Reshef, "Wages and human capital in the U.S. financial industry: 1909–2006," NBER Working Paper no. 14644 (Cambridge, MA: National Bureau of Economic Research, 2009); and Thomas Philippon, "The evolution of the US financial industry from 1860 to 2007: theory and evidence," working paper (New York: New York University, 2008). See also Thomas Philippon, "The future of the financial industry" *Stern on*

Finance (blog), NYU Stern School of Business (2008), http://sternfinance .blogspot.com/2008/10/future-of-financial-industry-thomas.html (accessed October 30, 2010).

17 U.S. Census Bureau, 2007 Economic Census, March 17, 2009, http://factfinder. census.gov/servlet/IBQTable?_bm=y&-geo_id=&-ds_name= EC0700CADV2&-_ lang=en; David Barboza, "Stream of Chinese textile imports is becoming a flood," *New York Times*, April 4, 2005.

18 Jeffry A. Frieden, *Debt, Development, and Democracy* (Princeton: Princeton University Press, 1991); on the bubbles, see especially 78, 160–164, and 209.

19 The literature on the East Asian crisis, and on the bubbles that preceded it, is massive. For a selection, see Wayne Arnold, "Monuments to Thai debt: real estate fiascoes rear their heads on Bangkok skyline," *New York Times*, February 23, 2000; Edison, Luangaram, and Miller, "Asset bubbles, leverage, and 'lifeboats' "; and Quigley, "Real estate and the Asian crisis."

20 Nominal output and employment data are from Tables 654 and 743, U.S. Census Bureau, *The 2010 Statistical Abstract*, http://www.census.gov/ compendia/statab/ (accessed December 28, 2010).

21 Hal Rothman, "Houses of cards," *Las Vegas Sun*, October 10, 2005, 5.

22 Economists use the term "bubble" in a very specific way, which differs from its more common general use. Technically, a bubble is a growing deviation of the asset price from that justified by the fundamentals, where the deviation is driven by (possibly rational) expectations of future price changes. In other words, the price of an asset might be "high" because everybody expects the price to rise in the future. In contrast, in general parlance—which we adopt here—bubbles are seen as booms in asset prices that might be driven by irrational or unrealistic expectations (such as overoptimism), or criminal behavior (such as Ponzi schemes).

23 The standard index of affordability effectively measures how many homeowners were paying more than 30 percent of disposable personal income in housing costs (mortgage payments, taxes, and insurance). *Builder* 29 (September 1, 2006). For an explanation and data on one traditional affordability index, see California Association of Realtors, Market Data, Housing Affordability Index—Traditional, http://www.car.org/marketdata/data/haitraditional/.

24 Karl Case and Robert Shiller, "Is there a bubble in the housing market?" *Brookings Papers on Economic Activity* no. 2 (2003): 299–362.

25 David Leonhardt, "Be warned: Mr. Bubble's worried again," *New York Times*, August 21, 2005, B1.

26 Raghuram Rajan, "Has financial development made the world riskier?" *European Financial Management* 12 (2006): 499–533 (quote on 502).

27 Stephen Mihm, "Dr. Doom," *New York Times Magazine*, August 17, 2008, 26. Even one of us (J. F.), normally wary of anything remotely related to forecasting, was clear enough about the dangers to say, in the summer of 2006, "The current imbalances are unsustainable . . . Any number of scenarios might follow from this; almost all the realistic ones involve a decline in the relative price of housing. . . . The resulting pressure on the mortgage market is likely to cause financial distress, which will exacerbate the general macro-

economic pressures on the middle classes. Whatever the preferred scenario one chooses for an end to the current imbalances, the process will create strains in the American macroeconomy—and in American politics." Jeffry A. Frieden, *Will Global Capitalism Fall Again? Bruegel Essay and Lecture Series* (Brussels: Bruegel 2006), 26.

28 Carmen Reinhart and Kenneth Rogoff, "Is the 2007 U.S. sub-prime financial crisis so different? An international historical comparison," NBER Working Paper no. 13761 (Cambridge, MA: National Bureau of Economic Research, 2008), 2.

29 Data available at "PACs by Industry," OpenSecrets.org, Center for Responsive Politics, http://www.opensecrets.org/pacs/list.php (accessed December 28, 2010).

30 See, for example, "4. Influence of the Housing Lobby on the Federal Tax Code," in "Top 10 Tax Stories of the Decade," *Commentary* (Tax Foundation), October 30, 2009, http://www.taxfoundation.org/news/show/25665.html##4.

31 Jessica Birnbaum, "Home builders halt campaign funds after setback," *Washington Post*, February 14, 2008, D1.

32 Tom Raum and Jim Drinkard, "Fannie Mae, Freddie Mac spent millions on lobbying," *USA Today*, July 16, 2008.

33 Atif Mian and Francesco Trebbi, "The political economy of the U.S. mortgage default crisis," NBER Working Paper no. 16107 (Cambridge, MA: National Bureau of Economic Research, 2010).

34 James Miller III, "Should homeowners worry?" *Washington Times*, January 7, 2005, A17.

35 Alan Reynolds, "No housing bubble trouble," *Washington Times*, January 8, 2005, http://www.washingtontimes.com/news/2005/jan/08/20050108-105440-9091r/?page=1.

36 Larry Kudlow, "The housing bears are wrong again: this tax-advantaged sector is writing how-to guide on wealth creation," *National Review* online, June 20, 2005, http://old.nationalreview.com/kudlow/kudlow200506201040.asp.

37 Prashant Gopal, "Former housing industry economist who famously said there was no housing bubble now admits he was wrong," *BusinessWeek*, January 5, 2009, http://www.businessweek.com/the_thread/hotproperty/archives/2009/01/former_housing.html.

38 Susie Mesure, "Financial sector grows to 30% of UK economy," *Independent*, August 21, 2004.

39 Judith Heywood, "Super-rich to push average price of London house to half-million pounds," *Times*, August 6, 2007; Jill Sherman, "Key workers are priced out of homes in most of Britain," *Times*, July 29, 2006.

40 Patrick Honohan, "Resolving Ireland's banking crisis," *Economic and Social Review* 40 (2009): 207–231.

41 *El Pais*, April 18, 2005.

42 With apologies to Carmen Reinhart and Kenneth Rogoff, *This Time Is Different* (Princeton: Princeton University Press, 2009).

43 As is made clear in the extensive evidence marshaled by Reinhart and Rogoff, *This Time Is Different*, their outstanding study of 800 years of financial crises.

44 Francisco Gil Díaz and Augustín Carstens, "Pride and Prejudice: The Economics Profession and Mexico's Financial Crisis," in Sebastian Edwards and Moisés Naím (eds.), *Mexico 1994: Anatomy of an Emerging-Market Crash* (Washington, DC: Carnegie Endowment, 1997), 189. At the time of the crisis Gil Díaz was vice governor of the central bank; Carstens, the general director of economic research.

45 Domingo Cavallo, "La tragedia argentina," July, 17 2002, 2, http://www.cavallo.com.ar/wp-content/uploads/9.pdf (first two quotes); Domingo Cavallo, "¿En qué sentido fue la Deuda Externa el detonante de la Crisis Argentina?" December 11, 2003, 8, http://www.cavallo.com.ar/wp-content/uploads/article%202.pdf (third quote).

46 For example, in Guillermo Calvo and Carlos Végh, "Inflation stabilization and nominal anchors," *Contemporary Economic Policy* 12 (1994): 35–45.

47 OECD, *Trade and Competitiveness in Argentina, Brazil and Chile: Not as Easy as A-B-C* (Paris: Organisation for Economic Co-operation and Development, 2004).

48 On explaining when governments maintain, or abandon, currency pegs, see Michael Klein and Nancy Marion, "Explaining the duration of exchange-rate pegs," *Journal of Development Economics* 54, no. 2 (1997): 387–404; Brock S. Blomberg, Jeffry A. Frieden, and Ernesto Stein, "Sustaining fixed rates: the political economy of currency pegs in Latin America," *Journal of Applied Economics* 8, no. 2 (2005). The question here is a bit more specific—when do governments go off currency pegs that are not sustainable. However, delay in abandoning a peg and the delay in slowing down an overheated economy have similar characteristics: both require that the government end something that is popular in the short run in order to protect the health of the economy in the long run. In this way, the circumstances are similar and implications of the literature on currency pegs are relevant.

49 I. M. Destler and C. Randall Henning, *Dollar Politics: Exchange Rate Policymaking in the United States* (Washington, DC: Institute for International Economics, 1989), 33.

50 See, for example, Jeffry A. Frieden, "Economic Integration and the Politics of Monetary Policy in the United States," in Robert Keohane and Helen Milner (eds.), *Internationalization and Domestic Politics* (Cambridge, UK: Cambridge University Press, 1996).

51 The evidence for this is far more than anecdotal. Carmen Reinhart and Vincent Reinhart, of the University of Maryland and the American Enterprise Institute, respectively, looked at hundreds of "capital flow bonanzas" over fifty years. Enrique Mendoza of the University of Maryland and Marco Terrones of the International Monetary Fund looked at forty-nine "credit booms" in the same period. Both studies—and many more—found that the bonanzas and booms drove up housing prices, stock prices, and the trade deficit. See Carmen Reinhart and Vincent Reinhart, "Capital flow bonanzas: an encompassing view of the past and present," NBER Working Paper no. 14321 (Cambridge, MA: National Bureau of Economic Research, 2008): 53–55; Enrique

Mendoza and Marco Terrones, "An anatomy of credit booms: evidence from macro aggregates and micro data," NBER Working Paper no. 14049 (Cambridge, MA: National Bureau of Economic Research, 2008): figures 9–12.

52 Some might include Alan Greenspan on the list of Fed chairs to have an academic background in economics. However, Greenspan was awarded a PhD in economics by New York University in 1977, at the age of fifty-one, immediately after serving three years as chairman of the Council of Economic Advisers. By most standards this would not constitute academic training in economics.

53 Benjamin Bernanke, "Permanent income, liquidity, and expenditure on automobiles: evidence from panel data," *Quarterly Journal of Economics* 99 (1984): 587–614.

54 Benjamin Bernanke, "The macroeconomics of the Great Depression: a comparative approach," *Journal of Money, Credit, and Banking* 27 (1995): 1–28; Benjamin Bernanke, "Non-monetary effects of the financial crisis in the propagation of the Great Depression," *American Economic Review* 73 (1983): 257–276; and Benjamin Bernanke and Harold James, "The Gold Standard, Deflation, and Financial Crisis in the Great Depression: An International Comparison," in R. Glenn Hubbard (ed.), *Financial Markets and Financial Crises* (Chicago: University of Chicago Press, 1991).

55 Benjamin Bernanke, "The economic outlook," Testimony before the Joint Economic Committee, U.S. Congress, Washington, DC, March 28, 2007.

Chapter 3: Risky Business Models

1 Peter Robison, "King County gets back less than half its money in failed SIVs," *Bloomberg*, October 23, 2009, http://noir.bloomberg.com/apps/news?pid=newsarchive&sid=aWkDmTv7Nwxo. See also Peter Robison, Pat Wechsler, and Martin Z. Braun, "Back-door taxes hit Americans with public financing in the dark," *Bloomberg*, October 26, 2009.

2 Orange County's plight was ironic, as the county had famously declared bankruptcy in 1994 due to bad investments in an earlier set of derivative assets that had gone sour. Andrew R. Sorkin, "Dealbook: another city where C.D.O. spelled trouble," *New York Times*, January 28, 2008.

3 Robison, Wechsler, and Braun, "Back-door taxes hit Americans."

4 Ben Bernanke, "The global saving glut and the U.S. current account deficit," Speech delivered at the Homer Jones Lecture, Federal Reserve Bank of St. Louis, St. Louis, April 14, 2005.

5 Maurice Obstfeld and Kenneth Rogoff, "Global imbalances and the financial crisis: products of common causes," Paper presented at Federal Reserve Bank of San Francisco Asia Economic Policy Conference, Santa Barbara, CA, October 18–20, 2009.

6 Alan Greenspan, "Federal Reserve Board's semiannual monetary policy report to the Congress," Testimony before the Committee on Banking, Housing, and Urban Affairs, U.S. Senate, Washington, DC, February 16, 2005.

7 Roger Craine and Vance L. Martin, "Interest rate conundrum," *B.E. Journal*

of Macroeconomics 9, no. 1 (2009). See also Veronica C. Warnock and Francis E. Warnock, "International capital flows and U.S. interest rates," *Journal of International Money and Finance* 28, no. 6 (2009): 903–919. Their estimate is that long-term interest rates were a 0.8 percentage point lower as a consequence of foreign purchases of Treasury securities.

8 One substrand of this view highlighted enhanced Federal Reserve inflation-fighting credibility. Since inflation expectations were anchored, that meant future expected short-term rates were lower, and that there was less risk associated with holding longer-dated securities; hence a smaller premium for holding long-term debt was required than in past episodes of recovery.

9 For an outstanding summary of modern banking, including the source of periodic crises, see Richard Grossman, *Unsettled Accounts* (Princeton: Princeton University Press, 2010).

10 The Depository Institutions Deregulation and Monetary Control Act of 1980 overrode preexisting state limits on interest rates; the Alternative Mortgage Transaction Parity Act of 1982 allowed adjustable-interest-rate mortgages; the Tax Reform Act of 1986 removed the deductibility of interest payments on consumer debt but continued to permit it for residential mortgages. Combined, these made it possible, and attractive, to both borrowers and lenders to write high- and variable-interest-rate mortgages to less creditworthy borrowers. Souphala Chomsisengphet and Anthony Pennington-Cross, "The origination of the subprime mortgage market," *Federal Reserve Bank of St. Louis Review* 88, no. 1 (2006): 31–56.

11 The example is drawn from Adam B. Ashcraft and Til Schuermann, "Understanding the securitization of subprime mortgage credit," Staff Report 318 (New York: Federal Reserve Bank of New York, 2008); the example uses the typical characteristics of the mortgages in the special purpose vehicle (SPV) Ashcraft and Schuermann discuss (of which more later).

12 In fact, a clause limits how much the interest rate can go up in any six-month period, so that it can rise more slowly than the London Interbank Offered Rate (LIBOR); we ignore this detail for the sake of a simpler illustration.

13 For origination data, see Paul Mizen, "The credit crunch of 2007–2008: a discussion of the background, market reactions, and policy responses," *Federal Reserve Bank of St. Louis Review* 90, no. 5 (2008): 531–567. For delinquency data, see Doris Dungey, "More Moody's subprime data," *Calculated Risk* (blog), October 4, 2007. http://www.calculatedriskblog.com/2007/10/more-moodys-subprime-data.html.

14 Dennis Overby, "They tried to outsmart Wall Street," *New York Times*, March 10, 2009.

15 Again, this example is drawn from Ashcraft and Schuermann, "Understanding the securitization of subprime mortgage credit"; we thank the authors for permission to use their example and to benefit from their clear explanation.

16 Fannie Mae was split into two parts, with one part privatized to remove the agency's debt from the federal government's balance sheet. The other part was transformed into a federally financed agency, the Government National Mortgage Agency (or Ginnie Mae), which enjoyed official guarantee.

17 David Goldstein and Kevin G. Hall, "Private sector loans, not Fannie or Freddie, triggered crisis," *McClatchy Newspapers*, October 12, 2008.

18 See figure 1.8 in IMF, *Global Financial Stability Report* (Washington, DC: International Monetary Fund, October 2008).

19 Capital requirements are not reserve requirements (which involve holding some assets in reserve against potential losses), but for our purposes they have a similar effect, of constraining bank lending.

20 An excellent summary is Viral V. Acharya and Matthew Richardson, "Causes of the financial crisis," *Critical Review* 21, no. 2–3 (2009): 195–210.

21 This example is taken from Viral V. Acharya and Philipp Schnabl, "Do global banks spread global imbalances?" *IMF Economic Review* 58, no. 1 (2010): 37–73.

22 For more details on the conduits, see Viral Acharya, Philipp Schnabl, and Gustavo Suarez, "Securitization without risk transfer," NBER Working Paper no. 15730 (Cambridge, MA: National Bureau of Economic Research, February 2010), http://nber.org/papers/w15730.pdf (accessed December 28, 2010).

23 Asset-backed commercial paper conduits, in structured investment vehicles, in auction-rate preferred securities, tender option bonds, and variable-rate demand notes, possessed assets of $2.2 trillion; assets financed overnight in repurchase agreements intermediated through a clearinghouse (triparty repo) grew to $2.5 trillion. Assets held in hedge funds grew to roughly $1.8 trillion. Assets of the (then) five major investment banks totaled $4 trillion. Total assets of the entire banking system were about $10 trillion. Statistics cited by Timothy F. Geithner, "Reducing systemic risk in a dynamic financial system," Speech at the Economic Club of New York, New York City, June 8, 2010.

24 Bradley Keoun, "Citigroup's $1.1 trillion of mysterious assets shadows earnings," *Bloomberg*, July 13, 2008.

25 For detailed description of the real estate mortgage-backed securities (MBSs) and collateralized debt obligations (CDOs), see Gary Gorton, "The panic of 2007," in *Maintaining Stability in a Changing Financial System: A Symposium Sponsored by the Federal Reserve Bank of Kansas City*, Jackson Hole, Wyoming, August 21–23, 2008 (Kansas City: Federal Reserve Bank of Kansas City, 2009).

26 Example from Michael Lewis, *The Big Short* (New York: W. W. Norton, 2010), chapter 2.

27 These agreements are those of the Basel Committee on Banking Supervision, which provides a forum for regular cooperation on banking supervisory matters. The Basel Committee is best known for its international standards on capital adequacy, as well as defining principles for banking supervision, and understandings regarding cross-border banking supervision. The Basel I and Basel II accords set capital standards; Basel II sought to refine the capital standards to account for risk, relying on credit rating agency measures and the statistical risk-assessment models that failed in the crisis of 2008. Organization of the Basel Committee is described at Bank for International Settlements, "About the Basel Committee," http://www.bis.org/bcbs/ (accessed December 28, 2010).

28 See discussion in Simon Johnson and James Kwak, *13 Bankers* (New York: Pantheon, 2010). Acharya and Richardson, "Causes of the financial crisis,"

argue that the main objective of these faulty ratings was to circumvent capital requirements, given that the main holders of the CDOs were other banks.

29 Effi Benmelech, "The credit rating crisis," *NBER Reporter* 1 (2010): 10.

30 For a good summary of the measures and their impact, see William Silber, "Why did FDR's bank holiday succeed?" *FRBNY Economic Policy Review* 15, no. 1 (2009): 19–30.

31 There are different definitions of "regulatory arbitrage." The one cited here is the exploitation of differences in regulatory regimes for different types of institutions and/or in different jurisdictions.

32 Barry Eichengreen, "Anatomy of a crisis," *VoxEU*, September 23, 2008, http://www.voxeu.org/index.php?q=node%2F1684. Barry Eichengreen, *Exorbitant Privilege: The Decline of the Dollar and the Future of the International Monetary System* (Oxford, UK: Oxford University Press, 2010), argues that the end of the Glass-Steagall Act left stand-alone investment banks such as Merrill Lynch in a regulatory vacuum—one that allowed them to overleverage, making them vulnerable during the crisis.

33 Barbara A. Rehm, "Countrywide to drop bank charter in favor of OTS," *American Banker* 171, no. 217 (November 10, 2006): 1–3.

34 Greg Ip and Damian Paletta, "Regulators scrutinized in mortgage meltdown states, federal agencies clashed on subprimes as market ballooned," *Wall Street Journal*, March 22, 2007, A1.

35 Stephen Labaton, "The reckoning: agency's '04 rule let banks pile up new debt," *New York Times*, October 3, 2008, http://www.nytimes.com/2008/10/03/business/03sec.html.

36 Joseph Polizzotto and David A. DeMuro, "Comments on proposed rule: alternative net capital requirements for broker-dealers that are part of consolidated supervised entities," March 8, 2004, http://www.sec.gov/rules/proposed/s72103/lehmanbrothers03082004.htm; Joseph Polizzotto is general counsel, and David A. DeMuro, global head of compliance and regulation, of Lehman Brothers.

37 Labaton, "Reckoning." "Big" is defined as institutions having more than $5 billion in assets.

38 The decision by the Securities and Exchange Commission (SEC) was also made to comply with the basic structure of the Basel II agreements, which set forth standards on capital requirements. However, it is unclear whether the decision had to be made with such haste. The Federal Reserve did not approve final rules for implementation of Basel II until November 2007. Board of Governors of the Federal Reserve System, Press Release, November 2, 2007, http://www.federalreserve.gov/newsevents/press/bcreg/20071102a.htm.

39 Details are in Acharya, Schnabl, and Suarez, "Securitization without risk transfer," 13–14.

40 A clear exposition of this is in Viral Acharya, Thomas Cooley, Matthew Richardson, and Ingo Walter, "Manufacturing tail risk: a perspective on the financial crisis of 2007–09," *Foundations and Trends in Finance* 4, no. 4 (2010): 247–325.

41 Alan Greenspan, "Risk transfer and financial stability," Speech to the Federal Reserve Bank of Chicago's Forty-First Annual Conference on Bank Structure, Chicago, May 5, 2005.

42 Thomas Philippon, "The evolution of the US financial industry from 1860 to 2007: Theory and evidence," Working Paper (New York: New York University, 2008). Philippon estimates that corporate financial services accounted for about 70 percent of total financial services in GDP.

43 Paul Krugman, "Making banking boring," *New York Times*, April 9, 2009.

44 Thomas Philippon and Ariell Reshef, "Wages and human capital in the U.S. financial industry: 1909–2006," NBER Working Paper no. 14644 (Cambridge, MA: National Bureau of Economic Research, 2009).

45 Matt Taibbi, "The great American bubble machine," *Rolling Stone*, July 13, 2009, http://www.rollingstone.com/politics/news/the-great-american-bubble -machine-20100405.

46 Ibid.

47 David Wessel and Thomas T. Vogel Jr., "Market watcher: arcane world of bonds is guide and beacon to a populist president—rally seen as endorsement of policy —and it helps economy as rates fall—but it could be a fickle friend," *Wall Street Journal*, February 25, 1993, A1.

48 This general thesis is laid out in detail in Johnson and Kwak, *13 Bankers*.

49 Dean Baker was warning of a bubble as early as 2002. See Dean Baker, "The run-up in home prices: a bubble," *Challenge* 45, no. 6 (2002): 93–119. Dean Baker and David Rosnick, "Will a bursting bubble trouble Bernanke? The evidence for a housing bubble" (Washington, DC: Center for Economic and Policy Research, 2005). See also Robert Shiller, "The bubble's new home," *Barron's*, June 20, 2005.

Chapter 4: The Death Spiral

1 Lori Montgomery, Neil Irwin, and David Cho, "A joint decision to act: it must be big and fast," *Washington Post*, September 20, 2008, A1.

2 The Case-Shiller indices are available at Standard & Poor's website: http:// www.standardandpoors.com/indices/sp-case-shiller-home-price-indices/en/ us/?indexId=spusa-cashpidff--p-us----.

3 Data available at *Zillow.com*: http://www.zillow.com/local-info/.

4 Gary Gorton, "The panic of 2007," in *Maintaining Stability in a Changing Financial System: A Symposium Sponsored by the Federal Reserve Bank of Kansas City*, Jackson Hole, Wyoming, August 21–23, 2008 (Kansas City: Federal Reserve Bank of Kansas City, 2009).

5 For origination data, see Paul Mizen, "The credit crunch of 2007–2008: a discussion of the background, market reactions, and policy responses," *Federal Reserve Bank of St. Louis Review* 90, no. 5 (2008): 531–567. For delinquency data, see Doris Dungey, "More Moody's subprime data," *Calculated Risk* (blog), October 4, 2007, http://www.calculatedriskblog.com/2007/10/more-moodys -subprime-data.html.

6 Doris Dungey, "We're all subprime now," *Calculated Risk* (blog), February 12, 2008, http://www.calculatedriskblog.com/2008/02/were-all-subprime-now .html.

7 Ben Bernanke, "The economic outlook," Testimony before the Joint Economic Committee, U.S. Congress, Washington, DC, March 28, 2007.

8 In addition to individual years of decline, there was a sustained decline in house prices over the 1929–1933 period. See the data for figure 2.1 in Robert J. Shiller, *Irrational Exuberance*, 2d ed. (Princeton: Princeton University Press, 2009).

9 Taleb defines a black swan as "an *outlier* . . . because nothing in the past can convincingly point to its possibility." See Nassim Nicholas Taleb, "Black swans and the domains of statistics," *American Statistician* 61, no. 3 (2007): 198–200. Nassim Nicholas Taleb, *The Black Swan: The Impact of the Highly Improbable* (New York: Random House, 2007).

10 Peter T. Larsen, "Goldman pays the price of being big," *Financial Times*, August 14, 2007, http://www.ft.com/cms/s/0/d2121cb6-49cb-11dc-9ffe -0000779fd2ac.html#axzz19HIZzeQ5.

11 In the postwar period, home prices dropped in 1964 and 1991. Calculations are based on data for figure 2.1 in Shiller, *Irrational Exuberance*, as updated by Shiller. In inflation-adjusted terms, home price declines were relatively common, with recent episodes in the mid-1970s, the early 1980s, and the early 1990s.

12 It is important to make a distinction between the modelers who ran the models, and understood the tenuous nature of the assumptions, and the executives who made the decisions regarding trades and holdings. Gillian Tett recounts how one statistical expert, worried that the models were underpricing the risk associated with the highest tranches, was pushed out of the Royal Bank of Scotland. Gillian Tett, *Fool's Gold* (New York: Free Press, 2009).

13 Robert L. Rodriguez, "Absence of fear," Speech to the CFA Society of Chicago, June 28, 2007.

14 Published in *The New Yorker*, February 9, 2009, 44; the cartoon is by Paul Noth.

15 Suzanne Kapner, "FBI to target mortgage fraud," *Financial Times*, June 11, 2010. "Fraud for Profit is sometimes referred to as 'Industry Insider Fraud' and the motive is to revolve equity, falsely inflate the value of the property, or issue loans based on fictitious properties." FBI, "Financial crimes report to the public: FY2006" (Washington, DC: Federal Bureau of Investigation, March 2007), 21, http://www.fbi.gov/publications/financial/fcs_report2006/ publicrpt06.pdf.

16 Dan Wilchins and Karen Brettell, "Factbox: how Goldman's ABACUS deal worked," Reuters, April 19, 2010. The SEC reports on its complaint at http:// www.sec.gov/news/press/2010/2010-59.htm (accessed December 29, 2010).

17 Quoted in Grace Wong, "Behind Wall Street's subprime fear index: understanding the ABX," *CNNMoney.com* (2007), http://money.cnn.com/galleries/2007/ news/0711/gallery.abx_index/index.html (accessed December 29, 2010).

18 The ABX is actually an index for credit default swaps, so it measures the cost of *insuring* these deals, not the deals themselves. There are different prices for different vintages of the index; the ones cited here for the 7-1 series, which reflects mortgages written in the second half of 2006. For more details, see Markus Brunnermeier, "Deciphering the liquidity and credit crunch," *Journal of Economic Perspectives* 23, no. 1 (2009): 77–100; and Gary Gorton, "Information, liquidity, and the (ongoing) panic of 2007," *American Economic Review* 99, no. 2 (2009): 567–572.

19 Effi Benmeluch and Jennifer Dlugosz, "The credit rating crisis," NBER Working Paper no. 15045 (Cambridge, MA: National Bureau of Economic Research, 2009).

20 Brunnermeier, "Deciphering the liquidity and credit crunch."

21 Joshua Coval, Jakub Jurek, and Erik Stafford, "The economics of structured finance," *Journal of Economic Perspectives* 23, no. 1 (2009): 3–25. The default correlation need only rise from 0.2 to 0.6 to turn an AAA tranche into junk.

22 This is the case of the ABACUS 2007-AC1 deal for which the SEC eventually sued Goldman Sachs. Hedge fund manager John Paulson bought credit default swaps that would pay off if the collateralized debt obligations originated by Goldman Sachs defaulted; however, Paulson did not actually buy any of the collateralized debt obligations involved in the ABACUS deal. See Steve R. Waldman, "Deconstructing ABACUS," *Interfluidity* (blog), April 25, 2010, http://www.interfluidity.com/v2/date/2010/04.

23 *BIS Quarterly Review*, June 2010, table 19.

24 Rene Stulz, "Credit default swaps and the credit crisis," *Journal of Economic Perspectives* 24, no. 1 (2010).

25 Joseph G. Haubrich and Deborah Lucas, "Who holds the toxic waste? An investigation of CMO holdings," Federal Reserve Bank of Cleveland Policy Discussion Paper no. 20 (Cleveland: Federal Reserve Bank of Cleveland, 2007). Commercial Bank was the largest single holder.

26 Coval, Jurek, and Stafford, "Economies of structured finance," 4.

27 Letter from Warren E. Buffett, Chairman of the Board, Berkshire Hathaway Inc., to the Shareholders of Berkshire Hathaway Inc., February 21, 2003, http://www.berkshirehathaway.com/letters/2002pdf.pdf.

28 "Bear Stearns execs to face financial crisis panel," *All Things Considered*, NPR, May 4, 2010.

29 Raghuram Rajan explained the incentives toward greater risk taking in Raghuram Rajan, "Global current account imbalances: hard landing or soft landing," Speech at the Crédit Suisse First Boston Conference, Hong Kong, March 15, 2005, http://www.imf.org/external/np/speeches/2005/031505.htm. The speech, also circulated as a paper, was widely dismissed at the time.

30 These numbers are based on table 1 in Gorton, "Information, liquidity, and the (ongoing) panic." The numbers actually refer to haircuts—the percentage that is subtracted from the par value of assets being used as collateral—in the market for repurchase agreements (repo market), but for ease of exposition we have presented them as directly related to asset-backed commercial paper (ABCP). Little accuracy is lost in the translation. See also Randall Dodd,

"Subprime: tentacles of a crisis," *Finance and Development* 44, no. 4 (2007); and Randall Dodd and Paul Mills, "Outbreak: U.S. subprime contagion," *Finance and Development* 45, no. 2 (2008).

31 Again, much of the actual action was in the market for repurchase agreements rather than in direct issues of commercial paper, but the effect is the same.

32 Mark Pittman, "Bear Stearns fund collapse sends shock through CDOs," *Bloomberg*, June 21, 2007, http://www.bloomberg.com/apps/news?pid=news archive&sid=a7LCp2Acv2aw&refer=home.

33 James Mackintosh and Ben White, "Goldman reclaims most of $2bn rescue funds," *Financial Times*, March 26, 2008.

34 Brunnermeier, "Deciphering the liquidity and credit crunch," provides an excellent summary of the chronology of events.

35 Roddy Boyd, "The last days of Bear Stearns," *Fortune*, March 31, 2008.

36 Minutes of the Board of Governors of the Federal Reserve System, March 14, 2008, http://www.federalreserve.gov/newsevents/press/other/other20080627a1 .pdf.

37 E. Scott Reckard, "Countrywide sued by state over lending," *Los Angeles Times*, June 26, 2008.

38 Christina Hoag, "Customers line up at IndyMac to withdraw money," *USA Today*, July 14, 2008.

39 Stephen Labaton, "Treasury acts to shore up Fannie Mae and Freddie Mac," *New York Times*, July 14, 2008.

40 Atif Mian, Amir Sufi, and Francesco Trebbi, "The political economy of the U.S. mortgage default crisis," NBER Working Paper no. 16107 (Cambridge, MA: National Bureau of Economic Research, 2010).

41 Barclays did eventually purchase Lehman's North American Investment Banking, Fixed Income and Equities Sales, and Trading and Research Operations. See Andrew R. Sorkin, *Too Big to Fail: The Battle to Save Wall Street* (New York: Viking, 2009). Britain's largest mortgage bank, HBOS, was under stress at the same time. The government brokered a merger with Lloyds Bank and eventually injected government funds. As it turns out, the Financial Services Authority (FSA) was right to be extremely wary of the Barclays transaction. Lehman had shifted $50 billion off its balance sheet using derivatives known as "repo 105." Francesco Guerrera, Henry Sender, and Patrick Jenkins, "Lehman file rocks Wall Street," *Financial Times*, March 12, 2010.

42 Damian Paletta, "Barney Frank celebrates free market day," *Real Time Economics* (*Wall Street Journal* blog), September 17, 2008, http://blogs.wsj.com/ economics/2008/09/17/barney-frank-celebrates-free-market-day/.

43 Phillip Swagel, "The financial crisis: an inside view," *Brookings Papers on Economic Activity* Spring 2009 (conference draft), 30, available online at http://www.brookings.edu/economics/bpea/~/media/Files/Programs/ES/ BPEA/2009_spring_bpea_papers/2009_spring_bpea_swagel.pdf.

44 William K. Sjostrom Jr., "The AIG bailout," *Washington and Lee Law Review* no. 66 (2009): 943–991.

45 Gretchen Morgenson, "Behind insurer's crisis, blind eye to a web of risk,"

New York Times, September 28, 2008, http://www.nytimes.com/2008/09/28/business/28melt.html.

46 As cited in ibid.; see also Sjostrom, "AIG bailout," 955–959.

47 Ben Bernanke, "American International Group," Testimony before the Committee on Financial Services, U.S. House of Representatives, Washington, DC, March 24, 2009, http://www.federalreserve.gov/newsevents/testimony/bernanke20090324a.htm.

48 See Congressional Oversight Panel, *January Oversight Report* (January 13, 2010), http://cop.senate.gov/documents/cop-011410-report.pdf.

49 Lilla Zuill and Jonathan Stempel, "AIG has $61.7 billion loss," Reuters, March 2, 2009, http://uk.reuters.com/article/idUKTRE5210SZ20090302.

50 Andrew Gowers, "Exposed: Dick Fuld, the man who brought the world to its knees," *Sunday Times* (London), December 14, 2008, http://business.timesonline.co.uk/tol/business/industry_sectors/banking_and_finance/article5336179.ece.

51 For the details cited here, see Bob Ivry, Christine Harper, and Mark Pittman, "Missing Lehman lesson of shakeout means too big banks may fail," *Bloomberg*, September 8, 2009, http://noir.bloomberg.com/apps/news?pid=newsarchive&refer=top_news&sid=aX8D5utKFuGA.

52 See ibid.; and Bob Ivry, Christine Harper, and Mark Pittman, "The freeze: the bankruptcy's ripple effect," *Bloomberg*, September 8, 2009.

53 Ivry, Harper, and Pittman, "Missing Lehman lesson."

54 Brian Swint and Jennifer Ryan, "King says Bank of England will act as recession seems likely," *Bloomberg*, October 22, 2008, http://noir.bloomberg.com/apps/news?pid=newsarchive&sid=anB9vLnBSBdk.

55 David Wessel, *In Fed We Trust: Ben Bernanke's War on the Great Panic* (New York: Crown Business, 2009), 229.

56 Paul J. Davies, "Half of all CDOs of ABS failed," *Financial Times*, February 10, 2009.

57 "Treasury's bailout proposal," *CNN Money*, September 20, 2008, http://money.cnn.com/2008/09/20/news/economy/treasury_proposal/index.htm.

58 Adam Davidson, "Bailout seeks broad new powers for Treasury chief," *Morning Edition*, NPR, September 23, 2008, http://www.npr.org/templates/story/story.php?storyId=94921462.

59 Newt Gingrich, "Before D.C. gets our money, it owes us some answers," *National Review* online, September 21, 2008, http://www.nationalreview.com/corner/170162/d-c-gets-our-money-it-owes-us-some-answers/newt-gingrich.

60 Robert Reich, "What Wall Street should be required to do, to get a blank check from taxpayers," Robert Reich's blog, 2008, http://robertreich.blogspot.com/2008/09/what-wall-street-should-be-required-to.html (accessed December 29, 2010).

61 Rasmussen Reports, "63% say Wall Street, not taxpayers, will benefit from bailout plan," October 3, 2008, http://www.rasmussenreports.com/public_content/business/federal_bailout/october_2008/63_say_wall_street_not_taxpayers_will_benefit_from_bailout_plan.

62 "U.S. chamber: votes against bailout are prelude to calamity," *The Hill*, September 29, 2008.

63 Robert Kuttner, "Paulson's folly," *American Prospect*, September 22, 2008, http://www.prospect.org/cs/articles?article=paulsons_folly.

64 Luke Mullins, "Sen. Jim Bunning: the bailout is un-American," *US News & World Report Money*, September 23, 2008, http://money.usnews.com/money/blogs/the-home-front/2008/09/23/sen-jim-bunning-the-bailout-is-un-american.html.

65 Jim Snyder, "A crushing failure for lobbyists," *The Hill*, September 29, 2008, http://thehill.com/homenews/news/16556-crushing-failure-for-lobbyists.

66 The end-2007 market capitalization was $19.9 trillion. Adjusting by the S&P price increase that occurred through August 2008 implies that market capitalization was $17.3 trillion. The 6.9 percent drop that day implies a $1.2 trillion loss. Capitalization statistics from World Federation of Exchanges, and S&P price change (close to close) from Yahoo Finance (accessed April 1, 2010).

67 Baird Webel and Edward Murphy, "The emergency economic stabilization act and current financial turmoil: issues and analysis," Congressional Research Service Report no. RL-34730 (Washington, DC: Congressional Research Service, November 25, 2008). Other provisions included an acceleration of timing to allow the Fed to pay interest on reserves, a suspension of mark-to-market in inactive markets, and some measures directed at easing mortgage relief for distressed homeowners.

68 Mian, Sufi, and Trebbi, "The political economy of the U.S. mortgage default crisis."

Chapter 5: Bailout

1 The talking points and commitment agreement were later obtained by Judicial Watch, and are available at http://www.judicialwatch.org/news/2009/may/judicial-watch-forces-release-bank-bailout-documents (accessed December 29, 2010).

2 Mark Landler and Eric Dash, "Drama behind a $250 billion banking deal," *New York Times*, October 15, 2008, http://www.nytimes.com/2008/10/15/business/economy/15bailout.html.

3 For a summary and assessment, see Pietro Veronesi and Luigi Zingales, "Paulson's gift," *Journal of Financial Economics* 97 (2010): 339–368. See also David Wessel, *In Fed We Trust: Ben Bernanke's War on the Great Panic* (New York: Crown Business, 2009), 238–399; and Phillip Swagel, "The financial crisis: an inside view," *Brookings Papers on Economic Activity* Spring 2009 (conference draft), available online at http://www.brookings.edu/economics/bpea/~/media/Files/Programs/ES/BPEA/2009_spring_bpea_papers/2009_spring_bpea_swagel.pdf.

4 Landler and Dash, "Drama behind a $250 billion banking deal."

5 The statements are at "President Bush Meets with G7 Finance Ministers to Discuss World Economy, October 11, 2008, White House, Washington, DC," G7/8

Finance Ministers Meetings, G8 Information Centre, http://www.g7.utoronto .ca/finance/fm081011-bush.htm.

6 Richard Woods and David Smith, "Gordon Brown gambles it all on rescue plan," *Sunday Times* (London), October 12, 2008, http://business.timesonline .co.uk/tol/business/economics/article4926735.ece.

7 As the International Monetary Fund put it, somewhat blandly, "If banks were to bring forward to today loss provisions for the next two years, before expected earnings, U.S. and European banks in aggregate would have tangible equity close to zero," adding in a footnote, "Bringing forward the expected writedowns for loans approximates a mark-to-market for the loan book." IMF, *Global Financial Stability Report* (Washington, DC: International Monetary Fund, April 2009), 35–36.

8 Swagel, "Financial crisis," 49.

9 Ian Katz, Scott Lanman, and Alison Fitzgerald, "Citigroup's $306 billion rescue fueled by pizza from Domino's," *Bloomberg*, November 25, 2008.

10 See James Kwak and Simon Johnson, *13 Bankers* (New York: Pantheon, 2010), 171.

11 "Adding up the government's total bailout tab," *New York Times*, February 4, 2009, http://www.nytimes.com/interactive/2009/02/04/business/20090205 -bailout-totals-graphic.html.

12 The two surveys are by Rasmussen Reports, "63% say Wall Street, not taxpayers, will benefit from bailout plan," October 3, 2008, http://www.rasmussenreports .com/public_content/business/federal_bailout/october_2008/63_say_wall_ street_not_taxpayers_will_benefit_from_bailout_plan; Rasmussen Reports, "56% oppose any more government help for banks," February 11, 2009, http://www.rasmussenreports.com/public_content/business/federal_bailout/ february_2009/56_oppose_any_more_government_help_for_banks.

13 Representative Marilyn Musgrave, "Debate on the Emergency Economic Stabilization Act of 2008," Speech on the House floor, September 29, 2008, http:// www.c-spanarchives.org/videolibrary/clip.php?appid=595264033.

14 Joseph Stiglitz, "Henry Paulson's shell game," *Nation*, September 26, 2008, http://www.thenation.com/article/henry-paulsons-shell-game.

15 Paul Krugman, "Wall Street Voodoo," *New York Times*, January 18, 2009, http:// www.nytimes.com/2009/01/19/opinion/19iht-edkrugman.1.19488316.html.

16 Ibid.

17 Rebecca Christie and Brendan Murray, "Paulson hit by investors as he seeks to halt crisis," *Bloomberg*, July 16, 2008, http://www.bloomberg.com/apps/ news?pid=newsarchive&refer=home&sid=aWssvqlta37Q.

18 In reality most open market operations are conducted by way of "repurchase agreements," such as when the Fed buys U.S. Treasury securities from a primary dealer who agrees to buy them back at some future date. The procedure described here, in which open market operations work by way of the purchase and sale of Treasury securities, would achieve the same effect of temporarily increasing the effective money supply, and is presented for the sake of simplicity (and because it is the process usually described in textbooks).

19 Peter Coy, "Rates: when zero is way too high," *BusinessWeek*, January 19, 2009.

20 Paul Krugman, "Optimal fiscal policy in a liquidity trap," *The Conscience of a Liberal* (*New York Times* blog), December 29, 2008, http://krugman.blogs.nytimes.com/2008/12/29/optimal-fiscal-policy-in-a-liquidity-trap-ultra-wonkish/.

21 Paul Krugman, "ZIRP," *The Conscience of a Liberal* (*New York Times* blog), December 18, 2008, http://krugman.blogs.nytimes.com/2008/12/16/zirp/.

22 The text of the Federal Reserve Act reads, "In unusual and exigent circumstances, the Board of Governors of the Federal Reserve System, by the affirmative vote of not less than five members, may authorize any Federal reserve bank, during such periods as the said board may determine, at rates established in accordance with the provisions of section 14, subdivision (d), of this Act, to discount for any individual, partnership, or corporation, notes, drafts, and bills of exchange when such notes, drafts, and bills of exchange are indorsed or otherwise secured to the satisfaction of the Federal Reserve bank." From Section 13.3, Federal Reserve Act [12 USC 343. As added by act of July 21, 1932 (47 Stat. 715); and amended by acts of Aug. 23, 1935 (49 Stat. 714) and Dec. 19, 1991 (105 Stat. 2386)].

23 Joseph Gagnon, Matthew Raskin, Julie Remache, and Brian Sack, "Large-scale asset purchases by the Federal Reserve: did they work?" Staff Report no. 411 (New York: Federal Reserve Bank of New York, 2010).

24 Ben Bernanke, "Remarks by Governor Ben S. Bernanke before the National Economists Club," Washington, DC, November 21 2002, http://www.federalreserve.gov/BOARDDOCS/SPEECHES/2002/20021121/default.htm.

25 Steve Matthews and Scott Lanman, "Fed's Bullard calls for resuming purchase of Treasuries if economy slowing," *Bloomberg*, July 29, 2010, http://www.bloomberg.com/news/2010-07-29/fed-should-resume-treasury-purchases-if-deflation-risk-grows-bullard-says.html.

26 Sewell Chan, "Within the Fed, worries of deflation," *New York Times*, July 29, 2010.

27 Bernanke, "Remarks by Governor Ben S. Bernanke before the National Economists Club."

28 Patrice Hill, "McCain adviser talks of 'mental recession,'" *Washington Times*, July 9, 2008, http://www.washingtontimes.com/news/2008/jul/09/mccain-adviser-addresses-mental-recession/.

29 Donald Luskin, "A nation of exaggerators: quit doling out that bad-economy line," *Washington Post*, September 14, 2008, http://www.washingtonpost.com/wp-dyn/content/article/2008/09/12/AR2008091202415.html.

30 From September 12, 2008 (the last trading day before Lehman's bankruptcy) to the stock market trough on March 6, 2009, the S&P 500 declined from 1251.7 to a low of 666.79.

31 For example, see Lawrence Christiano, Martin Eichenbaum, and Sergio Rebelo, "When is the government spending multiplier large?" NBER Working Paper no. 15394 (Cambridge, MA: National Bureau of Economic Research, 2009); Giancarlo Corsetti, André Meier, and Gernot Müller, "What determines government spending multipliers," May 2010, http://www.newyorkfed.org/

research/conference/2010/global/multipliers.pdf; Miguel Almunia, Agustín Benetrix, Barry Eichengreen, Kevin O'Rourke, and Gisela Rua, "From Great Depression to Great Credit Crisis: similarities, difference, and lessons," Paper presented at the 50th Economic Policy Panel Meeting, Tilburg, Netherlands, October 23–24, 2009.

32 Ryan Lizza, "Inside the crisis: Larry Summers and the White House economic team," *The New Yorker*, October 12, 2009.

33 CBO, "The effects of automatic stabilizers on the federal budget" (Washington, DC: Congressional Budget Office), May 2010, table 1; CBO, "Budget and economic outlook: Fiscal years 2010 to 2020" (Washington, DC: Congressional Budget Office, January 2010), table 1-3.

34 Phil Davis, "Believer in small government predicts 15-year depression," *Financial Times*, March 22, 2009, http://www.ft.com/cms/s/0/ee3e07f0-16b2 -11de-9a72-0000779fd2ac.html#axzz19LwLJlR1.

35 Barry Eichengreen, *Golden Fetters: The Gold Standard and the Great Depression, 1919–39* (Oxford, UK: Oxford University Press, 1992), 251.

36 The intellectual descendents of this view often fall into the Austrian school of economics, associated with Friedrich Hayek and Ludwig von Mises. The Austrians believe that credit cycles drive economic fluctuations; excessive credit creation inevitably leads to malinvestment, or unsustainable overinvestment in the wrong sectors.

37 Paul Krugman, "How did economists get it so wrong?" *New York Times Magazine*, September 6, 2009, 36–46.

38 Data from *Wall Street Journal* poll, available at http://wsj.com/public/resources/ documents/wsjecon0209.xls (accessed August 1, 2010).

39 Martin Feldstein, "The case for fiscal stimulus," *Project Syndicate*, January 26, 2009, http://www.project-syndicate.org/commentary/feldstein6/English.

40 The Congressional Budget Office subsequently revised upward the total cost of the package to $863 billion.

41 Paul Krugman, "Behind the curve," *New York Times*, March 8, 2009.

42 Elizabeth McNichol, Phil Oliff, and Nicholas Johnson, "Recession continues to batter state budgets: state responses could slow recovery" (Washington, DC: Center on Budget and Policy Priorities, July 15, 2010), http://www.cbpp .org/cms/index.cfm?fa=view&id=711.

43 Joshua Aizenman and Gurnain Pasrich, "On the ease of overstating the fiscal stimulus in the U.S. 2008–9," NBER Working Paper no. 15784 (Cambridge, MA: National Bureau of Economic Research, 2010).

44 See CBO, "Estimated impact of the American Recovery and Reinvestment Act on employment and economic output from January 2010 through June 2010" (Washington, DC: Congressional Budget Office, 2010).

45 Alan Blinder and Mark Zandi, "How the Great Recession was brought to an end" (2010), Table 8 http://www.economy.com/mark-zandi/documents/End -of-Great-Recession.pdf (accessed August 1, 2010).

46 Swap arrangements between the Fed and the European Central Bank and the

Swiss National Bank existed before September 2008, but they were limited in scope and amounts. From October 2008, the swap arrangement with the European Central Bank was substantially expanded, further arrangements were set up with the Bank of Japan, Bank of England, Bank of Canada, Reserve Bank of Australia, Sveriges Riksbank, Danmarks Nationalbank, Norges Bank, Reserve Bank of New Zealand, as well as the central banks of Brazil, Mexico, Korea, and Singapore. See Linda Goldberg, Craig Kennedy, and Jason Miu, "Central bank dollar swap lines and overseas dollar funding costs," NBER Working Paper no. 15763 (Cambridge, MA: National Bureau of Economic Research, 2010).

47 See comments in Craig Whitlock and Edward Cody, "Europe beginning to realize its lenders share in the blame," *Washington Post*, October 2, 2008.

48 A timeline of these international measures is available from the Federal Reserve Bank of New York, "Timelines of policy responses to the global financial crisis," http://www.newyorkfed.org/research/global_economy/policyresponses.html (accessed December 29, 2010).

49 See IMF, "Group of Twenty meeting of deputies, Jan 31–Feb 1, 2009, London, U.K.: note by the staff of the International Monetary Fund" (Washington, DC: International Monetary Fund, undated).

50 Table 2 from IMF, "Group of Twenty meeting of the ministers and central bank governors, March 13–14, 2009, London, U.K.: global economic policies and prospects: note by the staff of the International Monetary Fund" (Washington, DC: International Monetary Fund, undated).

51 U.S. figures for total value of goods and services relative to 2008Q2, from national income and product accounts.

52 Barry Eichengreen and Kevin O'Rourke, "A tale of two depressions," *VoxEU*, June 4, 2009.

53 Year-on-year growth rates, from Asian Development Bank (ADB), Asia Regional Integration Center. See also Deutsche Bank, "Global economic perspectives: financial conditions weakest since late '08" (New York: Deutsche Bank, June 23, 2010).

Chapter 6: Economy in Shock

1 One of us (J. F.) was in Brazil at the time and witnessed both the government statement and the outraged response on the streets of Rio de Janeiro.

2 Data on regional per capita GDP are in real terms, as calculated by Angus Maddison, available at Angus Maddison, *Statistics on World Population, GDP and Per Capita GDP, 1-2008 AD* (2010), http://www.ggdc.net/maddison/Historical_Statistics/vertical-file_03-2009.xls (accessed December 28, 2010). In the previous fifteen years Latin American per capita GDP rose over 48 percent; in the fifteen years after 1981, it was stagnant.

3 As in Maddison, *Statistics on World Population*; 1992–2002 per capita GDP grew barely 6 percent, at a pace less than one-sixth that of the previous decade.

4 Data are in real per capita GDP, as indicated by the Bureau of Economic Analysis, National Economic Accounts.

5 Anthony B. Atkinson, "Three questions about the global economic crisis and three conclusions for EU and Member State policy-makers," *ECFIN Economic Brief* 2 (Brussels: European Commission, June 2009).

6 Data for August 2010 kindly supplied by Andy Sum and Joseph McLaughlin. For earlier data, see Andrew Sum and Ishwar Khatiwada, "Labor underutilization problems of U.S. workers across household income groups at the end of the Great Recession" (Boston: Center for Labor Market Studies, Northeastern University, February 2010).

7 Corelogic, *Negative Equity Report Q2 2010* (Santa Ana, CA: Corelogic, August 26, 2010), http://www.corelogic.com/uploadedFiles/Pages/About_Us/ResearchTrends/CL_Q2_2010_Negative_Equity_FINAL.pdf.

8 Keith Jurow, "Housing isn't close to stabilizing," *MarketWatch*, September 22, 2010, http://www.marketwatch.com/story/story/print?guid=AD3D5EF8-C58A-11DF-BA89-00212804637C.

9 Data from Zillow.com, http://www.zillow.com/local-info/ (accessed August 9, 2010); Lita Epstein, "Underwater homes hold steady but likely to increase," *AOL Housing Watch*, August 31, 2010, http://www.housingwatch.com/2010/08/31/underwater-homes-hold-steady-but-likely-to-increase/; and "Report: 1 in 5 U.S. homeowners underwater," *MSNBC.com*, February 10, 2010, http://www.msnbc.msn.com/id/35335957/ns/business-real_estate/.

10 Daniel H. Cooper, "Impending U.S. spending bust? The role of housing wealth as borrowing collateral," Federal Reserve Bank of Boston Public Policy Discussion Paper no. 09-9 (Boston, MA: Federal Reserve Bank of Boston). Cooper's calculations indicate an 11 percent effect for a credit-constrained household, which would imply a reduction in debt-financed consumption of over $7000, spread over time.

11 See, for example, Optimal Benefit Strategies, *Jobs in Peril: Assessing the Impact of Increases in Defined Benefit Plan Funding Obligations on Employment during an Economic Recession* (Washington, DC: American Benefits Council, 2009); and Trade Union Advisory Committee to the Organisation for Economic Co-operation and Development, *Submission to the OECD Working Party on Private Pensions* (Paris: Organisation for Economic Co-operation and Development, March 2009).

12 Pew Center on the States, *The Trillion Dollar Gap: Underfunded State Retirement Systems and the Road to Reform* (Washington, DC: Pew Foundation, 2010).

13 Kara Scannell and Jeannette Neumann, "SEC sues New Jersey as states' finances stir fears," *Wall Street Journal*, August 19, 2010.

14 For a compendium of stories about budget cuts and layoffs in education, including those mentioned here, see National Education Association, "Teacher layoffs and school budget cuts," http://www.nea.org/assets/docs/newsclipslayoffs10.pdf (accessed October 22, 2010).

15 Ianthe Jeanne Dugan, "Facing budget gaps, cities sell parking, airports, zoo," *Wall Street Journal*, August 23, 2010, 1; Hal Weitzman and Nicole Bullock, "States of distress," *Financial Times*, August 9, 2010, 5.

16 For a more detailed discussion of this period, see Jeffry A. Frieden, *Global*

Capitalism: Its Fall and Rise in the Twentieth Century (New York: W. W. Norton, 2006), part II.

17 See, for example, Richard E. Holl, *From the Boardroom to the War Room: America's Corporate Liberals and FDR's Preparedness Program* (Rochester, NY: University of Rochester Press, 2005).

18 IMF, *World Economic Outlook* (Washington, DC: International Monetary Fund, October 2009), chapter 4. OECD, *Economic Outlook* 85 (Paris: Organisation for Economic Co-operation and Development, 2009), chapter 4, discusses how the deep and prolonged recession might affect the normal level of output (called potential GDP), and the associated impact on the natural rate of unemployment.

19 Carmen M. Reinhart and Kenneth S. Rogoff, "From financial crisis to debt crash," NBER Working Paper no. 15795 (Cambridge, MA: National Bureau of Economic Research, 2010). Manmohan Kumar and Jaejoon Woo, "Public debt and growth," IMF Working Paper no. 10/174 (Washington, DC: International Monetary Fund, 2010), examine a shorter, smaller sample, controlling for other factors, and find a similar result regarding debt and growth.

20 Data from Thomas Piketty and Emmanuel Saez, "Income Inequality in the United States, 1913–1998," in Anthony Atkinson and Thomas Piketty (eds.), *Top Incomes over the Twentieth Century: A Contrast between European and English Speaking Countries* (New York: Oxford University Press, 2007), 141–225. Data set available at http://elsa.berkeley.edu/~saez/TabFig2007.xls (accessed April 15, 2010).

21 William D. Cohan, "The Wall Street bonus in retreat," *Fortune*, March 16, 2009.

22 Michael Shnayerson, "Wall Street's $18.4 billion bonus," *Vanity Fair*, March 2009; Louise Story, "After off year, Wall Street pay is bouncing back," *New York Times*, April 25, 2009; Stephen Grocer, "Banks set for record pay," *Wall Street Journal*, January 14, 2010.

23 Simon Johnson, "The quiet coup," *Atlantic*, May 2009, http://www.theatlantic.com/magazine/archive/2009/05/the-quiet-coup/7364/.

24 Geoffrey Best, *Churchill: A Study in Greatness* (New York: Oxford University Press, 2003), 119. Ironically, within a few months of this, Churchill proceeded to put the country back on the gold standard, coming down firmly on the side of finance and against that of industry. But at least he (apparently) agonized over the choice.

25 IMF, *Global Financial Stability Report* (Washington, DC: International Monetary Fund, April 2010), table 1.2 and figure 1.11.

26 Ezra Vogel, *Japan as Number One* (Cambridge, MA: Harvard University Press, 1979).

27 Takeo Hoshi and Anil Kashyap, "The Japanese banking crisis: Where did it come from and how will it end?" *NBER Macroeconomics Annual 1999* (Cambridge, MA: MIT Press, 2000), 129–201; Thomas Cargill, Michael H. Hutchison, and Takatoshi Ito, "The Banking Crisis in Japan," in Gerald Caprio Jr., William C. Hunter, George G. Kaufman, and Danny M. Leipziger (eds.), *Pre-*

venting Bank Crises: Lessons from Recent Global Bank Failures (Washington, DC: World Bank, 1998).

28 Ricardo J. Caballero, Takeo Hoshi, and Anil Kashyap, "Zombie lending and depressed restructuring in Japan," *American Economic Review* 98, no. 5 (2008): 1943–1977.

29 Anil Kashyap and Takeo Hoshi, "Will the U.S. bank recapitalization succeed? Lessons from Japan," Paper presented at the Macroeconomic and Policy Challenges following Financial Meltdowns Conference, hosted by the IMF, Washington, DC, April 3, 2009.

30 Calculations based on IMF, *World Economic Outlook* (Washington, DC: International Monetary Fund, October 2009), data, through 2008.

31 The 2008 net government debt to GDP was approximately 100 percent.

32 Tim Curry and Lynn Shibut, "The cost of the savings and loan crisis: truth and consequences," *FDIC Banking Review* 13, no. 2 (2000); Frederic Mishkin, *The Economics of Money, Banking, and Financial Markets*, 9th ed. (New York: Prentice Hall, 2010), appendix 1 to chapter 11.

33 O. Emre Ergungor, "On the resolution of financial crises: the Swedish experience," Federal Reserve Bank of Cleveland Policy Discussion Paper no. 21 (Cleveland: Federal Reserve Bank of Cleveland, 2007); Carter Dougherty, "Stopping a financial crisis, the Swedish way," *New York Times*, September 22, 2008.

34 In April 2009, the Financial Accounting Standards Board (FASB), under pressure from Congress and the American Bankers Association, allowed banks greater flexibility in valuing their illiquid assets. This greater flexibility included using internal statistical models to value the assets. See Ronald D. Orol, "FASB approves more mark-to-market flexibility: panel passes measure unanimously; measure could boost bank profit," *MarketWatch*, April 2, 2009.

35 Some of these provisions are summarized in "Factbox: major U.S. financial regulation reform proposals," Reuters, July 15, 2010. Provisions that require regulatory action to be implemented are discussed in Douglas J. Elliott, *Financial Reform: Now It's up to the Regulators* (Washington, DC: Brookings Institution, July 12, 2010).

36 Douglas J. Elliott, "Another big step forward for the Basel III bank capital proposals" *Up Front Blog*, Brookings Institution, September 23, 2010, http://www.brookings.edu/opinions/2010/0913_basel_elliott.aspx?p=1.

37 Higher capital requirements would also make it more costly for a bank to become very large.

38 "Conservative leaders urge Senate to reject Dodd-Frank financial bailout legislation," *AmSpecBlog*, July 7, 2010, http://spectator.org/blog/2010/07/07/conservative-leaders-urge-sena.

39 Kelly William Cobb, "Dodd-Frank financial regulation bill is a massive taxpayer funded bailout. Period," Americans for Tax Reform, July 21, 2010, http://www.atr.org/dodd-frank-financial-regulation-bill-massive-a5235.

40 Simon Johnson, "Flawed financial bill contains huge surprise," *Bloomberg Businessweek*, July 8, 2010, http://www.businessweek.com/news/2010-07-08/

flawed-financial-bill-contains-huge-surprise-simon-johnson.html; Tom Keene, "Tom Keene's EconoChat," *Bloomberg Businessweek*, July 12–18, 2010.

41 CBO, "Budget and economic outlook: Fiscal years 2010 to 2020" (Washington, DC: Congressional Budget Office, January 2010), summary table 1.

42 Bob Corker, "Corker statement on unemployment benefits," *News Room*, June 25, 2010, http://corker.senate.gov/public/index.cfm?p=News&ContentRecord_id=5b20ac62-8ca7-4e47-a03e-69b55e937b14. Senator Corker's opposition temporarily halted a $33 billion bill, which eventually passed with some Republican support.

43 Representative Paul Ryan, on *Hardball* with Chris Matthews, July 26, 2010, http://www.youtube.com/watch?v=z09w9UY7uOM (accessed August 16, 2010). According to the Congressional Budget Office (CBO), only about $270 billion of the stimulus funds would remain unspent by the end of September 2010. Council of Economic Advisers, "The economic impact of the American Recovery and Reinvestment Act of 2009," fourth quarterly report (Washington, DC: Executive Office of the President, July 14, 2010); Pat Garofalo, "Wonk room: when pressed for a specific spending cut, Ryan goes after middle class tax benefits," *ThinkProgress*, July 27, 2010, http://wonkroom.thinkprogress.org/2010/07/27/ryan-stimulus-cuts/.

44 Emanuele Baldacci, Sanjeev Gupta, and Carlos Mulas-Granados, "How effective is fiscal policy response in systemic banking crises?" IMF Working Paper no. 09/160 (Washington, DC: International Monetary Fund, 2009).

45 CBO, "Budget and economic outlook" (January 2010), tables 1-3 and 3-3.

46 The Government Accountability Office (GAO) estimated the present value of the excess of costs over revenues for Medicare Part D at $8.4 trillion for the seventy-five-year horizon from January 2007 onward. GAO, *Financial Report of the United States Government, 2008* (Washington, DC: Government Accountability Office, 2009), 41.

47 CBO, "Long term budget outlook" (Washington, DC: Congressional Budget Office, June 2010).

48 In one estimate, using CBO projections of the president's budget submitted in 2010, foreign holdings of U.S. Treasuries rise from $4 trillion at the end of 2009 to about $18 trillion by 2020, and interest payments to foreigners on Treasury debt rise from about $100 billion to about $850 billion. John Kitchen and Menzie D. Chinn, "Financing U.S. debt: is there enough money in the world—and at what cost?" La Follette Working Paper no. 2010-015 (Madison: University of Wisconsin, August 2010).

49 As of June 2009, China's holdings of Treasury securities (long term and short term) were about $969 billion. U.S. Treasury, Federal Reserve Bank of New York, and Board of Governors of the Federal Reserve, *Report on Foreign Portfolio Holdings of U.S. Securities as of June 30, 2009* (Washington, DC: U.S. Treasury, 2010), 9. Henning Bohn notes that the United States is in a privileged position, with a historical AAA rating on its Treasury bonds, and the ability to issue debt to foreigners in its own currencies, and (currently) real interest rates less

than trend growth of GDP. Nonetheless, he notes that these privileges can be revoked if they are abused by running up too much debt. Henning Bohn, "The economic consequences of rising U.S. government debt: privileges at risk," CESifo Working Paper no. 3079 (Munich: CESifo, 2010), http://www.ifo.de/pls/guestci/download/CESifo%20Working%20Papers%202010/CESifo%20Working%20Papers%20June%202010/cesifo1_wp3079.pdf (accessed August 16, 2010).

50 Martin Wolf, "The political genius of supply-side economics," *ft.com/wolfexchange* (blog), July 25, 2010, http://blogs.ft.com/martin-wolf-exchange/2010/07/25/the-political-genius-of-supply-side-economics/.

51 Richard B. Freeman, "Are your wages set in Beijing?" *Journal of Economic Perspectives* 9, no. 3 (1995), 15–32.

52 Some scholars believe that the growing importance of computer-based skills has been central to driving down the wages of low-skilled workers. Others point to the decline of labor unions, a trend that reduced the bargaining power of unskilled laborers. These and other trends may have been as important as low-wage trade competition. See, for example, Paul Krugman, "Trade and wages, reconsidered," *Brookings Papers on Economic Activity* no. 1 (2008): 103–154; Robert Gordon and Ian Dew-Becker, "Selected issues in the rise of income inequality," *Brookings Papers on Economic Activity* no. 2 (2007): 191–215.

53 Drawn from the Chicago Council on Global Affairs' authoritative surveys of Chicago Council on Foreign Relations, *Global Views* (Chicago: Chicago Council on Foreign Relations, 2006), http://www.thechicagocouncil.org/UserFiles/File/POS_Topline%20Reports/POS%202006/2006%20Full%20POS%20Report.pdf (accessed August 9, 2010).

54 Steven N. Kaplan and Joshua Rauh, "Wall Street and Main Street: what contributes to the rise in the highest incomes?" *Review of Financial Studies* 23, no. 3 (2009): 1004–1050.

55 Capgemini, *World Wealth Report 2009* (2009).

56 AFL-CIO, "Workers' rights in the global economy," http://www.aflcio.org/issues/jobseconomy/globaleconomy/workersrights/ (accessed December 30, 2010).

57 Pew Global Attitudes Project, *World Publics Welcome Global Trade—But Not Immigration: 47 Nations Pew Global Attitudes Survey* (New York: Pew Research Center, 2007).

58 Pew Research Center for the People and the Press, *Free Trade Agreements Get a Mixed Review, Survey Reports* (New York: Pew Research Center, 2006); Chicago Council on Foreign Relations, *Global Views*. On international investment, when asked whether companies from Europe should be allowed to buy American companies, 26 percent of poorly educated low-income Americans said yes, compared with 69 percent of highly educated high-income Americans. This pattern held for firms from other countries, although Americans in general were less enthusiastic about foreign investment from Asia and the developing world: typically wealthier, better-educated people were two or three times as

likely to think the United States should be open to foreign capital than poorer, less educated people.

59 Pew Research Center for the People and the Press, *U.S. Seen as Less Important, China as More Powerful, Survey Reports* (New York: Pew Research Center, December 3, 2009).

60 CBO, "Federal debt and interest costs" (Washington, DC: Congressional Budget Office, December 2010).

61 Jeffry A. Frieden, "Sectoral conflict and U.S. foreign economic policy, 1914–1940," *International Organization* 42, no. 1 (1988).

62 Daniel Eran Dilger, "Apple: international numbers are absolutely killer," *Apple Insider*, July 20, 2010, http://www.appleinsider.com/articles/10/07/20/apple_international_numbers_are_absolutely_killer.html.

63 "Export or die," *Economist*, March 31, 2010; Diana Farrell, Susan Lund, Alexander Maasry, and Sebastian Roemer, *The US Imbalancing Act: Can the US Current Account Deficit Continue?* (San Francisco: McKinsey Global Institute, 2007).

Chapter 7: The World's Turn

1 Pat Leahy, "The €400 billion night," *Sunday Business Post*, September 27, 2009; Alan Ruddock, "Ireland Inc. faces uncertain future as banking crisis comes full circle," *Independent*, March 1, 2009; and for background, Patrick Honohan, "Resolving Ireland's banking crisis," *Economic and Social Review* 40, no. 2 (2009): 207–231.

2 Lisbeth Kirk, "Irish bank guarantee unfair, say competitors," *EU Observer*, October 1, 2008, http://euobserver.com/9/26840 (quote from British financier); "Some view Ireland's bank guarantee as devious," Associated Press, October 1, 2008, http://www.msnbc.msn.com/id/26979552/ (quote from British Bankers Association; http://news.sky.com/skynews/Home/Business/Ireland-Steps-In-To-Protect-Savings-By-Guaranteeing-Deposits-In-Six-Banks-But-UK-Bankers-Slam-Plan/Article/200810115110786.

3 What follows is based largely on Jeffry A. Frieden, *Global Capitalism: Its Fall and Rise in the Twentieth Century* (New York: W. W. Norton, 2006), chapter 8.

4 "Oh yeah? Herbert Hoover predicts prosperity," *History Matters: The U.S. Survey Course on the Web* (undated), http://historymatters.gmu.edu/d/5063 (quote from Hoover; accessed August 10, 2010); and Barry Ritholtz, "Great Depression quotes 1929 vs 2008," *Essays and Effluvia: The Big Picture* (March 19, 2009), http://bigpicture.typepad.com/writing/2009/03/great-depression-quotes-1929-vs-2008-1.html (quote from Hoover's secretary of labor).

5 Aurel Schubert, *The Credit-Anstalt Crisis of 1931* (Cambridge, UK: Cambridge University Press, 1991), 12–16.

6 Charles Kindleberger, *Comparative Political Economy: A Retrospective* (Cambridge, MA: MIT Press, 2000), 15–31.

7 Charles Kindleberger, *The World in Depression, 1929–1939* (Berkeley: University of California Press, 1973), 219.

8 Herbert Feis, *Europe the World's Banker, 1870–1914* (New Haven, CT: Yale University Press, 1930), 14.

9 John Kitchen and Menzie D. Chinn, "Financing U.S. debt: is there enough money in the world—and at what cost?" La Follette Working Paper no. 2010-015 (Madison: University of Wisconsin, August 2010), figure 2. U.S. Treasury debt, plus debt of Fannie Mae and Freddie Mac (put under federal government conservatorship in 2008), increased by roughly $5 trillion from 1999 to 2008. By fiscal year 2015, when output is projected by the Congressional Budget Office to have returned to potential GDP, federal debt held by the public will have increased by $5 trillion above fiscal year 2009 levels, according to CBO, "Budget and economic outlook: Fiscal years 2010 to 2020" (Washington, DC: Congressional Budget Office, January 2010).

10 Estimates based on projections from the CBO as calculated by Kitchen and Chinn, "Financing U.S. debt."

11 World Bank, *World Development Indicators* (Washington, DC: World Bank, 2010).

12 Nouriel Roubini, "Teaching PIIGS to fly," *Project Syndicate*, February 15, 2010, http://www.project-syndicate.org/commentary/roubini22/English .

13 Carmen M. Reinhart and Kenneth S. Rogoff, "Growth in a time of debt," NBER Working Paper no. 15639 (Cambridge, MA: National Bureau of Economic Research, 2010).

14 On Iceland, see Willem H. Buiter and Anne Sibert, "The Icelandic banking crisis and what to do about it," *CEPR Policy Insight* no. 26 (London: Centre for Economic Policy Research, 2008); Anne Sibert, "The Icesave dispute," *VoxEU*, February 13, 2010, http://www.voxeu.org/index.php?q=node/4611; Jon Danielsson, "The saga of Icesave," *CEPR Policy Insight* no. 44 (London: Centre for Economic Policy Research, 2010); Jon Danielsson and Gylfi Zoega, *The Collapse of a Country*, 2d ed. (London: London School of Economics, March 12, 2009); Thorvaldur Gylfason, "Eleven lessons from Iceland," *VoxEU*, February 13, 2010, http://www.voxeu.org/index.php?q=node/4612.

15 The first reference we have found to this is in "Foreign news: Whose mercy?" *Time*, February 17, 1947, http://www.time.com/time/magazine/article/ 0,9171,778971,00. html#ixzz0iIEf4Flu.

16 Patrik Jonsson, "America's 'other' auto industry," *Christian Science Monitor*, December 5, 2008; Jennifer Freedman, "Americans' 'hypocrisy' in auto rescue spurs me-too trading ire," *Bloomberg*, November 22, 2008.

17 Global Subsidies Initiative, "Will government bailouts lead to trade wars?" (undated), http://www.globalsubsidies.org/en/subsidy-watch/analysis/will -government-bailouts-lead-trade-wars (accessed April 2010).

18 Again, this is not to say that deficits and surpluses are in themselves technically unsustainable. So long as lenders are willing to lend, and borrowers to borrow, capital flows of this sort could go on forever. The point, however, is that effects of further massive increases in debt levels are unlikely to be politically sustainable, as neither borrowing nor lending societies appear willing to resume pre-2008 levels of capital flows. A related point is that the capital

flows of the past decade are almost entirely from poor to rich countries, or among rich countries; while the latter can be defended on some grounds, the former is hard to justify economically.

19 Carmen M. Reinhart and Kenneth S. Rogoff, "The aftermath of financial crises," *American Economic Review Papers and Proceedings* 99, no. 2 (2009): 466–472.

20 Simon J. Evenett (ed.), *Unequal Compliance: The 6th GTA Report* (London: Centre for Economic Policy Research, 2010).

21 Wayne M. Morrison, *China-U.S. Trade Issues* (Washington, DC: Congressional Research Service, 2010).

22 Andrew Batson, Ian Johnson and Andrew Browne, "China talks tough to U.S.," *Wall Street Journal*, March 15, 2010, A1, A19.

23 Edward Wong and Mark Landler, "China rejects U.S. complaints on its currency," *New York Times*, February 5, 2010, A1.

24 For one prominent argument to this effect, see Dani Rodrik, "The real exchange rate and economic growth," *Brookings Papers on Economic Activity* no. 2 (2008), 365–412.

25 Hal Weitzman and James Politi, "Business attitudes harden in face of competition," *Financial Times*, March 24, 2010, 3.

26 Doug Palmer, "Lawmakers press for action on Chinese currency," Reuters, March 15, 2010. The extent of the undervaluation is hotly debated. See Yin-Wong Cheung, Menzie D. Chinn, and Eiji Fujii, "The Illusion of Precision and the Role of the Renminbi in Regional Integration," in Koichi Hamada, Beate Reszat, and Ulrich Volz (eds.), *Prospects for Monetary and Financial Integration in East Asia: Dreams and Dilemmas* (London: Edward Elgar, 2009), for a discussion; and Yin-Wong Cheung, Menzie D. Chinn, and Eiji Fujii, "Measuring Misalignment: Latest Estimates for the Chinese Yuan," in Simon Evenett (ed.), *The US-Sino Currency Dispute: New Insights from Economics, Politics and Law* (London: VoxEU/CEPR, 2010), for recent estimates.

27 This is the sense in which some argue simply that Americans should have no problem with a depreciated renminbi; if the Chinese want to sell Americans their goods so cheaply, why not accept the deal? True as this may be, it ignores the *political economy* of the relationship, which is dominated by the interests of American producers who are harmed by Chinese competition.

28 Wong and Landler, "China rejects U.S. complaints on its currency," A1.

29 Batson, Johnson, and Browne, "China talks tough to U.S.," A1, A19.

30 Olivia Chung, "Wen hints at yuan move," *Asia Times*, March 16, 2010, http://www.atimes.com/atimes/China_Business/LC16Cb01.html.

31 Geoff Dyer and James Politi, "China asks US groups to back it on currency," *Financial Times*, March 16, 2010, http://www.ft.com/cms/s/0/560e9992-30cc-11df-b057-00144feabdc0.html.

32 Michael Schuman, "Why the China-U.S. trade dispute is heating up," *Time*, September 14, 2009, http://www.time.com/time/business/article/0,8599,1922155,00.html.

Chapter 8: What Is to Be Done?

1 From 1998 to 2001, the cyclically adjusted budget balance was positive. CBO, "Budget and economic outlook: Fiscal years 2010 to 2020" (Washington, DC: Congressional Budget Office, January 2010).

2 The percentages given represent publicly held federal debt as a share of GDP at 2001Q1 and 2009Q1, respectively. Over the past century, the debt-to-GDP ratio has averaged about 35 percent.

3 Emanuele Baldacci, Sanjeev Gupta, and Carlos Mulas-Granados, "How effective is fiscal policy response in systemic banking crises?" IMF Working Paper no. 09/160 (Washington, DC: International Monetary Fund, 2009).

4 According to the Congressional Budget Office, the impact from allowing the 2001 and 2003 tax cuts to expire is $312 billion in fiscal year 2015, while the impact from allowing the Alternative Minimum Tax (AMT) to take effect is $103 billion. Kathy A. Ruffing and James R. Horney, "Where today's large deficits come from" (Washington, DC: Center for Budget and Policy Priorities, February 17, 2010), http://www.cbpp.org/files/12-16-09bud.pdf. The impact of allowing the AMT to take full effect would be widespread: In 2010, 27 million taxpayers would see an average tax increase of $3900. The effect would be even larger in 2011 if the 2001 and 2003 Bush tax cuts are not extended; see Jay Heflin, "Lawmakers looking at a one-year AMT fix," *The Hill*, July 6, 2010.

5 David Stockman, "Four deformations of the apocalypse," *New York Times*, July 31, 2010, 9.

6 Figures are for 2003. See James M. Bickley, "Value-added tax: a new U.S. revenue source?" Congressional Research Service Report no. RL33619 (Washington, DC: Congressional Research Service, August 22, 2006), table C-1. The corresponding percentages as a share of GDP are 6.4, 7, and 2.1.

7 See CBO, "The effects of adopting a value added tax" (Washington, DC: Congressional Budget Office, February 1992); and James M. Bickley, "Value-added tax as a new revenue source," Issue Brief no. 91078 (Washington, DC: Congressional Research Service, June 14, 2005).

8 George Will, "The perils of the value added tax," *Washington Post*, April 18, 2010, http://www.washingtonpost.com/wp-dyn/content/article/2010/04/16/AR2010041603993.html.

9 John D. McKinnon, "U.S. weighs tax that has VAT of political trouble," *Wall Street Journal*, July 11, 2010.

10 The Government Accountability Office estimated the present value of the excess of costs over revenues for Medicare Part D at $8.4 trillion for the seventy-five-year horizon from January 2007 onward: GAO, *Financial Report of the United States Government, 2008* (Washington, DC: Government Accountability Office, 2009).

11 There are special waivers to the pay-as-you-go (PAYGO) rule for certain bills; for instance, the American Recovery and Reinvestment Act was passed without having to conform to the PAYGO rule because it was an emergency measure.

12 Current PAYGO provisions are not statutory but pertain to House and Senate

rules; Bill Heniff Jr., "Budget enforcement procedures: Senate pay-as-you-go (PAYGO) rule," Congressional Research Service Report no. RL31943 (Washington, DC: Congressional Research Service, January 12, 2010). Table 2 highlights, for instance, several amendments to the State Children's Health Insurance Plan (SCHIP) and the American Recovery and Reinvestment Act (ARRA) that were not approved in part because of the PAYGO provision.

13 From CBO, "Social Security policy options" (Washington, DC: Congressional Budget Office, July 2010), summary table 1. For discussion, see the CBO report, as well as Center for Retirement Research, *The Social Security Fix-It Book*, revised ed. (Boston: Center for Retirement Research, 2009); and National Academy of Social Insurance, *Fixing Social Security: Adequate Benefits, Adequate Financing* (Washington, DC: National Academy of Social Insurance, 2009).

14 CBO, "Budget and economic outlook: fiscal years 2010 to 2020" (January 2010), tables 1-3 and 3-3. Up until 2035, the aging of the population accounts for most of the increase in health care costs; thereafter, cost growth due to inflation and more expensive medical technologies is projected to be an increasing factor. See box 1-2 in CBO, "Long term budget outlook" (Washington, DC: Congressional Budget Office, June 2010).

15 These "curves" include the federal budgetary commitment to health care, national health care expenditures, and premiums charged for health insurance. See CBO, "Letter to the Honorable Max Baucus: different measures for analyzing current proposals to reform health care" (Washington, DC: Congressional Budget Office, October 30, 2009). The most relevant curve from the federal budgetary perspective is the first, although the second is also important to the extent that resources wasted in the health care sector cannot be used for other purposes, including consumption of other goods.

16 The percentages are based on household credit market debt from Fed *Flow of Funds*, divided by personal income, both seasonally adjusted. Commercial and Industrial Loans at All Commercial Banks, from Federal Reserve H.8 release.

17 In 1997, the elimination of the capital gains tax on house sales further reduced the effective tax on housing investment. The impact of this provision is described in Vikas Bajaj and David Leonhardt, "Tax break may have helped cause housing bubble," *New York Times*, December 19, 2008. The calculations of effective tax rates are presented in IMF, "Debt bias and other distortions: crisis-related issues in tax policy," Fiscal Affairs Department paper (Washington, DC: International Monetary Fund, June 12, 2009). See also Dennis J. Ventry Jr., "The accidental deduction: a history and critique of the tax subsidy for mortgage interest," UC Davis Legal Studies Research Paper no. 196 (Davis: University of California, November 2009).

18 GAO, "Home mortgage interest deduction: despite challenges presented by complex tax rules, IRS could enhance enforcement and guidance," Report to the Joint Committee on Taxation, GAO-09-769 (Washington, DC: Government Accountability Office, July 29, 2009).

19 James R. Hines, "Taxing consumption and other sins," *Journal of Economic Perspectives* 21, no. 1 (2007): 49–68.

20 One of the key criticisms of the value added tax is that it is regressive, hitting poorer households disproportionately hard. This could be addressed by exempting certain goods, such as food and housing. CBO, "Effects of adopting a value added tax." Alternatively, a refundable tax credit allocated to each person could be implemented.

21 Income tax revenues have become increasingly volatile as they have become increasingly sourced from higher-income taxpayers, who tend to receive proportionately more nonwage income. See Edmund L. Andrews, "Surprising jump in tax revenues is curbing deficit," *New York Times*, July 9, 2006.

22 Carmen M. Reinhart and Vincent R. Reinhart, "Capital flow bonanzas: an encompassing view of the past and present," NBER Working Paper no. 14321 (Cambridge, MA: National Bureau of Economic Research, 2008).

23 Gretchen Morgenson, "Future bailouts of America," *New York Times*, February 13, 2010. As of April 2010, the Treasury Department estimated the cost of supporting Fannie Mae and Freddie Mac at $87 billion. See "New cost estimate for bank bailouts: $87 billion," Associated Press, April 23, 2010. The CBO estimates the ten-year total subsidy cost at $389 billion. See CBO, "CBO's budgetary treatment of Fannie Mae and Freddie Mac," Background Paper (Washington, DC: Congressional Budget Office, January 2010), table 2.

24 See CBO, "Budget and economic outlook: Fiscal years 2010 to 2020" (January 2010), box 1-2: recent activity in the Troubled Asset Relief Program.

25 Combines Pension Benefit Guaranty Corporation, Federal Deposit Insurance Corporation, and U.S. Department of Agriculture crop insurance programs; U.S. Treasury, *Financial Report of the U.S. Government* (Washington, DC: U.S. Treasury, February 26, 2009), note 18. Other liabilities total up to $271.9 billion (note 19, excluding international monetary liabilities). U.S. House Budget Committee, "Contingent liabilities: more bailouts to come?" (Washington, DC: U.S. House of Representatives, August 4, 2009), http://www.house.gov/budget_republicans/press/2007/pr20090804contliab.pdf.

26 Simon Johnson, "Testimony to Senate Budget Committee, hearing on A Status Report on the U.S. Economy" U.S. Senate, Washington, D.C., August 3, 2010. In his definition of contingent liabilities, Johnson included decreased tax revenues as well as explicit bailout costs and higher interest payments associated with financial crisis–induced recessions.

27 Willem Buiter, "Lessons from the global financial crisis for regulators and supervisors," Paper presented at the 25th anniversary workshop "The Global Financial Crisis: Lessons and Outlook" of the Advanced Studies Program of the Institut für Weltwirtschaft, Kiel, Germany, on May 8–9, 2009, http://www.nber.org/~wbuiter/asp.pdf.

28 See David Greenlaw, Jan Hatzius, Anil Kashyap, and Hyun S. Shin, "Leveraged losses: lessons from the mortgage market meltdown," U.S. Monetary Policy Forum Report no. 2, February 2008, http://research.chicagobooth.edu/igm/events/docs/MPFReport-final.pdf.

29 Markus Brunnermeier, "Deciphering the liquidity and credit crunch," *Journal of Economic Perspectives* 23, no. 1 (2009): 77–100; and M. Brunnermeier, A. Crocket, C. Goodhart, A. D. Persaud, and H. Shin, "The fundamental

principles of financial regulation," *Geneva Reports on the World Economy* 11 (London: Centre for Economic Policy Research, 2009).

30 Some proposals require posting collateral, and requiring mark to market, rather than merely establishing exchanges. Implementing this reform would entail creation of a central clearinghouse that would guarantee performance. It is not clear that implementing this proposal would lead to a more stable system; see Satyajit Das, " 'Swap tango'—a derivative regulation dance: part 2," *Eurointelligence*, March 4, 2010.

31 Samuel Hanson, Anil K. Kashyap, and Jeremy C. Stein, "A macroprudential approach to financial regulation," *Journal of Economic Perspectives* 25, no. 1 (2011): 3–28.

32 For discussion of implementation, see Rafael Repullo, Jesus Saurina, and Carlos Trucharte, "Mitigating the procyclicality of Basel II," in Mathias Dewatripont, Xavier Freixas, and Richard Portes (eds.), *Macroeconomic Stability and Financial Regulation: Key Issues for the G20* (London: Centre for Economic Policy Research, 2009).

33 For example, the credit rating agencies had a role in the financial crisis. The financial reform legislation directs the regulators to study various approaches to separate the issuer from selecting a particular rater. One proposal is for the government to select the rater, while still forcing the issuer to pay. This setup would overcome the conflict-of-interest problem.

34 Provisions that require regulatory action to be implemented are discussed in Douglas J. Elliott, *Financial Reform: Now It's up to the Regulators* (Washington, DC: Brookings Institution, July 12, 2010).

35 Brunnermeier, Crocket, Goodhart, Persaud, and Shin, "Fundamental principles of financial regulation," discuss the history of the Basel Committee's work and recommend reforms to Basel II.

36 Bank for International Settlements, "The Group of Governors and Heads of Supervision reach broad agreement on Basel Committee capital and liquidity reform package," press release, July 26, 2010, http://www.bis.org/press/p100726.htm.

37 Basel Committee on Banking Supervision, "Group of Governors and Heads of Supervision announces higher global minimum standards," press release, September 12, 2010.

38 Washington has already clashed with the Europeans over capital standards. Washington had hoped to get tougher capital standards, but the Europeans were resistant. In the end, the criteria for what constituted the highest-quality capital (Tier 1 capital) were weakened.

39 As represented by the Institute for International Finance. See D. J. Elliott, *Basel III, the Banks, and the Economy* (Washington, DC: Brookings Institution, 2010).

40 J. Goldfarb, "U.S. has much to prove on new bank capital rules," Reuters, September 23, 2010.

41 L. Di Leo, "Fed gets more power, responsibility," *Wall Street Journal*, July 16, 2010, http://online.wsj.com/article/SB10001424052748703722804575369072934590574.html.

42 J. Taylor, *Getting off Track: How Government Actions and Interventions Caused, Prolonged, and Worsened the Financial Crisis* (Stanford, CA: Hoover Institution Press, 2009).

43 The Fed does not control the entire panoply of interest rates, including those on longer-term securities or those on private debt. Moreover, it is difficult to explain the entire rise in housing prices using only monetary policy. See E. L. Glaeser, J. D. Gottlieb, and J. Gyourko, "Can cheap credit explain the housing boom?" NBER Working Paper no. 16230 (Cambridge, MA: National Bureau of Economic Research, 2010).

44 Addressing these asset price booms could be undertaken either by monetary policy—raising interest rates in the face of an asset price boom—or by regulatory policy. The means by which the goal of "pricking bubbles" is achieved should be determined on the basis of which route is more effective.

45 A big part of the American borrowing binge is attributable to the American need for oil; of the $392.4 billion trade deficit the United States ran in 2009, $253.4 billion was accounted for by oil imports. Part of a rebalancing program should involve reducing dependence on imported energy.

46 Industries experiencing greater growth in domestic demand include services, health services, electronic and telecommunications equipment, and office machinery. See R. Feenstra and C. Hong, "China's Exports and Employment," in R. Feenstra and S.-J. Wei (eds.), *China's Growing Role in World Trade* (Chicago: Chicago University Press, 2010).

47 E. Prasad, "Rebalancing growth in Asia," NBER Working Paper no. 15169 (Cambridge, MA: National Bureau of Economic Research, 2009).

48 A. Kroeber, "Economic rebalancing: the end of surplus labor," *China Economic Quarterly* 14, no. 1 (2010): 35–46; and M. Chinn, B. Eichengreen, and H. Ito, "Rebalancing global growth," Paper prepared for the World Bank's Re-Growing Growth Project, 2010.

49 EIA, *Annual Energy Outlook, 2010* (Washington, DC: Energy Information Administration, 2010).

50 These figures are based on a calculation using 2009 prices and quantities. In that year, the United States imported about $267.4 billion worth of petroleum and petroleum-related products, equal to about 70 percent of the trade deficit. Assuming a gasoline price elasticity of between 0.3 to 0.9, a $1 per gallon tax on gasoline (then averaging $2.40/gallon) would reduce annual petroleum imports by $43.2 to $117.2 billion. The elasticity range is from CBO, "The economic costs of fuel economy standards versus a gasoline tax" (Washington, DC: Congressional Budget Office, 2003).

51 While the year and a half after Lehman's collapse witnessed relatively little increase in the conventional protectionist measures, there has been a substantial increase in the number of requests for protection, which are working their way through the system in various countries; see S. Evenett, "Have long-established patterns of protectionism changed during this crisis? A sectoral perspective," *Global Trade Alert*, October 2009. Furthermore, protection in the form of country-specific bailouts and subsidies is on the rise; the most obvious example is the state aid to automobile manufacturers; see S. Evenett

and F. Jenny, "Bailouts: How to Avoid a Subsidies War," in S. Evenett and R. Baldwin (eds.), *The Collapse of Global Trade, Murky Protectionism, and the Crisis: Recommendations for the G20* (London: Centre for Economic Policy Research, 2009).

52 L. G. Kletzer and H. F. Rosen, "Easing the Adjustment Burden on US Workers," in C. F. Bergsten (ed.), *The United States and the World Economy: Foreign Economic Policy for the Next Decade* (Washington, DC: Institute for International Economics, 2005); and H. F. Rosen, "Strengthening trade adjustment assistance," Policy Brief no. 08-02 (Washington, DC: Peterson Institute for International Economics, 2008).

53 From P. Blustein, *And the Money Kept on Rolling In (and Out): Wall Street, the IMF, and the Bankrupting of Argentina* (New York: PublicAffairs, 2005).

Chapter 9: Conclusion

1 It has become common to blame economists, or economics, for a failure to forecast the collapse. This is profoundly unfair and simply mistaken. As we have demonstrated, there was close to a consensus among mainstream economists after 2003 that the macroeconomic imbalances were likely to cause serious problems. To be sure, this did not amount to a precise prediction of exactly what would happen and when; but nobody faults a doctor who warns a patient that he is in grave risk of suffering a heart attack but cannot provide its precise date or nature. Economic analysis did a reasonably good job of projecting that the country's macroeconomic course would end badly.

2 These estimates are based on Congressional Budget Office projections. The cumulative loss from 2007Q4 to 2014Q4 is $3.87 trillion (in 2009 dollars). The per capita cumulative loss is $12,454, or approximately $50,000 for a family of four. Other estimates of output loss are reported in IMF, *World Economic Outlook* (Washington, DC: International Monetary Fund, October 2009), chapter 4.

INDEX